HISTORICAL
ATLAS OF
BRITAIN

THE END OF THE MIDDLE AGES
TO THE GEORGIAN ERA

HISTORICAL ATLAS OF BRITAIN

THE END OF THE MIDDLE AGES TO THE GEORGIAN ERA

JEREMY BLACK

SUTTON PUBLISHING

For
Kristopher Allerfeldt
A good companion on Devon walks

First published in the United Kingdom in 2000 by
Sutton Publishing Limited · Phoenix Mill
Thrupp · Stroud · Gloucestershire · GL5 2BU

British Library Cataloguing in Publication Data
A catalogue record for this book is available from the British Library

ISBN 0 7509 2128 5

Endpapers: Detail from Christopher Saxton's map of England and Wales, 1579. Saxton followed his county maps with maps of all England and Wales, first, in 1579, to a small scale and then, in 1583, a large-scale wall map that occupied 1.7 × 1.5 metres and was made up of twenty sheets. Saxton's work marked a major advance in English cartography although, with their absence of keys and of coordinates of latitude and longitude, they were not advanced by continental standards.

Frontispiece: Anonymous manuscript map of the British Isles, 1534–46, the earliest known surviving non-Ptolemaic map of the British Isles from the sixteenth century to show latitude and longitude: degrees calculated from a western prime meridian, probably that of the Azores. It is more accurate in its depiction of Scotland than the maps that accompanied Ptolemy's *Geography*, but is still very inaccurate for the outline of Wales and Ireland. It marks Hampton Court.

Typeset in 10/14pt Sabon
Additional mapping, typesetting and origination by
Sutton Publishing Limited
Printed and bound in France by
Imprimerie Pollina s.a., Luçon, France n°L80973

Contents

William Cecil, Lord Burghley's, hand-coloured copy of a map of Devon, from the first national atlas compiled by Christopher Saxton. Saxton started his survey in 1574 and the resulting maps, bound into a single volume, were published in 1579. Burghley added his own notes to the margins, recording, for example, on the map of Dorset possible invasion sites. Burghley, Secretary of State to Elizabeth I, was sent proof copies of the maps.

List of Maps

List of Illustrations

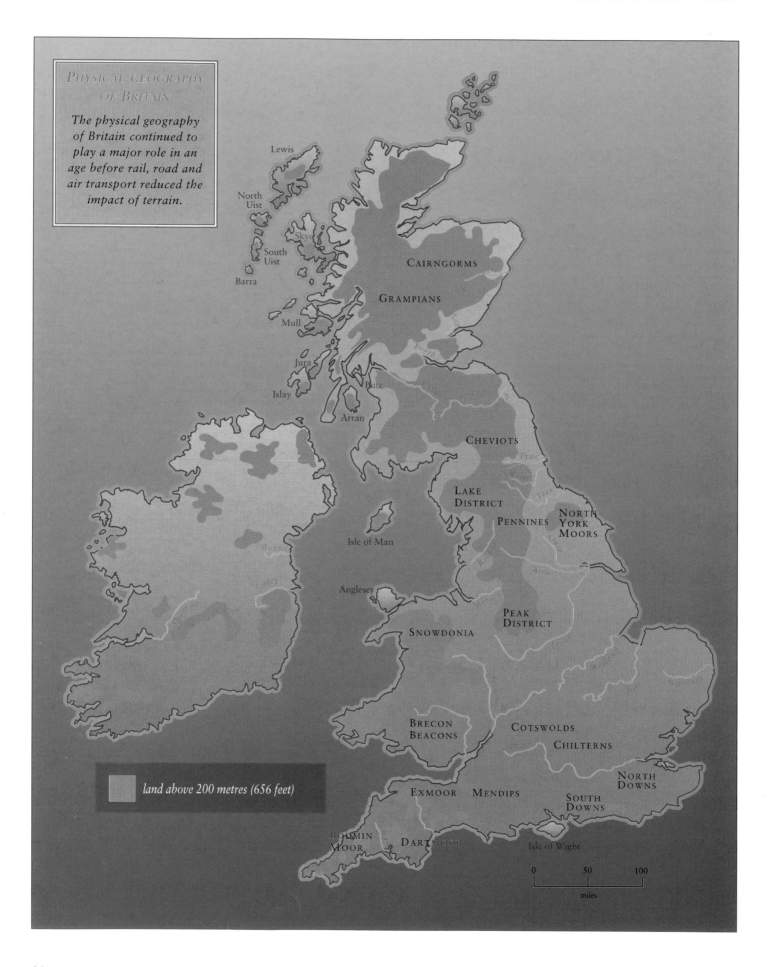

PHYSICAL GEOGRAPHY
OF BRITAIN

The physical geography of Britain continued to play a major role in an age before rail, road and air transport reduced the impact of terrain.

Lewis

North
Uist

Skye

South
Uist

Barra

Mull

Jura

Islay

Bute

Arran

CAIRNGORMS

GRAMPIANS

Forth

CHEVIOTS

Tyne

Wear

Tees

LAKE
DISTRICT

PENNINES

NORTH
YORK
MOORS

Ribble

Ouse

Aire

Boyne

Liffey

Isle of Man

Mersey

Anglesey

PEAK
DISTRICT

Trent

SNOWDONIA

Wash

Wye

BRECON
BEACONS

COTSWOLDS

CHILTERNS

NORTH
DOWNS

BODMIN
MOOR

DARTMOOR

EXMOOR

MENDIPS

SOUTH
DOWNS

Isle of Wight

land above 200 metres (656 feet)

0   50   100

miles

Preface

To present the exciting and complex history of early modern Britain within the possibilities offered by the requirements of this historical atlas is a fascinating challenge. As in any book, the number of maps and photographs and the length of the text permitted are far too limited, but the combination of the three provides a chance to offer an exciting interaction of ideas and images.

I have chosen when mentioning sites from the period to concentrate on properties that are accessible to the public. This has led me to focus on the National Trust (NT) and the National Trust for Scotland (NTS) which own an extraordinary range of properties from this period. They are frequently visited, and are also well known through film and television. Thus, Elizabethan Montacute in Somerset and two Georgian properties, Saltram in Devon and Mompesson House in Salisbury, were both extensively used for the film of Jane Austen's novel *Sense and Sensibility*. Lyme Park in Cheshire appears in the BBC version of her novel *Pride and Prejudice*, while Little Moreton Hall in Cheshire was the location for the television adaptation of Daniel Defoe's novel *Moll Flanders*. Many Trust properties have almost iconic status as images of their age. This is true, for example, of the Elizabethan splendour of Hardwick Hall and of the Georgian gardens at Stourhead and Studley Royal. Equally there are many fascinating NT and NTS possessions that are less famous but equally deserving of attention. One of the pleasures of working on this book was that it led me to visit and revisit many of them. There is also much of importance to Britain's heritage that does not belong to the Trust, not least the churches of the period. Therefore it is necessary to balance mention of Trust properties with those outside its care.

Nigel Aston, Richard Brown, Grayson Ditchfield, Malcolm Gaskill, Bill Gibson, Richard Griffiths, Paul Harvey, Rosemary Horrox, Ann Hughes, Helen Jewell, Harald Kleinschmidt, Murray Pittock and Nigel Saul most helpfully commented on all or part of earlier drafts. I am grateful for the encouragement, friendship, and support of Christopher Feeney at Sutton Publishing. Sarah Moore at Sutton Publishing saw the book through the difficult stages of publication. I have benefited much from the opportunity to test out ideas in lectures given for the Oxford University Department for Continuing Education, the University of Virginia Alumni Summer School at Oxford, and the University of Cambridge Summer School.

This work draws on my own research, and on the work of others, especially the excellent studies published in numerous local history publications, many of which are unfairly neglected. Space does not permit me to mention even a small fraction, but those interested in this book would benefit from reading such works as the *Transactions of the Birmingham and Warwickshire Archaeological Society*, the *Journal of the Royal Institution of Cornwall*, the *Transactions of the Cumberland and*

Westmorland Antiquarian and Archaeological Society, Derbyshire Miscellany, the *Devon Historian*, the *Proceedings of the Dorset Natural History and Archaeological Society*, the *Bulletin of the Durham County Local History Society*, the *Essex Journal*, the *Hatcher Review*, the *Transactions of the Historic Society of Lancashire and Cheshire*, the *Transactions of the Leicestershire Archaeological and Historical Society*, the *Leicestershire Historian*, the *Manchester Region History Review*, the *Journal of the Merioneth Historical and Record Society*, *Northamptonshire Past and Present*, *The Nottinghamshire Historian*, *Oxoniensia*, *Notes and Queries for Somerset and Dorset*, *Sussex History*, *Tyne and Tweed*, *Warwickshire History*, the *Transactions of the Worcestershire Archaeological Society*, the *Yorkshire Archaeological Journal* and *York Historian*. Their shorter counterparts, such as *Cake and Cockhorse* (the journal of the Banbury Historical Society), and *Wychwoods History*, are also very useful. In addition, I am also fortunate, as editor of *Archives*, the journal of the British Records Association, since 1989, and as general editor of the Macmillan series *British History in Perspective*, to have kept in touch with first-rate work in many fields.

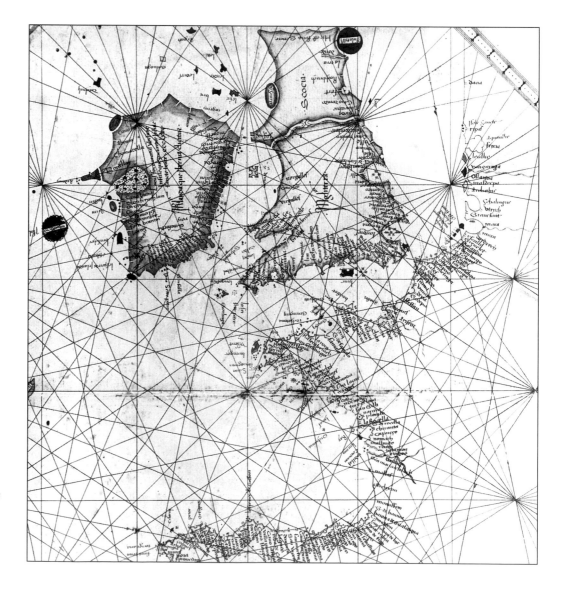

Part of a map by Grazioso Benincasa, drawn at Venice in 1469. Such maps were portolan charts, derived from the Italian word portolano *which means written sailing directions. These charts were a guide to anchorages and sailing directions. They were a testimony to the importance of trade links with the Mediterranean. Much of this was in the hands of foreign merchants, but, as with trade to the Baltic, English merchants had come to play a greater role.*

Introduction

Space, Distance – they look the same on historical and modern maps. They are apparently established and measured by the scale, a comforting suggestion that the past is but a prelude to the present. But they are not the same. Maps of Britain in 1600 and today may employ the same projection, alignment and scale, but they cover different experiences of space, and contrasting meanings of travel. Space and distance are not just a matter of the number of hours it takes to get from, say, Newcastle to Banbury, but also the attitudes of mind that are created by the nature of travel and the effects of these attitudes on how distance is perceived. Concepts of time and space formed parameters to our mentalities and to our ancestors'. In the period covered by this book there was a sense that the world was becoming at once larger and more manageable: in 1776 the British were able to land a large expeditionary force on Staten Island and James Cook was on his final voyage to the Pacific. Yet in 1776 the style of journeys and the concepts of space and time were more similar to the situation 225 years earlier than 225 later.

So to look at a modern map of Britain in 1600 or 1750 is to look at a record not of smooth journeys interrupted only by occasional delays – less than two hours now from London to Exeter by train, only one from London to Newcastle by plane – but rather, to attempt to understand lengthy journeys made unpredictable and hazardous by a multitude of circumstances. These included theft and violence, breakdowns in equipment – axles snapping and horses bolting – and accidents caused by poor road surfaces.

In addition, these road surfaces were unreliable. They were greatly affected by rain, especially on clay soils. Travel through the Weald posed particular problems, but heavy clays, for example in south Essex and the Vale of Berkeley (Gloucestershire), also created difficulties. Furthermore, standards of road maintenance were low. Upkeep was largely the responsibility of the local parish, and the resources for a speedy and effective response to deficiencies were lacking – medieval merchants (among the main sufferers from dreadful roads) left money for repairs in their wills. The situation did not improve greatly in the sixteenth or seventeenth centuries. Travel was not much easier in 1700 than it had been in 1500. Horses were the same, ships were still wooden and wind-powered, most roads were still dirt tracks, and the impact of the weather had not changed. In his play *She Stoops to Conquer* (1773), Oliver Goldsmith wrote of a journey 'it is a damned long, dark, boggy, dirty, dangerous way'.

The slowness of land travel, the difficulty of moving bulk goods by land, other than by river, and Britain's island character, ensured that trade and travel by sea were more important than today. On land, a network of regular and reliable long-distance wagon services did not develop until the seventeenth century. But the situation was even worse at sea than it was on the roads. Shipwreck, and the problems of storm-tossed or, in

Sir John Luttrell emerging from the sea, 1550, at Dunster Castle by Hans Eworth, an Antwerp painter. The vulnerability of wooden ships is clearly depicted.

contrast, becalmed journeys, engaged the imagination of the age; as can be seen from the role of storms and shipwrecks in such Shakespeare plays as *The Tempest, The Merchant of Venice, Twelfth Night, A Winter's Tale,* and *The Comedy of Errors.* Jonathan Wilson, a Cumbrian Quaker and malt dealer, recorded in July 1726: 'I set forward towards Cork . . . but I met with contrary wind and was driven into Wales and so after four days came home again and stayed about a week at home and so set sail again and met with contrary winds again and was driven upon the coasts of Ireland near the mountains of Newry . . . but after six days at sea got safe and well to Dublin.' The storms of the 1720s also drove George I ashore near Rye on his return from Hanover and he sheltered at Lamb House. Winter voyages were harshest, and this was true not only of long journeys but also of the numerous shorter trips that were so important for trade and transport, such as those in the Bristol Channel.

Coastal charts were frequently imperfect, and lighthouses absent or inadequate. At Dunster Castle close to the Bristol Channel there is an allegorical portrait dated 1550 of Sir John Luttrell depicting him emerging half-naked from a storm-tossed sea, while in the background sailors abandon a sinking ship. Lundy's reefs claimed many ships in the Bristol Channel. The construction of the Old Light on Lundy, a major lighthouse completed in 1820, was long overdue. To add to a seaman's problems, accurate time-keeping (and thus navigation) was very difficult without the instruments that were to be developed later in the period.

The pervading sense, as far as travel and distance were concerned, was one of uncertainty; an uncertainty, in comparison with modern life, that was captured most vividly by the abrupt shift from light to darkness. The modern world can overcome the latter with electric lighting and, as far as travel and distance are concerned, navigation systems, but, in the early modern period, the dark was a world of uncertainty, danger and menace. This was especially true for the traveller literally unable to see his route:

The west yet glimmers with some streaks of day;
Now spurs the lated traveller apace,
To gain the timely inn.

(Macbeth, III, iii, First Murderer)

More generally, the dark was a world outside human understanding and control. Macbeth's evil is measured by his willingness to call on the dark to cover the murder of Banquo:

Come, seeling Night,
Scarf up the tender eye of pitiful Day,
And, with thy bloody and invisible hand,
Cancel, and tear to pieces, that great bond
Which keeps me pale! – Light thickens; and the crow
Makes wing to th' rooky wood;
Good things of Day begin to droop and drowse
Whiles Night's black agents to their preys do rouse.

(III, ii)

This was a world of nightmare, in all senses 'unenlightened'. The role of the dark in the life of the imagination was both aspect and product of a more generalised sense of fear. This was a world of malevolence, where the Devil and witches were real, part of the varied legions of evil. The witches brought on stage in *Macbeth* operate in the dark. James VI of Scotland and I of England, for whose court the play may have been written, wrote against witches and was believed to be the target of their diabolical schemes, although he later recanted his opinions and, if anything, became a force for moderation in their treatment. An earlier king of Scotland, James III, had in 1479

Dunster Castle, Somerset. The original fortifications were built for the Mohuns to whom the manor was granted after the Norman Conquest. From 1376 until it was given to the National Trust in 1976, the castle was held by the Luttrells. It was the major fortified position on the Somerset coast of the Bristol Channel. Dunster Castle also literally towered over the surrounding countryside.

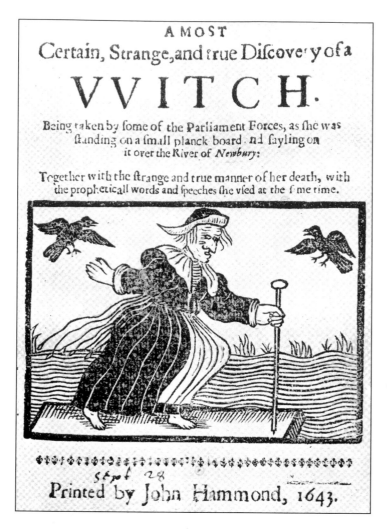

A MOST
Certain, Strange, and true Difcovery of a
VVITCH.

Being taken by fome of the Parliament Forces, as fhe was
ftanding on a fmall planck-board and fayling on
it over the River of *Newbury:*

Together with the ftrange and true manner of her death, with
the propheticall words and fpeeches fhe vfed at the fame time.

Printed by John Hammond, 1643.

A Most Certain, Strange and true Discovery of a Witch, 1643. Belief in witchcraft, astrology and providentialism were all aspects of the interaction of human and sacred space, and of the extent to which this interaction was continual, and thus a subject for regular report and commentary. News helped to explain life. It was a counterpart to a religious culture that put a greater stress than prior to the Reformation on explanation, not least through the use of the vernacular and of print. Providential tales attracted entrepreneurial publishers. News was also presented in a partisan fashion. Although the last recorded witch trial in England occurred in 1717, popular views proved more intractable.

accused his brother, the Earl of Mar, of witchcraft. Several witches were accused of melting a wax image of James, and were burned. Thirty-eight years earlier, Eleanor Cobham had been accused of using a witch to entrap her husband, Humphrey, Duke of Gloucester, and with hiring an astrologer to melt a wax image of Henry VI in order to kill him and obtain the throne for his uncle, her husband.

News of witches was spread in the new culture of print, in learned treatises, chap-books, printed ballads, and engravings, for example, in Reginald Scot's *The Discoverie of Witchcraft* (1584) (although Scot was a vehement sceptic), George Gifford's *A Dialogue Concerning Witches and Witchcraftes* (1593) and John Cotta's *The Triall of Witchcraft* (1616); and in accounts of trials, such as the *Most strange and admirable discoverie of the three Witches of Warboys* (1593) and *The Witches of Northamptonshire* (1612). The last reported an episode that allegedly happened to William Avery and his sister Elizabeth Belcher, who had been bewitched because she had hit a witch:

> Riding homewards in one coach, there appeared to their view a man and a woman riding both upon a black horse. Master Avery having spied them afar, and noting many strange gestures from them, suddenly . . . cried out . . . That either they or their horses should presently miscarry. And immediately the horses fell down dead.

Whereupon Master Avery rose up praising the grace and mercies of God that had so powerfully delivered them, and had not suffered the foul spirits to work the uttermost of their mischief upon men made after his image, but had turned their fury against beasts.

Concern about witches bridged elite and populace, and church and state; although there was a contrast between the category of witchcraft imposed by the law and less defined traditional religious and folklore beliefs. The frequency of curses in disputes and the concern to which they gave rise focused attention on the power of bewitchment. Accusations of witchcraft arose from a range of causes, including refusals of charity, but fear of real evil was at the core of allegations: it was believed possible to cause harm to person and property using magical means, as part of a rejection of society and Christianity.

Such evil and malevolence seemed the only way to explain the sudden pitfalls of life (described by Thomas Hobbes in his *Leviathan* (1651) as 'nasty, brutish and short'), the fatal accidents and tragic illnesses that snuffed out life with brutal rapidity. To keep away such fates, it was necessary to turn to white magic, both the teachings and practices of Christianity, and the semi- (or not at all) Christianised magical beliefs that brought meaning, comfort and a precarious safety to many. Many, especially, but not only, prior to the Protestant Reformation, relied on lucky charms and travelled to sacred sites, such as springs – holy wells were especially numerous in Wales.

White magic and science were not polar opposites. In medieval, and later, thinking alchemy and astrology were intellectual pursuits and science; whereas, in the value judgment of the period, 'magic' was the technique either of the humble (wise women) or of the suspect (ritual magicians). In 1456–7, the government licensed groups of prospectors to continue their efforts to transmute base metal into bullion: but alchemy, alas, was not to be a substitute for taxation. Belief in astrology, alchemy and the occult continued throughout the period, and was especially strong in the early seventeenth century. His alchemical enthusiasm led to Henry Percy, 9th Earl of Northumberland (1564–1632) being known as the 'wizard earl'. Far from being considered ridiculous, such beliefs had a rationality in contemporary terms that helped to make them central to ways of understanding the world. The publications of popular astrologers, such as William Lilly, author of *The Starry Messenger* (1645), sold tens of thousands of copies. Interest in the occult was still very much part of the intellectual repertoire of the virtuosi of the Royal Society of London for the Promotion of Natural Knowledge founded in 1660, and even Sir Isaac Newton had alchemical interests.

Such beliefs did not decline in impact until the eighteenth century, but that decline should not be exaggerated. Very large numbers of astrological works were still being sold in the 1790s. The press also repeated popular superstitions that reflected a belief in the occult. *Drewry's Derby Mercury* of 10 September 1775 noted of a fatal accident in Staffordshire: 'it is very remarkable that a bird hovered over the head of the deceased for a considerable time'. This could have been providential and thus quite in keeping with Protestant theology. By then, 'polite' society not only no longer believed in witches but treated belief as superstition and the practice of white witchcraft as fraudulent. The last recorded witch trial in England occurred in 1717 and the Witchcraft Act of 1736 banned accusations of witchcraft and sorcery. This was a product of an important cultural shift in the period, which eventually resulted in mankind acquiring a much greater control over its environment.

The church had originally set its face against any systematic 'scientific' enquiry, on the grounds that man was only intended to know the mind of God as interpreted by itself. Early Protestants similarly, although rejecting the role of the church , believed that all necessary knowledge was to be found in the scriptures. Francis Bacon, however, suggested in the early seventeenth century that God actually intended man to recover that mastery over nature which he had lost at the Fall: it was (along with the

Sir Isaac Newton, 1642–1727, by Antonio Verrio. The image of science to his contemporaries, Newton acquired a totemic significance thanks to the attention devoted to him. Presented as a scholar who had brought understanding of nature to humanity, he thus freed men from fear. For example, he demonstrated that comets were integral to nature, not portents. Popularised by Voltaire in the 1730s, Newton also achieved a great European reputation.

Francis Bacon, 1561–1626, painted towards the end of his life. An intellectual, lawyer and politician, who rose thanks to the favour of James I, becoming Lord Chancellor in 1618, although he was impeached for bribery in 1621. He helped advance English discussion of scientific method with his Advancement of Learning *(1605) and his* Novum Organum *(1620).*

Protestant Reformation) part of the preparation for the Second Coming. Thus scientific enquiry became not only a legitimate pursuit, but almost a religious duty for the devout Protestant. This idea became immensely influential among the English and Dutch intelligentsia of the mid- and later seventeenth century, and had major long-term impact in preparing the way for the so-called Scientific Revolution.

The menace of the dark is an important aspect of the misleading nature of maps for they present everything as if it were fully lit. In twilight and at night, space shrank to the shadowy spots lit by flickering lights. This is difficult to understand when visiting surviving houses from the period, and easiest to do so only if they lack electric lights and are kept dark to protect tapestries, as with the Edgcumbe house at Cotehele. Even then, we do not get the effect of candlelight. For the poor of any neighbourhood the great houses would have been the only places where there was any real measure of light after dusk. At night, sight was a privilege of the rich, and Britain was a dark country speckled with glimmers of light.

Season was another limitation on the applicability of maps. Journeys that could be undertaken in the summer might be impossible in winter. Spring thaws and autumn floods could also bring problems, especially by sending rivers into spate, making them impossible to ford, and flooding low-lying areas, such as the Somerset Levels and the Fens. Boats were more important than bridges in crossing rivers and the numerous estuaries on the country's indented coastline. Ferries across the Bristol Channel – from Sully near Cardiff to Uphill in Somerset and from Beachley to Aust – moved cattle and other products. The stone for Castle Ward, built above Strangford Lough in County Down in 1762–70, was shipped from England. Many settlements and country houses, for example Antony House in Cornwall, were best approached by sea. Water – both the sea and inland waters – had far more of an impact on people's lives than is the case today. Many towns that today lack quays and wharves were ports. Langport in Somerset was a *sea* port. Fishing was far more widespread than in the twentieth century.

The importance of waters focused attention on bridges. The seven-arched medieval stone bridge over the Tyne at Newcastle was a crucial feature of the city's position. The same was true of Gloucester and the River Severn. London Bridge remained the lowest crossing point on the Thames and there was no road crossing of the Tamar downriver of Gunnislake until the Tamar Bridge at Saltash was opened in 1961.

The flood-defence measures that seek to contain the stormy sea and modern rivers mostly date from the last 150 years. Most rivers in the early modern period were shallower, had broader courses with lower banks, and were thus readier to flood. More generally, rivers and mountains featured strongly in the sense and awareness of terrain of people before the motor age, and were important features of medieval and early modern route maps.

There were other problems for travellers on the level of day-to-day subsistence. Acquiring both food and accommodation could be very difficult. In 1780 Mary Montagu-Douglas-Scott reached Worksop:

> . . . a dirty inn:
> The meat was very tough and bad,
> and mother storm'd like any mad,
> But forced 'half pleased to be content',
> We munched our meat and on we went.

Modern maps offer no expression of the problems of distance in the past, and of the particular attitudes that arose as a result. Modern maps, whether of motorways, railways or air routes, tend to ignore both. The Pennines and other crucial features of topography are lost. What can the Chilterns mean to an age that can blast a hole through them, as with the M40 at Stokenchurch? The same is true of less prominent features, such as Failand ridge which is carved by the M5 east of Clevedon, or the boggy high moors west of Huddersfield crossed by the M62.

The Classical front of Castle Ward, County Down. This eighteenth-century mansion has opposing façades in different styles, the west front is Classical, and the east front Gothic. Grassland and trees came up close to the house in the characteristic style of the period. In such houses, there were frequently grand rooms on the first floor.

Sowing and harrowing from the Roxburghe Ballads. *Agriculture was reliant on human and animal labour. The absence of mechanised means for breaking the soil ensured that ploughing was arduous, especially on the clay soils of the English Midlands. The birds that ate the seed were a major problem. The harvest was the key factor in individual, communal and national fortunes, the only other developments proving of comparable potential importance – epidemic disease, warfare and religious change – being episodic.*

Distance also implied difference. In the preface to his *Eneydos* (1490), William Caxton recounted a tale of London boatmen who stopped in Kent and could not make themselves understood because the Kentish dialect was so strong. One farmer's wife thought they were French because their language was so strange.

The world not only looked, but was, very different in winter and summer. This was a matter not only for travellers but also for those in the world of work. The seasonal round of agriculture set a rhythm, creating a world that was very different to ours, which is based on fairly constant tasks framed by a human timetable. The course and success of the harvest were crucial to rural life and human limitations were cruelly exposed in agriculture. Animal diseases, such as the cattle plagues of 1749–50 and 1769–70, had a devastating effect. The primitive nature of veterinary science ensured that the response to disease could not be preventive. Instead, animals had to be slaughtered. (Although it should be noted that the British turned to the same remedy in the 1990s to deal with cattle disease.) Farmers lived close to their stock, often under the same roof, as in the Fleece Inn near Evesham, and the killing of the animals was not 'sanitised' in some distant abattoir. Arable farming was also difficult and unpredictable,

and both ways of working the land involved far more human effort than has been necessary since effective mechanical aids were introduced. Plant stocks had not been scientifically improved to resist disease and adverse weather conditions, and increase yields. Tasks such as sowing, harrowing and harvesting were affected by the weather.

Industry was also influenced by the time of the year, making both employment and the nature of work seasonal. Frozen waterways denied watermills power, as did summer drought; water power was also required for bellows and hammers, such as those in the Wealden iron works. In the 'little ice age' of the seventeenth century the climate deteriorated, reducing growing and working seasons, only for temperatures to rise in the early eighteenth century.

Seasonal conditions also hit the river traffic that was so important to the economy, and that can be so difficult to grasp from modern maps, because our understanding of a river on a map is very different to the way it was used and viewed in the early modern period. Rivers combined to form trading systems that covered much of the country. In the West Midlands, the Severn was navigable as far as Bewdley, near Kidderminster, the Stratford Avon almost up to Warwick,

The Cotswold Games. The frontispiece of Annalia Dubrensis *(1636) recording the Whitsuntide Cotswold Games organised by Robert Dover. Founded as a protest against Puritanism, the games included cudgel-playing, horse-racing, hunting and walking on the hands. The games died out during the Civil War but were revived under Charles II and continued until 1852.*

the Wye to Hereford, and the Lugg to Leominster. All these waterways combined to enhance the importance of the Severn system and thus of the nearby major seaport, Bristol. However, Scotland and Wales were far worse served by inland waterways than lowland England.

Fairs and markets registered seasonal rhythms too. Such occasions were crucial to the flow of goods and people and thus to economic activity. Industrial production is frequently misrepresented if shown in terms of static plant and processes, for most manufacturing involved a degree of out-work and assembly, or, at least, of the movement of raw materials. In addition, transhumance – the movement of animals to summer and winter pastures – linked upland and lowland areas, while, more generally, there was a close interdependence between areas of difference. This was true both of the economy as a whole, and of regional and local economies. Thus the moorlands of Dartmoor and Exmoor had important commercial relationships with nearby parishes.

Map of Scotland, seventeenth century, Miliaria Scotia. Although it was less extensive than in England in the sixteenth and seventeenth centuries, the mapping of Scotland, nevertheless, greatly improved. In place of a contorted shape, there was a more accurate depiction of the coastline, although the Highlands remained poorly mapped. In the mid-sixteenth century John Elder and Lawrence Nowell both produced maps of Scotland. The proximity of Scotland to Ulster emerges clearly from this map.

Maps, whether modern, historic (old), or historical (modern maps depicting the past), record and re-create a reality, but one that is a less than complete account of life. This is even more true once we consider the mental maps of the period. These are difficult to re-create, not least because we tend to understand past people in our own terms and not in theirs. This is especially true of religion. The sense of direct providential intervention, of a daily interaction of the human world and wider spheres of good and evil, of heaven and hell, of sacred places and saintly lives, is one that is today heavily constricted by secularism and science. In the early modern period, doubt was far less common. Life and public morality were framed in terms of the struggle between good and evil. Thus the 'maps' that counted were those of the route to salvation, whether pre-Reformation pilgrimage journeys, or the *Pilgrim's Progress* (1678) of John Bunyan's allegory, or less defined, but still potent, journeys.

The world of good and evil was extensively depicted prior to the Reformation, especially in wall paintings, mystery plays, and, more generally, traditional oral culture. The coopers' pageant in the 1415 York Corpus Christi play showed 'Adam and Eve and a tree between them, a serpent deceiving them with apples, God speaking to them and cursing the serpent, and an angel with a sword casting them out of Paradise'. The

Reformation ensured that good and evil became more literary and less oral or visual, but that did not diminish the need for people to understand their world in terms of the struggle between the two. The journey to an earthly perdition and a hellish end was extensively rehearsed by commentators, both the explicitly religious and the 'secular' – for example William Hogarth's mid-eighteenth-century morality series of engravings,

Detail from a 1591 map of Chelmsford by John Walker, an estate surveyor, as part of a survey of the manor of Bishop's Hall. The nature of individual plots emerges clearly, as does the proximity of fields. Most sixteenth-century towns were the size of modern villages.

*Scene in the madhouse from
A Rake's Progress by William
Hogarth, 1735. It shows a lunatic
drawing lines of longitude on the
walls of a madhouse. The engraving
was originally published in 1735
and then republished in 1763,
'retouched by the Author', just as a
method for measuring longitude at
sea was finally discovered, although
word of the discovery had clearly
not reached Hogarth. Hogarth
(1697–1764) produced moral satires
and depicted depravity from within
a Christian view of vice and
morality.*

*The great avenue of megaliths at
Avebury, Wiltshire. The leading
antiquarian William Stukeley
believed it to be a 'Temple of the
British Druids'.*

including *The Rake's Progress*, *The Apprentice's Progress* and *Before and After*. While not maps in conventional terms, such works were intended both to depict and to offer guidance on the routes of life. This was even more true of admonitory prints set in a landscape, such as the Methodist image *The Tree of Life* (*c*. 1770), which brought both the Heavenly City and the 'Bottomless Pitt' into the picture.

Such 'maps' seem a long way from those we are familiar with, but they were important to contemporaries who did not need our route and street guides. Distant, also, are the secret schemas of the period, such as the masonic and druidical beliefs that affected the design of the Circus at Bath (1754–64) by John Wood. What could be mapped as 'rational' townplanning in fact reflects a complex of beliefs about the appropriate ordering of life. Druidical beliefs and patterns were of considerable interest in the eighteenth century. The leading antiquarian of the period, William Stukeley (1687–1765) believed Avebury to be a 'Temple of the British Druids' and wrote on the subject. He also published on druidical influences at Stonehenge, and laid out a 'temple of the Druids' near to his home in Grantham.

Thus, when we consider the maps and mapping of early modern Britain and, more generally, its history, it is important to remember that there were other schemas that were important guides to the life and thought of the people of the period.

ONE

The End of the Middle Ages

All historical periods are artificial constructions, and most are the creations of commentators living well after the time in question. How in 1450 or 1500 was someone supposed to know that they were living at the close of the Middle Ages? There was a sense of history, of past, present and future as different, but there was little sense of history as progress. Time was framed by Christian history, human society was to be transformed when God chose at the Millennium, and this was understood not as a date in the human calendar, but as the rule of saints before the end of time.

Within the span of history on earth, it was difficult to feel much confidence in progress or the future. The remains of the former prestige but subsequent ruin of the Roman world were stark evidence that what came later was not better. Even within the confines of recent British history, the epidemic of bubonic plague in the Black Death of 1348–9 had led to a massive fall in the population: by approximately a third. Fresh attacks of plague followed in 1361–2, 1369 and 1375, and it continued to recur thereafter. The fall in population left many deserted or shrunken villages and hit agriculture. The lynchets that permitted the cultivation of steep slopes were abandoned. The pattern of ridge and furrow in modern pasture shows the extent of ploughland that was returned to grazing. Some of this was low-grade due to the neglect of pasture, especially in marginal land – there was not the manpower to weed effectively. Farmhouses, barns, ditches, fences and walls fell into disrepair and soil improvement through marling appears to have dwindled. Rents fell. By 1355 the lord's profit from the Worcestershire manor of Clent had fallen from £4 a year to £1 10 shillings (£1.50), 'by reason of the pestilence'. The trade at most markets and fairs declined. As their rural hinterlands encountered serious problems, towns, such as Canterbury, declined. There was, however, some urban growth, for example at the port of Southampton. Nevertheless, in so far as a cyclical theory of history appeared appropriate, Britain was on a downward part of the cycle. Cyclical theories were often developed by those experiencing decline.

There was no sense, therefore, that the world, or Britain, was moving towards a different, let alone better, future, one that would draw to a close the recent centuries. Yet, by 1600 the situation had obviously altered. There had been major changes. Choosing between them involves a prioritisation that reflects modern suppositions, but, in choosing to focus on any individual change, it is possible to qualify the rate or

Map of Europe by Gerard Mercator (1512–94), c. 1554, showing Britain as a stage between Europe and North America. Mercator printed a map of the British Isles in Duisburg in 1564 and an English edition of his atlas was published in 1636. Mercator's projection, produced in 1569, treated the world as a cylinder, keeping angles and thus bearings accurate in every part of the map, a crucial tool for navigation. Mercator placed Europe at the top centre of his projection.

impact of change. Nevertheless, it is clear that the combination of Protestantism and the Reformation, with printing and the sustained demographic (population) expansion of the sixteenth century, greatly altered life.

Important as these changes were, however, they had less impact, particularly in terms of cartography, than the 'discovery' of the wider world. The inhabitants of the Americas, sub-Saharan Africa, and Asia did not need to be 'discovered', and the discovery did them (especially the first two) much harm. As far as the Europeans were concerned, however, their exploration was indeed a pursuit of discoveries, which forced them to come to terms both with new worlds and with the sense of a 'brave new world' (*Tempest*). It became apparent that traditional learning was limited, and thus flawed, and that the ancients – the Greeks and the Romans – were not omniscient. This was made bluntly clear by the need to draw totally new maps and also by the development of the new, Mercator projection of the world. Geography became a subject of study in England. Exploration contributed powerfully to a sense that time brought novelty, that it could be profitable, and that the past could and should be parted with. Change and novelty became less pejorative terms, although they still had negative connotations for many.

These 'discoveries' affected a society still trying to adapt to the economic and social strains that had followed the Black Death. Yet it would be inappropriate to concentrate simply on problems. Alongside the most obvious theme in any consideration of fifteenth-century Britain – a variety that primarily reflected the possibilities of local agricultural environment – there was prosperity and expansion as well as problems.

In the short term, in England, the fall in population caused by the Black Death brought an attempt to reimpose labour services, in place of the pre-plague situation when a rising population had made it sensible for lords to collect their rents in cash and hire cheap labour, thus encouraging the spread of the money economy. This attempted reimposition of labour service was unsuccessful. The absence of population growth resulting from endemic plague made it possible for peasants to exploit demands for labour, and they were helped by the decline of serfdom and the resulting increase of fluidity in tenurial, if not social, relations. Labour-rents were commuted into money payments, and this increased the penetration of the money economy into the rural world. The higher level of wages allowed workers more leisure time: drinking socially in alehouses became more widespread and increased legislation against games was prompted by the same trend.

Labour shortages also encouraged a shift to pastoral farming, which required fewer workers. Across much of England, especially in the Midlands, landlords enclosed some of their land for sheep farming and stock keeping, leading to rural depopulation and deserted villages (see p. 37). The general increase in stock farming meant that meat eating spread further down the social scale. As a result of rural depopulation, the conversion of tilled land to pasture was made an offence by Parliament in 1489, but that did not end the shift. Exports of woollen cloth to the continent brought too much prosperity, especially to East Anglia and also to London, through which 70 per cent of cloth exports were passing by 1500.

HENRYS IV AND V

This predominantly rural society was headed, and largely owned, by a landed aristocracy and gentry that spent much of the fifteenth century at war or under the threat of war. From the outset, there was conflict. In England, Henry, Duke of Lancaster, seized the crown from his cousin Richard II in 1399, establishing the Lancastrian line on the throne. The imprisoned Richard was murdered in Pontefract Castle the following year, but Henry IV (1399–1413) found that his debatable claim to the throne – he was descended from a younger son of Edward III (1327–77) – and his reliance on violence encouraged others to act against him. The dead Richard challenged the legitimacy of his rule. In Wales, Owain Glyn Dŵr (Owen Glendower) rose against English control in 1400, just over a century after it had been finally imposed on the Principality. Three years later, the Percys, a mighty magnate family who wielded great power in the north of England and had helped Henry IV depose Richard II, rebelled and allied with Glyn Dŵr. Henry IV defeated and killed the Percy heir, 'Hotspur', Sir Henry Percy, at the battle of Shrewsbury on 21 July 1403, but Hotspur's father, Henry, 1st Earl of Northumberland, rebelled again in both 1405 and 1408, before being defeated and killed on Bramham Moor on 20 February 1408.

The defeat of the Percys led to their estates being declared forfeit. Warkworth Castle was battered into submission by royal cannon in 1405, and given to John, Duke of Bedford, the son through whom Henry IV sought to run the north. Glyn Dŵr lost ground in 1408, and, with support for the rebellion ebbing, disappeared in 1415.

Henry IV thus saw off his opponents, but this had taken several years, and his reign served as a reminder of the precarious nature of the English state. He was the first king to speak English as his first language rather than French. Henry not only had to face French attacks on his possessions in Aquitaine (south-west France) and Wales, Scottish attack, and the fragmentation of the English position in Ireland, but also an attempt to divide England itself. In 1405 Glyn Dŵr had agreed with Northumberland and Edmund Mortimer to depose Henry and split his realm. Mortimer, who married Glyn Dŵr's daughter, was the uncle and namesake of the young Edmund, 5th Earl of March, who had a claim to the throne and was in Henry IV's custody.

Henry V, c. 1387–1422, king from 1413. A young and bellicose king who had played a major role, while Prince of Wales, in helping Henry IV against his opponents, from 1415 he pursued his claim to the French throne. He died before the difficulty of this task became apparent. He developed the navy but was responsible for heavy taxation.

The division of the realm was not the preferred route for rebels. Both in England and Scotland, critics generally sought to influence policy in, or take over, the entire realm. In both England and Scotland, such schemes rested on aristocratic factionalism and an ability and willingness to resort to rebellion. Rebellion was the consequence of exceptional strains in the polity or the ambitions and desires of a maverick individual who was likely to end up politically isolated, because rebellion was seen as an aberration from the desired norm of cooperation between king and lords. Henry V (1413–22) felt it appropriate to restore the Percys in 1416, and in 1417 Henry, 2nd Earl of Northumberland, was made Warden of the East Marches, a crucial figure in the defence of the border with Wales.

Henry IV's eldest son, the young and vigorous Henry V, strengthened both state and dynasty. Internal threats to his authority were weak and speedily suppressed. But he quelled them through fighting, ensuring that success in war was seen as crucial to stability. In 1414 Henry crushed a conspiracy organised by Sir John Oldcastle, a member of the radical anti-clerical Lollard movement – religious orthodoxy was important to Henry's image, and contributed to his success. The following year, on the eve of Henry's invasion of France, a conspiracy to overthrow him in favour of the 5th Earl of March was betrayed to him by the intended beneficiary. The domestic stability of the remainder of the reign was the context allowing military success abroad, but, even so, dynastic insecurity had not been completely banished.

Invading Normandy in 1415, Henry captured the port of Harfleur and, thanks in large part to the skills of his longbowmen, smashed a French army at Agincourt. The French force, bigger than Henry's own, was mostly composed of dismounted men of arms who were no match for the English archers. This success encouraged Henry to press on. In 1417–19, he conquered Normandy, allied with the powerful Duke of Burgundy, and laid claim to the French throne, as his great grandfather Edward III had done. The weak Charles VI of France betrothed his daughter Catherine to Henry, and, by the Treaty of

Warkworth Castle, seen from outside the west curtain (left). The Percy family's Northumberland stronghold was taken by Henry IV's troops in 1405 and handed to the king's son John, Duke of Bedford, to act as a base from which he could control the north. Above is the Grey Mare's Tail Tower.

Troyes of 21 May 1420, recognised Henry as regent during his reign. According to the terms of this document, Henry and his heirs were to inherit France on Charles's death.

Henry had no sense that the Channel should act as a boundary to his authority. Although identifying with the cult of St George and presented essentially as an assertor of Englishness in Shakespeare's *Henry V*, the king himself followed his predecessors since William I's conquest in 1066 in envisaging a realm that spanned the Channel. Normandy seemed closer to his centre of power in southern England, and a more attractive prospect for operations and expansion, than the margins of his possessions in the British Isles. There was also a sense of a great tradition to be maintained and fame to be gained. The rulers of England had held Normandy until John lost it in 1204. Edward III had invaded France, winning great fame and having his claims to much of the country accepted. Edward and his eldest son, the Black Prince (who was Richard II's father), had won spectacular victories at Crécy (1346) and Poitiers (1356). By winning fresh triumphs, Henry V would assert a continuity that could help to legitimise his position in England.

Charles VI's son, the Dauphin, refused, however, to accept the Treaty of Troyes. Henry had to fight on, and, on 31 August 1422, besieging Meaux, he died (possibly of dysentery), leaving most of France unconquered, and Parliament critical at the likely cost of conquest and unhappy with the idea that England should have to pay for the assertion of Henry's control over his French subjects. Had Henry lived longer he might have created a new polity, as well as bringing much prestige to the House of Lancaster, but asserting control over all France was a formidable task well beyond the demands of winning and holding Normandy.

HENRY VI AND THE LOSS OF FRANCE

Henry V's son, Henry VI (1422–61, 1470–1), became king although he was only nine months old. Hereditary succession was more important than meritocratic monarchy (rule by the member of the royal family best suited to the task): the latter offered neither legitimacy, nor stability. The first three decades of the new reign were overshadowed by failure in France. Never before had there been such a consistent run of defeats and, as with earlier monarchs beaten in France – most obviously John (1199–1216) and Henry III (1216–72) – or in Scotland – Edward II (1307–27) – foreign defeat was followed by domestic opposition. Defeat led to a loss of prestige and a slackening of the process by which patronage and success enabled the monarchy to elicit the support of clients.

Initially, the English forces in France under the direction of the regent, Henry VI's uncle, John, Duke of Bedford, had some success, including an important victory at

The descent of Henry VI as king of England and France from St Louis of France (top centre), through the French kings (left) and English kings (right). Henry's claim to the throne could not prevail over military defeat.

Verneuil in 1424, although Scottish troops greatly helped the French in the 1420s. However, a charismatic peasant, Joan of Arc, inspired the new king, Charles VII, and, in what was to be the turning point of the war, broke the English siege of Orléans in May 1429. The English were heavily beaten at Patay in June. Charles was crowned king at Reims that July, and, although Henry was crowned at Paris in 1430, and the captured Joan burned as a witch in 1431, the English impetus in France had been lost. The last sustained attempt by a ruler of England to become a major power on the continent collapsed. In 1435 Henry was abandoned by the powerful Duke of Burgundy, who had been a crucial ally, and Bedford died. Henry lost Paris in 1436 and Maine in 1444. Charles VII was now stronger, his army with its train of cannon more advanced. It conquered Normandy and Gascony in 1449–51, defeating the English archers at Formigny in April 1450. An English counter-offensive in Gascony, where there had been a rebellion against French rule, was smashed at Castillon in 1453, the last battle of the Hundred Years War.

France had gone. Calais was held until 1558, and the Channel Islands are still under the British crown, but the link with France created by William the Conqueror

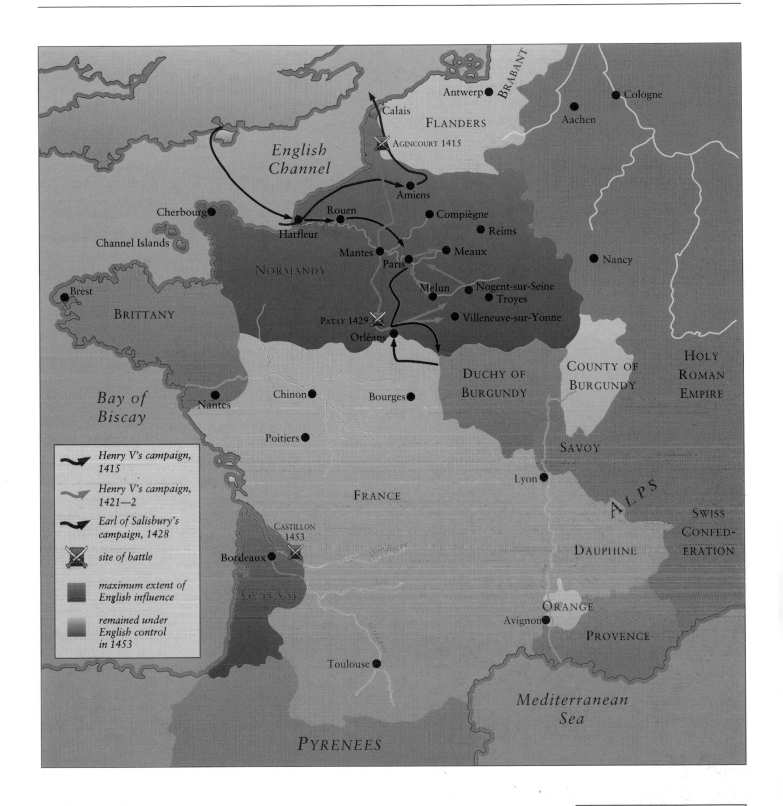

Henry V's campaign, 1415

Henry V's campaign, 1421–2

Earl of Salisbury's campaign, 1428

site of battle

maximum extent of English influence

remained under English control in 1453

in 1066 was severed. There were to be further invasions of France, by Edward IV (1461–83), Henry VII and Henry VIII, but the nature of English history had changed. Thereafter, England had a more insular character, and this was to be important to its later domestic and international development. Until first William III (1689–1702) and then the Hanoverians (1714–1837), relations with the continent became a matter of foreign policy, not the pursuit of the continental dominions of the ruler of England.

CAMPAIGNS OF THE HUNDRED YEARS WAR

Despite the efforts under his successor, Henry V's conquests proved very ephemeral.

THE WARS OF THE ROSES, 1450–87

Defeat abroad was followed by crisis at home, the lengthiest period of internal conflict in English history – 1455–71 and 1483–7. The origin of this civil warfare can be traced to particular circumstances, specifically the struggle for the throne between the families of Lancaster (Henry VI) and York, but internal conflict was not unique to England in this period. Indeed the struggles in France involving the Valois kings, the kings of England, and the dukes of Burgundy, that lasted until the death of Charles the Bold of Burgundy in 1477, were more serious and disruptive than those in England. In Scotland two rival factions within the royal family competed for control from 1384. This led to much instability and violence. James I (1394–1437, r. 1406–37) was captured by the English while en route to France as a child, and was held for nineteen years before being returned in 1424. James only gained power in 1425 by bringing down the former regent, his uncle, the Duke of Albany. Albany and his relatives were seized and beheaded. James then reimposed royal control in the Highlands, summoned a parliament in Inverness in 1427, executed recalcitrant chiefs and strengthened the royal power. In 1429 and 1431, however, James had to campaign against the Lord of the Isles in the Highlands. James was murdered in his bedchamber in an attempted coup in 1437.

IACOBVS · 2 · D · GRATI REX · SCOTORVM ·

James II of Scotland, 1430–60, king from 1437. Much of his reign was a struggle against the aristocratic families that dominated both his minority and the localities. Having overcome his domestic rivals, James was killed when his attempt to exploit the Wars of the Roses miscarried.

James II (1430–60, r. 1437–60) faced civil war between aristocratic factions during the 1440s. This was the politics of kidnappings and sudden executions, such as those of the members of the faction of Sir Alexander Livingstone in 1450. James stabbed William, 8th Earl of Douglas, to death in 1452 while the latter was under the king's safe-conduct, and then went on to break Douglas power in the Borders. The Douglas castle at Threave surrendered in 1455 in the face of a 'great bombard [cannon]'. James II was killed in 1460 when hit by a flying wedge dislodged by the discharge of a cannon bombarding Roxburgh Castle, the major English position in Scotland. The castle fell soon after.

From 1479, James III (1451–88, r. 1460–88) faced serious aristocratic opposition led by his brothers, and he was killed by rebels in 1488 after his defeat at Sauchieburn, close to Bannockburn. Scotland also suffered from the consequences of its support for France. English monarchs stirred up opposition. After Henry VI was given shelter in Scotland following his defeat at Towton in 1461, Edward IV encouraged the rebellion of John, 11th Earl of Ross in 1462. In 1482–3 Edward sought to replace James III with the latter's brother, Albany. Like England, Scotland was a violent society in which blood-feuds were important. Alexander Irvine, 5th Laird of Drum from 1457 to 1493, was dismissed as Sheriff of Aberdeen and sent to prison for waging a private war. Later, he got into trouble first for ambushing and killing two men and then for murdering and dismembering a chaplain, Sir Edward Macdowall, in Drum Castle.

So England's internal strife was not unique. And, as in Scotland, the calibre of the monarch and his ability to take command of a political situation made complex by competing aristocratic factions was important. Henry VI was not up to the task, and the contrast between him and the heroic image, political adroitness and skilful determination of his father was striking. The number of peers of royal blood was a potential problem, and in Richard, Duke of York (descended from Edward III's second and fourth surviving sons), Henry (descended from the third), faced a member of the royal family who felt that his status entitled him to more recognition. Henry's position was weakened by his inability to establish unity among the nobles, but so also was York's.

There had been factional rivalries throughout Henry VI's lengthy minority, and, during these years, leading nobles became used to ruling the country. The mutual dislike of his uncle, Humphrey, Duke of Gloucester, and great-uncle, Bishop Henry Beaufort, hindered government, and led to Parliament being held at Leicester in 1426, not at London where there was much sympathy for Duke Humphrey. The difficult situation led to an instruction to MPs not to carry weapons. Many, instead, brought bludgeons, leading to the gathering being termed 'the Parliament of battes'. Duke Humphrey remained a major source of dissension and instability until his death in 1447.

Force and the threat of force came to play a greater role in local and national politics. In 1442–3 Henry Percy, 2nd Earl of Northumberland, attacked the estates of John Kemp, Archbishop of York, in pursuit of a quarrel with him. Furthermore, this was not a case of violence only at the margins of the realm. Another example of a victim of violence at the heart of the realm was Ralph, Lord Cromwell of Tattershall Castle, Lord Treasurer and a landlord who essentially sought peace. In 1449 he was unsuccessfully attacked when about to enter a Council meeting, and, four years later, the wedding party of his niece Maud and Sir Thomas Neville of the powerful north of England family was ambushed by the Nevilles' rivals, the Percys, and a band of 700 men.

The political crisis became more serious in 1450, when the unpopular chief minister William de la Pole, 1st Duke of Suffolk, who had been criticised in Parliament the previous year, was impeached there, banished, and then murdered on a boat in the Channel. Then in June 1450, the outbreak of Cade's Rebellion in Kent reflected anger about extortion by manorial officials, widespread hostility to the government, and its inability to control areas near the centre of government. The rebels beat a royal army at Sevenoaks, seized London, and killed unpopular officials, before being evicted by the citizens and defeated. That year, there were also major disturbances in south and west England. The volatile state of the country highlighted Henry's deficiencies, while the loss of France ensured that the aristocracy no longer had a useful foreign outlet for their aggression. York used the occasion of Cade's Rebellion, which he was rumoured to have encouraged, to return from Ireland and demand changes in the government. Then in August 1453 Henry's mental and physical collapse led to York being made Protector. The king's far from total recovery in the winter of 1454–5, however, gave the court party, under Edmund Beaufort, 2nd Duke of Somerset, the opportunity to turn against York.

As enmity and mistrust within the aristocratic elite increased, there was a resort to force. From 1453 the Nevilles and the Percys waged a small-scale war in Yorkshire. On 22 May 1455 York clashed with Somerset at the first battle of St Albans. York won. In

The Lady Chapel, St Alban's Cathedral. The battle of St Albans on 22 May 1455 was a victory for the Yorkists: they captured Henry VI and killed the Duke of Somerset and Henry Percy, Earl of Northumberland.

THE SCOTTISH CIVIL WARS 1400–1460

Although not as well known as the Wars of the Roses in England, fifteenth-century Scotland suffered much civil conflict. Aristocratic factionalism clashed with royal authority.

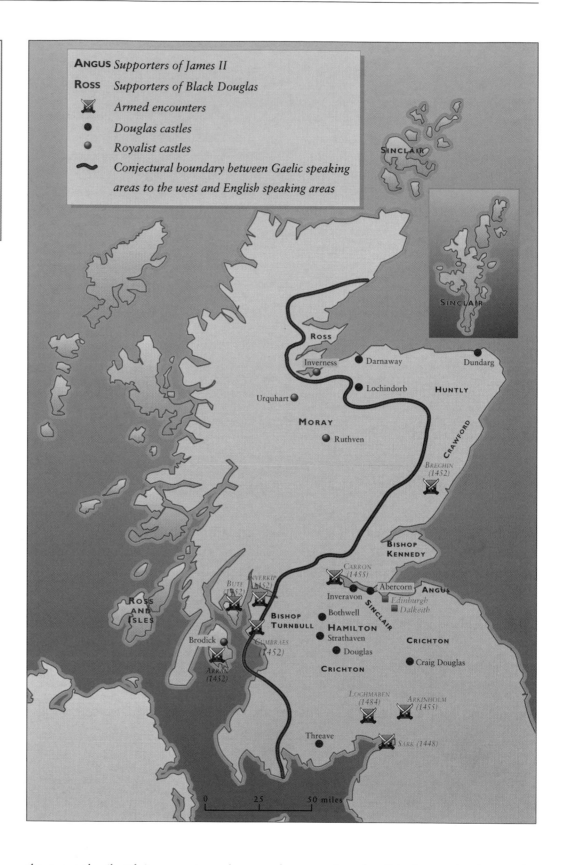

ANGUS *Supporters of James II*

ROSS *Supporters of Black Douglas*

✗ *Armed encounters*

● *Douglas castles*

● *Royalist castles*

〜 *Conjectural boundary between Gaelic speaking areas to the west and English speaking areas*

SINCLAIR

SINCLAIR

ROSS

Inverness

Darnaway

Dundarg

Urquhart

Lochindorb

HUNTLY

MORAY

Ruthven

CRAWFORD

BRECHIN (1452)

BISHOP KENNEDY

CARRON (1455)

BUTE (1452)

INVERKIP (1452)

Abercorn

ANGUS

Inveravon

SINCLAIR

Edinburgh

Dalkeith

ROSS AND ISLES

BISHOP TURNBULL

Bothwell

HAMILTON

Strathaven

Brodick

CUMBRAES (1452)

Douglas

CRICHTON

Craig Douglas

ARRAN (1452)

CRICHTON

LOCHMABEN (1484)

ARKINHOLM (1455)

Threave

SARK (1448)

0   25   50 miles

the event the 'battle' was not much more than a series of political assassinations – the Yorkists picking off their rivals. But given that those rivals were in the company of the king, it was as shocking as a full-scale battle, if not more so. Somerset and Henry Percy, 2nd Earl of Northumberland, were killed and Henry captured. This did not bring stability. York lost control of the government in 1457 and fighting resumed between the Percys and Nevilles. Fresh clashes between Yorkists and Lancastrians occurred in 1459, and, at Blore Heath on 23 September, the Nevilles under Richard, 1st Earl of Salisbury, routed the royal troops. However the Yorkists were less successful in fighting at Ludlow, and a partisan Lancastrian parliament meeting in Coventry that November attainted the leading Yorkists.

In 1460 there was once again a dramatic shift. At the battle of Northampton on 10 July, the Lancastrians were defeated, several of their leaders killed and Henry captured again. Having hitherto professed his loyalty to Henry, York now transformed the situation by claiming the throne. This was very much the last resort after a decade in which he had been politically marginalised. York was recognised as heir, but the unpopular and determined French queen, Margaret of Anjou, was not prepared to see the disinheritance of her son, Edward. She attacked, defeated and killed York at Wakefield on 29 December 1460: his severed head was adorned with a paper crown.

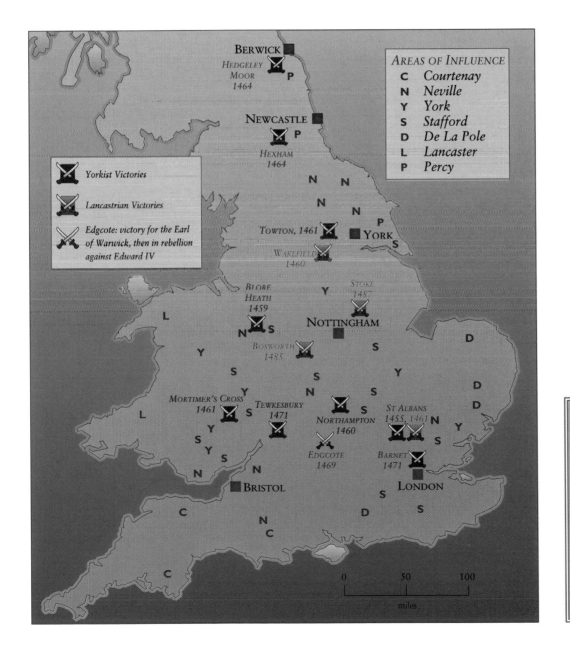

AREAS OF INFLUENCE

C Courtenay
N Neville
Y York
S Stafford
D De La Pole
L Lancaster
P Percy

Yorkist Victories

Lancastrian Victories

Edgcote: victory for the Earl of Warwick, then in rebellion against Edward IV

BERWICK

HEDGELEY MOOR 1464 P

NEWCASTLE P

HEXHAM 1464

TOWTON, 1461   YORK

WAKEFIELD 1460

BLORE HEATH 1459   STOKE 1487

NOTTINGHAM

BOSWORTH 1485

MORTIMER'S CROSS 1461   TEWKESBURY 1471   ST ALBANS 1455, 1461

NORTHAMPTON 1460

EDGCOTE 1469   BARNET 1471

BRISTOL   LONDON

0   50   100

miles

BATTLES OF THE WARS OF THE ROSES

The battles of the Wars of the Roses were far flung, although some areas, such as much of Wales, saw less conflict than others. The importance of London helped lead to battles nearby. Sieges played a smaller role in the wars than battles.

The Lilburne Tower, built in about 1325, at Dunstanburgh Castle, Northumberland. The Lancastrian fortress was besieged in 1462 and 1464.

York's ambitious and able eldest son, Edward, next claimed the throne, as Edward IV (1461–83). He was a more charismatic figure than his father. Margaret defeated Richard Neville, Earl of Warwick, the King-Maker, then a key Yorkist, at St Albans on 17 February 1461, and recovered Henry, but London defied her and she retreated north, seeking Scottish assistance with the promise of Berwick in return. At Towton, during a heavy snowstorm on Palm Sunday, 29 March 1461, the Lancastrians were heavily defeated in what was the largest and bloodiest battle ever fought in England – up to 60,000 men were involved: the number of casualties is not known. The thoroughness of Edward's victory allowed his coronation as Edward IV and brought the submission of all but the most committed Lancastrians, although it took several years before outlying parts of the realm were brought under Yorkist control. Dunstanburgh Castle, on the Northumbrian coast, was besieged in 1462 and 1464 and badly damaged. The castle, a Duchy of Lancaster fortress, was surrendered by Sir Ralph Percy in 1462 on condition he remained in control, but he swiftly betrayed Edward. In 1464, after the Lancastrian army in the north was defeated at the battles of Hedgeley Moor (25 April) and Hexham (14 May), Dunstanburgh fell to the King-Maker. His brother John was installed in the Percy estates. (Henry Percy, 3rd Earl of Northumberland, had been killed at Towton.) Other Lancastrian families also lost estates. Dunster Castle was transferred from the Luttrells to the Herberts, and not regained until after the accession of Henry VII.

Edward IV was able to restore a measure of order until he fell out with Warwick by 1469. They clashed over diplomacy and, more pointedly, over Edward's favour for the Woodvilles, relatives of the queen who challenged Warwick's dominance at court. After defeating and capturing Edward at Edgecote on 26 July 1469, Warwick seized power, but he could not maintain his authority and in 1470 he fled to France. In France, Warwick was reconciled with the exiled Margaret of Anjou and committed himself to the restoration of Henry – one of the most striking realignments in the opportunistic politics of the period, demonstrating that power rather than principle dominated some aristocratic strategies.

With French help, Warwick and his son-in-law, Edward's disloyal brother, George, Duke of Clarence, invaded in 1470. Edward was deposed and forced to flee into exile, and Henry was restored. The whirligig of fortune brought Edward back again in 1471. Having invaded with Burgundian help, he defeated and killed Warwick in thick fog at Barnet, and defeated Margaret at Tewkesbury. Henry's captured son, Edward, Prince of Wales, was killed after Tewkesbury, thus weakening Lancastrian prospects, while Henry, imprisoned in the Tower of London, was also butchered.

These ruthless killings helped return a measure of stability for Edward's regime, but there were still risings in the country and problems within the ruling house. Distrust led to killing within the royal family. Clarence had betrayed Warwick and rejoined Edward in 1471, but was sentenced to death in 1478 for treason. He was killed in the Tower, according to contemporaries drowned in a butt of malmsey wine.

Edward died at forty in 1483, solvent, but too early to leave his elder son, Edward V (1483), as an adult successor. Unlike in 1422, when the far younger Henry VI had been left to grow up as king while a strong regent directed affairs, there was a disputed succession. Edward IV's surviving brother, Richard, Duke of Gloucester, fearful of a Woodville takeover, moved swiftly. He seized power in April 1483, declaring his nephews, Edward V and Richard, Duke of York, bastards, and sending them to the Tower. Removed from view, they swiftly disappeared and their fate has long been cause for controversy. However, given Richard's brutal and decisive character, the example of his brother's ruthlessness, and the murderous nature of politics in this period, it is likely that they were killed. Contemporaries believed that they were dead and, otherwise, it would have been inconceivable for a rank outsider like Henry Tudor, son of Margaret Beaufort, the heiress of the illegitimate Lancastrian line, to seem a viable figurehead for opposition.

Richard III (1483–5) had ability and determination, and inspired trust up to the time of his usurpation, but not thereafter. He had invaded Scotland successfully in 1482 and regained Berwick, so his record was

good. But his seizure of the throne divided the Yorkists, and Richard was left with only a slender base of support. This was shown in October 1483 when the Woodvilles and Henry, 2nd Duke of Buckingham, who had played a major role in Richard's seizure of the throne, rebelled. Richard moved swiftly, dispersing the rebels, most of whom made their peace or escaped abroad. Buckingham was beheaded. Richard Edgcumbe of Cotehele escaped his nemesis by fooling his pursuers that the cap he had thrown into the river with a stone in it marked the spot of his death while fleeing across the Tamar. Cotehele then became the southern base of one of Richard's northern allies, Edward Redmane of Levens and Harewood.

Richard III was unable to consolidate his position before the next challenge to his authority was mounted in 1485. Thanks to the killing of Henry VI and his son Edward, Henry Tudor was now the Lancastrian claimant, although he had no real title to the throne and was not an issue until Richard III's usurpation blew the succession wide open. At Christmas 1483, Henry promised to marry Elizabeth of York, daughter of Edward IV. This helped to give him credibility in Yorkist eyes.

Invading through Wales in 1485 with the help of French and Scottish troops, Henry had little support in England, but Richard was similarly bereft. At the battle of Bosworth, Richard was abandoned by the Stanleys (an important family who had

The south front of Cotehele, Cornwall. Richard Edgcumbe, supporter of the Duke of Buckingham's rebellion, abandoned his home as Richard III's men moved to disperse the rebels. Edgcumbe pretended to drown in the River Tamar. In fact, he escaped to Brittany, joined Henry Tudor and fought for him at Bosworth.

Richard III, 1452–85, king from 1483. This portrait was faithfully copied between 1516 and 1522 from an original made during Richard's reign. The fourth son of Richard of York, he rose to prominence thanks to the instability created by the Wars of the Roses, but the narrow basis of his support proved fatal when Henry Tudor invaded in 1485. Richard's reputation has remained very controversial to this day. Shakespeare's negative portrayal was particularly influential.

brought their troops to the battlefield). Northumberland's troops did not fight. Unlike Edward IV, Richard did not escape his challengers. The killing of Richard at Bosworth, following on the earlier deaths of much of the House of York – the Princes in the Tower, Clarence, and Richard's only son, Edward, who had died in April 1484 – helped Henry to establish his position. Clarence's son, Warwick, was still alive and Henry made sure he had possession of him before entering London. Other key followers of Richard were swiftly removed. Sir Henry Trenowth, who had chased Edgcumbe at Cotehele, was now in turn driven into the sea at Bodrugan's Leap by Edgcumbe, who had fought for Henry at Bosworth. Henry's marriage to Elizabeth of York in 1486 helped to unify the two factions, a process symbolised by the replacement of the white rose of York and the red rose of the Beauforts (and maybe of Lancaster) by the Tudor rose.

This was not, however, the end of the Wars of the Roses. There were still rebellious Yorkists, although relatively few, and they, and hostile foreign rulers, supported the cause of two impostors, Lambert Simnel and Perkin Warbeck. The former claimed to be Clarence's son and was then held in the Tower; the latter said he was the younger of the two princes, who were, in fact, probably killed in the Tower on Richard's orders. Simnel was defeated at Stoke – the last battle of the Wars of the Roses – on 16 June 1487, and given a job as a turnspit in the palace kitchen. In the same battle, one of the major supporters of the rising, John De La Pole, Earl of Lincoln, who had a good claim to the throne as eldest son of John, 2nd Duke of Suffolk, and Edward IV's sister Elizabeth, was killed. Warbeck was captured in 1497 and hanged in 1499. The importance attributed to Warbeck's and Simnel's conspiracies was a testimony to Henry VII's insecurity. In a sign of this, money was being spent on York's town wall in 1487. Stoke was a hard fought battle, and larger than Bosworth, and Henry knew from Richard's fate that kings could be overthrown all too easily. If Simnel had won Stoke a Yorkist bandwagon might have begun to roll.

Bosworth is popularly held to mark the close of the Middle Ages in England. Its significance can be exaggerated, but the establishment of Henry VII and the Tudor dynasty is an appropriate point to take stock. By bringing the Wars of the Roses to a close, Henry helped to bring a measure of greater unity to the kingdom. Over the previous decades, civil strife had contributed to, as much as it had stemmed from, a serious crisis, both in law and order and, more generally, in royal governance.

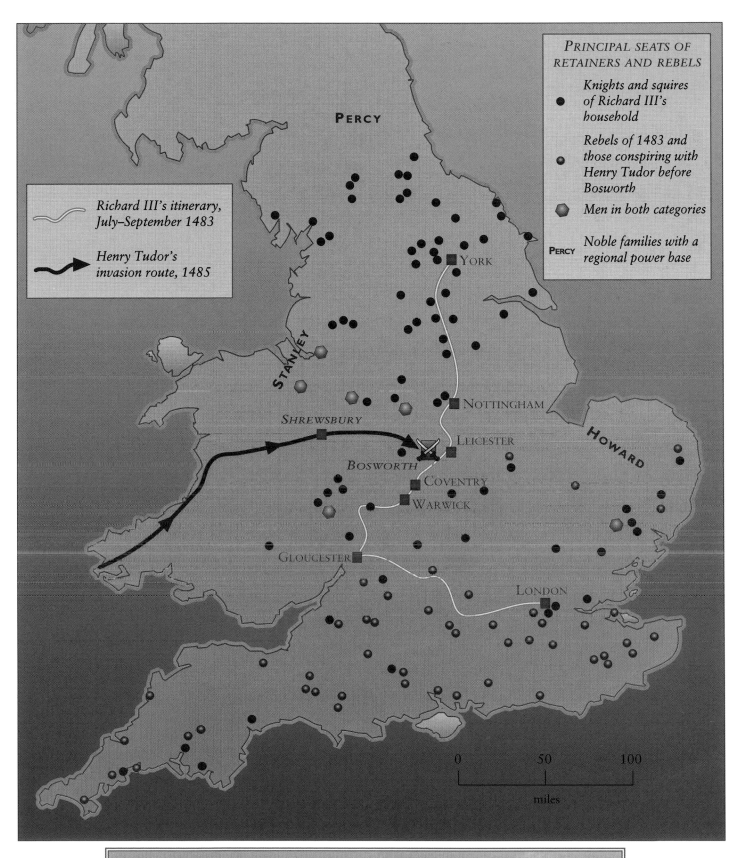

PRINCIPAL SEATS OF RETAINERS AND REBELS

● *Knights and squires of Richard III's household*

◉ *Rebels of 1483 and those conspiring with Henry Tudor before Bosworth*

⬡ *Men in both categories*

PERCY *Noble families with a regional power base*

~~~ *Richard III's itinerary, July–September 1483*

➤ *Henry Tudor's invasion route, 1485*

PERCY

STANLEY

HOWARD

YORK

NOTTINGHAM

SHREWSBURY

LEICESTER

BOSWORTH

COVENTRY

WARWICK

GLOUCESTER

LONDON

0   50   100

miles

THE ROAD TO BOSWORTH

Richard III's support base was limited, a consequence of his background and policies.

27

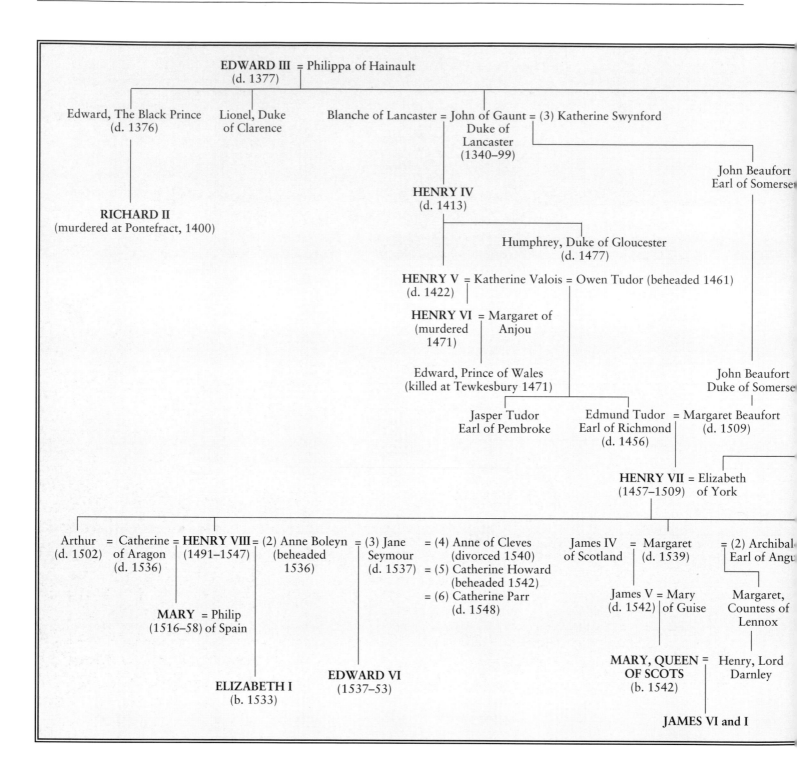

Aristocratic factionalism had been more important than Parliament and other national institutions of government. Although it is difficult to capture in maps, the unity of the kingdom was eroded considerably. The factions might centre their activities on control of the kingdom and none sought to break away from it, but the reliance of the monarchs on powerful aristocratic allies made it difficult to control them. Instead, aristocrats took over local government. Henry VI and Edward IV allowed power in the Palatinate of Durham to pass to the junior branch of the Nevilles. Ralph, 2nd Earl of Westmorland, the leader of this branch, engaged in private warfare with his uncles

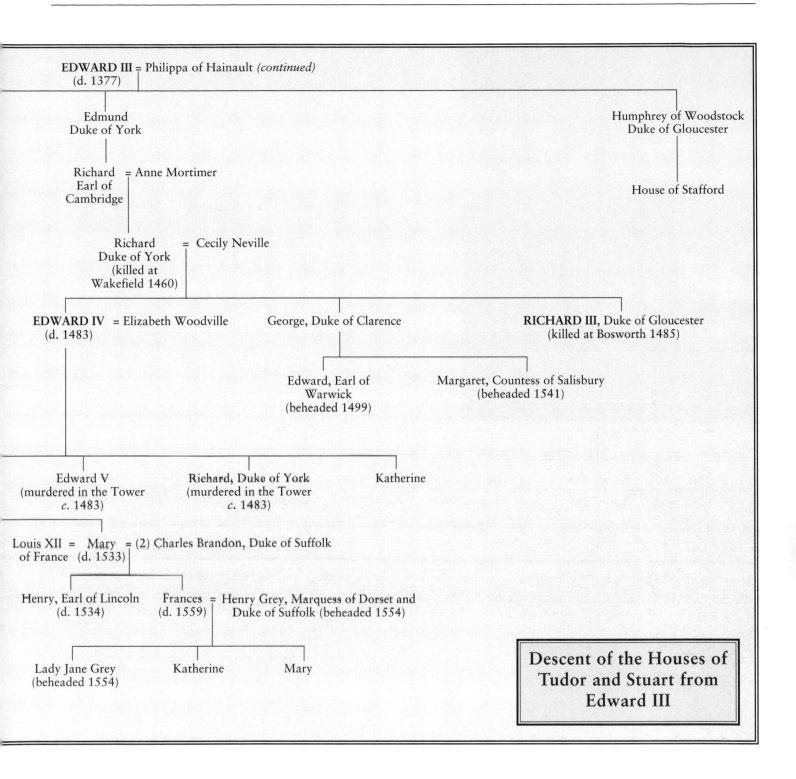

EDWARD III = Philippa of Hainault *(continued)*
(d. 1377)

Edmund
Duke of York

Humphrey of Woodstock
Duke of Gloucester

Richard = Anne Mortimer
Earl of
Cambridge

House of Stafford

Richard = Cecily Neville
Duke of York
(killed at
Wakefield 1460)

EDWARD IV = Elizabeth Woodville   George, Duke of Clarence   **RICHARD III**, Duke of Gloucester
(d. 1483)   (killed at Bosworth 1485)

Edward, Earl of   Margaret, Countess of Salisbury
Warwick   (beheaded 1541)
(beheaded 1499)

Edward V   Richard, Duke of York   Katherine
(murdered in the Tower   (murdered in the Tower
c. 1483)   c. 1483)

Louis XII = Mary = (2) Charles Brandon, Duke of Suffolk
of France   (d. 1533)

Henry, Earl of Lincoln   Frances = Henry Grey, Marquess of Dorset and
(d. 1534)   (d. 1559)   Duke of Suffolk (beheaded 1554)

Lady Jane Grey   Katherine   Mary
(beheaded 1554)

> **Descent of the Houses of Tudor and Stuart from Edward III**

(children of his grandfather Ralph, 1st Earl, by his second marriage), over the Middleham estates which had been left to them through the influence of their mother. Such disputes could affect politics at the 'centre'.

Henry VI and Edward IV, like their two predecessors, spent little time in the north, in part a consequence of the decline in importance of relations with Scotland since the times of Edwards I, II and III. Edward IV relied on aristocrats whose power he had developed, especially Lord Hastings, his Chamberlain, and William Herbert of Raglan, made Earl of Pembroke, although less totally than Henry VI had done: in the latter's

The gatehouse at Oxburgh Hall, Norfolk. Built in 1482 by Sir Edmund Bedingfield, the design of the manor testified not only to the status of its owner but also to the need of the propertied to rely on their own resources rather than on the power of royal government.

case, the Dukes of Suffolk and Somerset played crucial roles. Edward had created new jurisdictions under aristocratic control: three new lordships for the already powerful Herberts in Wales, and the Duke of Norfolk's liberty in East Anglia. Such jurisdictions were not undermined until an Act of Parliament in 1536, although it is important not to exaggerate the degree of aristocratic autonomy and the extent to which it threatened stability. The Duke of Norfolk was not particularly powerful, and after the death of John, the 4th Duke, in 1476, Edward IV married the heiress, Anne, to his infant second son, Richard, Duke of York, and absorbed the duchy into the crown estate.

Blood feuds, such as that between the houses of Beaufort and York, and struggles for regional dominance, such as that in the north between the Nevilles and the Percys, and smaller, but still intense disputes elsewhere, were scarcely conducive to stable government. Warwick's brother, George Neville, became Archbishop of York in 1465. Having made John Neville Earl of Northumberland, Edward IV then found that he could not rule effectively without Percy help, and in 1470 he restored the earldom to the Percys. John Neville was killed at the battle of Barnet where Warwick the King-Maker died. As Duke of Gloucester, the future Richard III reimposed governmental control over much of the north, including County Durham – but he was the northern heir of the junior Nevilles by his marriage to Anne Neville.

County families frequently owed their position and success to aristocratic patrons. In some counties, such as Cheshire and Derbyshire, there were no dominant magnates other than the crown, and links between the gentry were crucial. In other areas, powerful magnates dominated the situation: for example, William de la Pole, 1st Duke of Suffolk, and his son, also William, the 2nd Duke, in East Anglia; the Courtenay earls of Devon in Devon; the Beauchamp earls of Warwick, and then Richard Neville, Earl of Warwick, successively, in Warwickshire; and Lord Stanley in the north-west. This aristocratic leadership was even more marked in Scotland. The course of the civil wars affected these power bases. When Henry, Duke of Lancaster, became king in 1399, the Lancastrian power base in the north became a valuable support for the crown, but the fate of the dynasty also affected the power base. Leicestershire was dominated by the Beaumonts until 1460, when John, Viscount Beaumont, was killed at the battle of Northampton and William, Lord Hastings was established by the Yorkists as the local magnate. Hastings came to control government across much of the Midlands, and was thus able to raise troops, including a crucial 3,000 men for Edward IV in 1471. At least nineteen of his retainers became sheriffs in Derbyshire, Leicestershire, Staffordshire and Warwickshire between 1461 and 1487.

Local landowners were granted control of royal estates and castles, and the situation did not cease with the advent of the Tudors. William Ludlow, a king's serjeant, but also a Wiltshire landowner and MP for Ludgershall, was appointed Keeper of the royal manor and castle at Ludgershall for life in 1433. Henry Bridges was appointed Keeper in 1510, a post renewed to his son for a forty-year term in 1539.

Moats and defensive walls encircled new manor houses of the period, such as Great Chalfield Manor in Wiltshire which was completed in 1480. In 1482 Sir Edmund Bedingfield, an East Anglian landowner, was given a licence by Edward IV to 'build,

Tattershall Castle

What survives of Tattershall Castle in the flat fen country of east Lincolnshire is the work of Ralph, 3rd Baron Cromwell (1393–1456), who from 1433 to 1443 was Henry VI's Lord Treasurer. A veteran of Agincourt, who had also been a negotiator at the Treaty of Troyes and present at the trial and burning of Joan of Arc, Cromwell was an ally of the Beauforts who used the large income from his government posts to build status, not only at Tattershall but also on his other medieval estates at South Wingfield Manor, Derbyshire, and Collyweston, Northamptonshire. Cromwell also lived in state with a household of at least 100 people in Tattershall. The Great Tower was built of brick, then a relatively novel and therefore prestigious building material. It was probably as much for show as for defence, but the combination of the tower, moats and gatehouses with Cromwell's large retinue would have made it a formidable position. Nevertheless, the comforts of Tattershall were a sign that Cromwell expected to live peaceably in this fairly inaccessible part of eastern England.

The east front of the tower of Tattershall Castle built about 1440 by Ralph Cromwell, with moat and bridge.

Determined in pursuit of his own interests, as he showed in a prominent, long-standing dispute with another veteran, Sir John Gra, over a manor, Cromwell was implicated in encouraging York and the Nevilles, his relatives by marriage, to attack Henry VI at the first battle of St Albans. He died shortly after, but the subsequent fate of the estate reflected the disruption of the period, although the castle itself was undamaged. Cromwell died childless, much of his estate was bequeathed for religious and educational purposes (including an endowment to pay for 3,000 masses to be said in his name), his two Yorkist nephews by marriage both died in the Wars of the Roses, and Tattershall was confiscated by the crown after the battle of Barnet in 1471.

make and construct walls and towers with stone, lime and gravel, around and below his Manor of Oxburgh in the County of Norfolk, and enclose that Manor with walls and towers of this kind; also embattle, crenellate, and machicolate [create openings in parapets from where stones, etc. could be dropped on attackers] those walls and towers'. Such features were a claim to status and a product of what it was thought a nobleman's residence ought to look like. They were also a testimony to the need of the

Elizabeth of York, 1465–1503, eldest child of Edward IV. In her youth she was the tool of dynastic schemes, marriages being planned to George Neville, Duke of Bedford (1469), and to the Dauphin of France (1478). Her marriage with Henry VII (1486) helped consolidate his position on the throne.

propertied to rely on their own resources and local alliances, rather than on the power of royal government. The extent to which the fortified features in late medieval domestic architecture were defensive has been questioned, and it is clear that they were in part a mark of status, but they also affirmed strength in local politics.

The smaller houses often drew on the architectural language of castles, a notable example being Tattershall Castle, a fortified tower built in about 1440 for Ralph, Lord Cromwell, the Lord Treasurer of England. Castles such as Elmley in Warwickshire, held by the Beauchamps from about 1130 to 1446, were both a symbol and a reality of regional power, although there were few sieges in the Wars of the Roses: it was a conflict of battles. Less prominent families also built castles. A castle at Oxwich, a possession of the Mansels, one of the leading Glamorgan gentry families, was first specifically mentioned in 1459.

However, periods of actual conflict were fairly short (months or years rather than decades), and, by continental standards, England was peaceful. There was no equivalent to the advances in fortification technique seen in Italy in the late fifteenth century, nor to the massive expenditure on urban fortifications seen in much of Europe. Town defences in England were useful, but they could not prevent trouble. Exeter was walled, but that did not prevent the Earl of Devon from occupying the city in 1455, ransacking the houses of opponents and breaking into the cathedral.

Baronial conflicts did not suddenly cease when Henry VII came to the throne in 1485, and it is difficult to avoid a sense of *déjà-vu* when considering the power and goals of John Dudley, 1st Duke of Northumberland, in the 1550s and the suspicions cast upon successive Howards and Dudleys under Henry VIII and Elizabeth. Both York and Dudley were mistrusted and neither was the norm, but it is significant that such figures could be thrown up long after the Wars of the Roses were over.

Chance played a major role in politics and in maintaining stability. This was also shown in royal marriages. Henry VII's union with Elizabeth of York was critical to the cementing of the new Tudor dynasty. But for two other marriages, England again might have faced the possibility of a 'Roses'-style war of aristocratic ambition. The first of these unions was between Henry VII's daughter Mary and James IV of Scotland; this was to result in the Stuart succession of James I of England and VI of Scotland. The second, more tenuously, was the marriage of Charles I's sister Elizabeth to Frederick V, Elector Palatine of the Rhine: Elizabeth and Frederick's daughter Sophie became the wife of Ernest, Elector of Hanover, and this was instrumental in the latter house's succession to the British Throne in 1714.

Yet, for all its similarity to the earlier period there was also a change in the late fifteenth century. Strong royal authority was an eventual consequence of the collapse of order in the 1450s and 1483–5. The first beneficiary of the Wars of the Roses had been Edward IV, who offered a return to stable government. Henry VII then benefited from Richard III's demonstration that order was vulnerable. The end of civil war in England in 1487, and the consolidation of royal authority in Scotland under James IV (1473–1513, r. 1488–1513), who, in 1493, enforced his power in the distant Hebrides, provided opportunities for developments that had earlier been inhibited by decades of strife.

TWO

Early Modern Society

The society of Tudor England, and, to a lesser extent, of sixteenth-century Wales and Scotland, can be glimpsed more readily than that of the previous century. Partly thanks to printing, a rise in literacy and population, more extensive governmental activity, and the nationalisation of the church, records, both private and State, are more copious, a situation that very much extends to maps. There are also more surviving buildings, especially secular buildings, than for the previous century, and more of the material culture, the world of things.

Thanks both to the greater use and development of vernacular languages, rather than Latin, and also through the literature of the period, especially the oft-seen and cited works of William Shakespeare (1564–1616), the people seem more close and more vivid than their predecessors. The use of English was a fifteenth-century development that was pushed further under the Tudors when it became the language of authority and of a culture that still echoes today. In addition, thanks to more lifelike and more numerous portraits, for example by Holbein, we can see Tudor courtiers as we cannot see their fifteenth-century predecessors.

Yet there are still many features of the society of the period that are not readily apparent. First, and foremost, came the rise of population, which can be charted although, prior to the first national census of 1801, all figures must be approximate. The English population had remained low from the Black Death to the early sixteenth century, but it then more than doubled – from under 2.5 million to over 4 million by 1600 and about 5 million by 1651 – before entering another period of stagnation that lasted until the 1740s. The population of Scotland also rose – to about 1 million by 1650 – and that of Wales from about 226,000 in the 1540s, to about 342,000 in 1670. These aggregate figures, however,

Illustration from Rösslin's textbook The Byrthe of Mankynde (translated by Thomas Ranalde, 1554) shows a birthing chair being used and a horoscope being cast.

Inside the gatehouse of the Black Gate, Newcastle upon Tyne. Medieval fortifications continued to play a prominent role in the sixteenth-century townscape. In Newcastle, the castle, much of the walls and the parish churches were preserved, although there had been development of a friary site. Until after the Civil Wars, the walls largely delimited the town. The seventeenth century saw the construction of prominent secular buildings, the rebuilding of the Guildhall and Exchange (1655–8) and the new Mansion House (1691).

conceal often terrifying unpredictability and much misery. James IV of Scotland (1473–1513) had six legitimate children, but only one survived infancy. Sir George Graham, a Cumbrian landlord, died 'of a fever' in 1658, at the age of thirty-three, leaving six children under the age of six. His wife remarried, to a widower, Sir George Fletcher MP, who already had five children, but whose first wife had died in childbirth. Yet the new couple had four more children and the second husband died aged sixty-seven, indicating the variety of demographic fortune. Although the upper classes were likely to live longer, vulnerability to death and disease crossed social boundaries.

Although the analysis of past population trends is far from easy, it seems clear that the increase in population was due largely to a fall in mortality, not least the retreat of the plague. This became less frequent, though there were further virulent outbreaks, as in 1499–1500, 1518, 1538, 1563, 1603, 1605, 1625 and 1636. Local, as well as national, consequences could still be catastrophic. About one-fifth of the population of Manchester died in 1605. Newcastle had outbreaks in 1589, 1636 and 1675, with reported deaths respectively of 1,727, 5,037 and 924 out of a population of about 9,000 in 1548 and 16,000 in about 1665.

A population increase like that in Newcastle was only possible thanks to migration from rural areas, which was indeed important to all cities. These rural areas could not only be hard hit by disease, but also by bad harvests, such as those in north Scotland in the 1690s. Even when the plague retreated, other diseases quickly replaced it. The 1660s 'plague' in Eyam, Derbyshire, was in fact anthrax, although no less virulent for the diagnosis.

A rise in fertility stemming from a small decrease in the average age of women at marriage was probably also important in pushing up the population in the sixteenth century. The absence of artificial contraceptives (although, thanks to *coitus interruptus* and infanticide, not of contraception), and the general abstinence from sexual intercourse before betrothal, ensured that the average age of marriage was crucial to fertility. Infanticide was employed as a form of post-birth contraception.

The rise in population dramatically altered the circumstances of the bulk of the population. After the Black Death, labour shortages had led to comparatively high wages which, combined with relatively stable prices and low rents, offered a bearable standard of living to the majority of the working population and their dependants. It gave rise to a 'moral economy' designed to ensure that populations were fed by local harvests before surpluses were sold for profit.

The sixteenth-century population increase, started and fuelled inflation, and led to a rise in consumer demand, so that food prices rose faster than wages. The demand for food caused agricultural land rents to rise proportionately more than wages; and the resulting situation hit both tenants and those with little or no land. Agrarian capitalism became more intense. Landlords tried to increase the yield of their customary estates or to destroy the system of tenure on customary terms; and only occasionally did tenants combine to resist their landlords in the courts. Entry fines and rent were increased, and customary tenants bought out or evicted, in order to make way for fixed-term leases. Much of the peasantry lost status, and became little different from poorly paid wage labourers. Economic expansion from the 1480s could not provide employment for the rising numbers of poor; while economic change lessened labour security, for example through guild membership, and, instead, ensured that casual labour became even more common. This exacerbated insecurity. Furthermore, the poverty of the bulk of the population depressed demand for manufactured goods, a conclusion also later made by the 'pessimists' when considering parliamentary enclosure in 1780–1830.

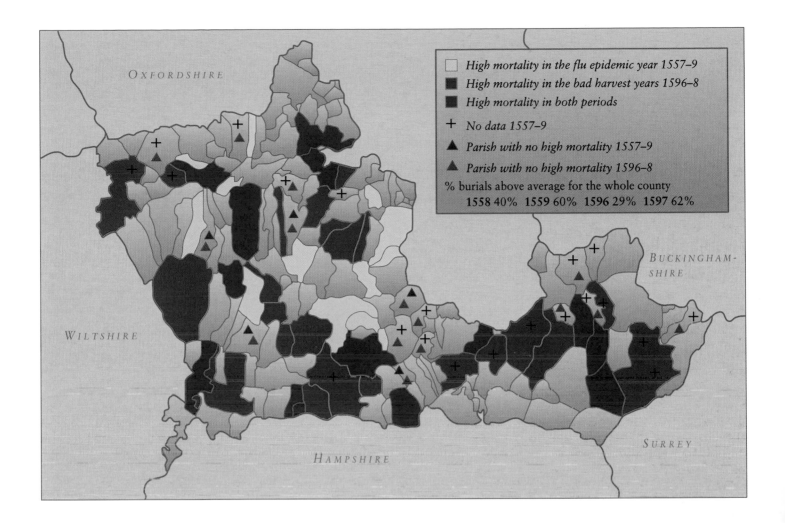

High mortality in the flu epidemic year 1557–9
High mortality in the bad harvest years 1596–8
High mortality in both periods
+ No data 1557–9
▲ Parish with no high mortality 1557–9
▲ Parish with no high mortality 1596–8
% burials above average for the whole county
1558 40% 1559 60% 1596 29% 1597 62%

OXFORDSHIRE

BUCKINGHAM-SHIRE

WILTSHIRE

SURREY

HAMPSHIRE

The growing numbers of paupers and vagrants greatly concerned the government, although for law-and-order far more than for humanitarian reasons. Poverty pressed on the neighbourliness within the parish community that was important to social cohesion, and to the maintenance of order. A number of Acts of Parliament sought to control the problem. The 1495 Act Against Vagabonds and Beggars was followed by a series of Poor Laws – passed in 1531, 1536, 1572, 1598 and 1601 – that extended local responsibilities. Compulsory poor rates were introduced in 1572, and in 1598 the relief of poverty was made the task of the individual parish. This reflected the limitations of central government and the local nature of health, welfare and education provision. The restricted scope of national government's ability to help its subjects in their day-to-day needs, however, contrasted with the willingness to reach into the localities to seize church wealth in the 1530s and 1540s (see pp. 61–3).

Poor relief distinguished between the deserving and the undeserving poor, a distinction made by those in power, as they struggled to contain the situation and were driven to regulate, and thus define, it. Children, the elderly and the ill fell into the first category, able-bodied men into the second. This distinction was strongly made from the late fourteenth century, when the demographic collapse, after the Black Death, and the difficulty in finding workers led to a strong sense that the able-bodied could easily find employment and must therefore be lazy or greedy or both if unemployed. Thus the model was established before the Tudor period during which work genuinely was not as

EPIDEMICS IN BERKSHIRE IN THE SIXTEENTH CENTURY

Poor harvests led to greater losses through disease as the poor were hit by malnourishment. The terrible harvests of 1555 and 1556 were followed by a disastrous epidemic, probably of influenza. This pattern was repeated in the 1590s, as bad harvests from 1594 onwards led to high death rates, especially in the winter and in the late spring when food was scarce and costly.

The central tower, Durham Cathedral, dating from after about 1465 with the higher stage built c. 1483–90. Many of the Dean and Chapter's tenants joined the Northern Rising in 1569, in response as much to economic as to religious grievances.

easy to come by. The able-bodied were treated harshly, their inability to find work ignored in favour of the notion that they were reprehensible rogues and vagabonds. In 1504 the Scottish Parliament banned begging by the able-bodied. Poor relief for those deemed worthy was far from generous. Towns such as Ipswich spent much on food and entertainment for civic feasts, while care for the poor was allocated frugally. However, from the mid-sixteenth century there was formal recognition of the able-bodied worker unable to find paid work, i.e. the labouring poor.

Economic change, and the impact of the market for food and wages, led to anxiety – an aspect of the remoulding of society under the impact of population increase and the Reformation. For much of the population, there was scant prospect of advancement and social mobility was to be feared. Economic pressure led to widespread malnutrition among the poor and to some starvation. Most folktales centred on peasant poverty, and, in many, the desire for an unending source of food played a major role. Malnutrition stunted growth, hit energy levels, and reduced resistance to ill-health. Poor diet encouraged colon parasitic infection, hepatitis and salmonella. The poor were also colder than their more affluent contemporaries and more commonly in the dark.

Bad harvests and disruptive changes in the rural economy could make the situation volatile, taking misery to the point of desperation. The severe winter of 1740–1 led to a doubling of theft figures in Lindsey in Lincolnshire, and, more generally, crime rates, at least in part, appear to have been related to economic circumstances.

The same was true of more general breakdowns of law and order, although these were frequently seen as attempts to impose traditional norms of behaviour, the 'moral economy', on those who were portrayed as changing society. The bad harvests of the 1590s and early 1600s led to rural disturbances, notably the Midlands rising of 1607 which affected Leicestershire, Northamptonshire and Warwickshire. They may also have been responsible for the increased reference to debt in Essex wills of the period. Landlords who vigorously sought to raise their incomes were unpopular. Many tenants of the Dean and Chapter of Durham joined the Northern Rising of 1569 as a response to their economic as much as their religious policies. Seventy years later, church tenants in the county organised resistance to their landlords' agrarian policies. More generally, enclosure of common land by landlords led to bitterness. (Enclosure was the process of (re)organising land into private holdings by reorganising communal holdings.) It reflected a decline in paternalism, a new relationship between 'employer' and labour, and a search for profit that hit the poor, especially if it was designed, as it often was, to further a switch from arable to pastoral farming, and, therefore, to drive people from the land. Enclosure riots were frequent, especially, but not only, in the Midlands. At Osmington in Dorset in 1624 new hedges were torn down and an effigy of the landlord was hanged; hardly indicative of social subordination. Economic pressures helped to dissolve deference as well as paternalism.

Landlord attacks on customary tenant rights in Cumbria led in 1621 to a critical public meeting and a resolution to resist the process. In 1622 James I wrote to the Bishop of Carlisle, complaining about 'tumultuous and evil-disposed persons, unlawful assemblies . . . and seditious libels'. A group of lords brought an action in Star Chamber against the tenants, but, in the event, the legal resistance of the well-organised and ably led tenants blunted the assault and the judges found for the customary rights. There was popular opposition, especially in the 1620s and 1630s, to drainage schemes in the Fens, Hatfield Chase and the Somerset Levels that threatened to extend arable farming at the expense of traditional lifestyles. At Wicken Fen in Cambridgeshire, drainage on behalf of William, 1st of the Russell dukes of Bedford led to popular resistance. The disruption of the Civil War provided an opportunity to overthrow enclosures, as in County Durham in early 1642. In addition, across the country, poaching reflected the limitations of social subordination. The young Shakespeare was allegedly brought up for poaching before Sir Thomas Lucy in his hall at Charlecote, and subsequently satirised him as Justice Shallow in *The Merry Wives of Windsor* (an imperfect draft was printed in 1602 but the play is probably earlier).

Although food and enclosure riots were feared by the elites, there was no social explosion in England, Scotland or Wales prior to the Civil Wars. Indeed, it is ironic that rebellion, when it came, was by the social elites, first in Scotland in 1638 and then in England and Wales in 1642. Instead of any revolution by the poor, there was a steady pressure of official and social constraints on the weaker members of the community. These constraints reflected and sustained social norms and the distribution of power, and are impossible to map. They included measures against bridal pregnancy and illegitimacy, the insistence, in opposition to folk practices, on

In 1629 the villagers of Bassingham, south-west of Lincoln, submitted this petition in favour of enclosure. They complained about the fact that their stock had a long walk to the pasture because of the open fields. Bassingham was eventually enclosed by Act of Parliament; it was not one of the older private enclosures.

Wicken Fen, Cambridgeshire, a view of Drainer's Dyke, which is probably the oldest to run across the Sedge Fen. It dates from the seventeenth century. Drainage on behalf of William, 1st of the Russell Dukes of Bedford, prompted popular resistance.

a formal church wedding as the only source of a valid marriage, and attempts in some parishes to prevent the poor from marrying and having children. Illegitimacy was regarded as morally unacceptable and as likely to cause a burden on the poor rates. Church wardens presented people to the church courts for a wide variety of moral offences, including adultery and selling alcohol at the time of church services. Lay religious observance was seen as central to morality.

The enforcement of ecclesiastical sanctions underlined the nature of power in society and the public nature of Christian sanctions. It also reflected the sense that religion and morality were not separate from each other, nor jointly separate from secular life, nor spheres in which individual free will could play a role. At Wimborne Minster in Dorset in the 1590s, presentments included 'the widow Sanders' for keeping 'a youth in her house' (a breach of public propriety) and two men for conspicuously ignoring the demands of religious conformity; William Lucas 'for playing of a fiddle in the time of God's service', and Christopher Sylar 'for sitting by the fire in the sermon time and when we asked him if he would go to the church he said he would go when he listeth'.

Justices of the peace and constables maintained a parallel jurisdiction to the church courts, that was firmly enforced with physical punishments. Parishes had their stocks and whipping posts. Most crime was petty theft, and most petty theft was the poor stealing from the poor.

The practice of the law favoured the rich. As Shakespeare suggested in *King Lear* (*c.* 1605), the poor had less access to justice:

> Through tatter'd clothes small vices do appear;
> Robes and furr'd gowns hide all. Plate sin with gold,
> And the strong lance of justice hurtless breaks;
> Arm it in rags, a pigmy's straw doth pierce it.

In his pamphlet *Work for Armourers* (1609), the playwright Thomas Dekker condemned enclosures and the treatment of the poor. The poor were definitely cut off from the growing comfort that characterised the wealthier sections of the community, with their finer, sometimes sumptuous, clothes, and larger and healthier dwellings. The tax assessments of the better off were low and, as landlords, they benefited from the rising agricultural demand that stemmed from a growing population, either by farming on their own demesne or by raising rents. This helped to sustain the consumption

Montacute and the Wealth of the Phelips

One of the best preserved of Elizabethan mansions is Montacute in Somerset. Constructed in the 1590s for Sir Edward Phelips, a successful lawyer and MP, the house was built on land sold by the crown after the dissolution of the nearby monastery, as were many other mansions of the period. The Phelips were 'new men', the first identifiable ancestor of the builder being his great-grandfather Thomas, who in the 1460s rose in the service of the Brooke family from yeoman to gentleman. His son Richard became a royal official and MP, and survived accusations of extortion and oppression of the tenants of the Grey family's estates for which he was Surveyor-General. Richard Phelips found it difficult to satisfy the Exchequer with his accounts as lessee of the Customs of Poole. Richard's son, Thomas, was involved in a prison escape, but, thereafter, he followed a career as office-holder and MP. His youngest son, the future Sir Edward of Montacute, cemented the family's rising position in the West Country.

Ability, sharp practice and connections were all crucial to the Phelips family. By these means they sought, like other families who made their way in government, commerce or the law, to establish a landed position. The family had made its money through office-holding and the law, like Sir William Cordell, who built Melford Hall on the manor that had belonged to the abbey of Bury St Edmunds, and Sir Richard Shuttleworth, who built Gawthorpe Hall in Lancashire in the 1600s. These men did not fund the construction of their great houses off the backs of sheep as did many other rising families of the period, for example the Spencers of Althorp, and Walter Jones, a successful wool merchant, who bought the estate of Chastleton and built Chastleton House in c. 1610–12.

Montacute is a masterpiece in oolitic limestone, glowing in summer evenings. It was intended to impress. Its splendour proclaimed status. The master mason was almost certainly William Arnold, who also worked for George Luttrell at Dunster. Status and wealth were prominently displayed inside. Armorial stained glass and elaborate screen and oak panelling adorned the Great Hall; armorial glass and an ornate plaster frieze and ceiling decorated the Great Chamber. The inventory drawn up at the death of Edward's son, Sir Robert (1586–1638), listed gold and silver plate which alone was valued at £470, equivalent to about £10,000 in 2000.

View of the exterior of Montacute House, Somerset, a glittering Elizabethan mansion, built in the 1590s for Sir Edward Phelips. The west front was altered in 1780, by a Phelips descendant.

Hardwick Hall, Derbyshire, is one of the most impressive examples of surviving Elizabethan 'prodigy' houses, built with a royal visit in mind. The layout takes account of the needs of the travelling court.

patterns of the wealthy. The land market expanded greatly as a consequence of the Dissolution of the monasteries in the 1530s, and the Dissolution also provided major opportunities for building. Nevertheless, conspicuous consumption could lead to serious problems, and many aristocrats had to sell land, particularly in 1590–1610. Wealth and the drive for status were tapped by James I when in 1611 he invented the title of Baronet as a way to raise money at a price of £1,085.

Sir Richard Robartes not only became a baronet in 1621 and in 1625 paid £10,000 to become Baron Robartes of Truro, but also in 1620 bought the estate of Lanhydrock and began building a new house. One of the most obvious manifestations of elite consumption was the building or renovation of a large number of mansions, although much of the building of the period has been swept aside or obscured, often due to subsequent construction. Wallington in Northumbria, for example, survives as the eighteenth-century home of the Blacketts, but, on the site, their predecessors, the Fenwicks, had built a stone house before the mid-sixteenth century. Dunham Massey survives as it was left in 1758 by George, 2nd Earl of Warrington, not as the Tudor house built by Sir George Booth. In the 1690s William Blathwayt totally transformed the Tudor house at Dyrham Park. Osterley Park, remodelled by Robert Adam in 1761, was earlier a Tudor house. Lyme Park was transformed by the Venetian architect Giacomo Leoni in the 1720s, but much of what had been built in the 1590s remained untouched. Leoni also built Clandon Park to replace an earlier Elizabethan house.

Much still survives from the sixteenth century, however. One of the most splendid examples is Hardwick Hall in Derbyshire, described by contemporaries as 'more glass than wall'. Built for Bess of Hardwick, it was almost certainly designed by Robert Smythson, an outstanding English architect who was also largely responsible for Longleat. Both are examples of the so-called Elizabethan 'prodigy houses', built with an eye to royal progresses and with the needs of a visiting court reflected in their layout. ('Prodigy' comes from the Latin *prodigium* – out of the ordinary.) Fountains Hall and Chastleton House, were probably designed by Smythson. Charlecote Park, with its fine chimneys, was visited by Queen Elizabeth I in 1572. Ironically, she built nothing of importance herself.

Many more modest but still impressive country houses survive from the Elizabethan period. Examples include Melford Hall in Suffolk, Benthall Hall and Wilderhope Manor in Shropshire, and Eastbury House, now surrounded by a Barking housing estate. Many such Tudor houses were timber framed with close studding. Their interior layout reflected the growing division between 'private' and 'public' space. These houses also reflected the expansion of the number of gentlemen in the period. The gentry benefited from their access to education, their under-assessment for taxation, and their role in the law, and in the agricultural and industrial expansion of the period.

Building was not restricted to Elizabeth's reign. Major houses were constructed earlier in the century, for example The Vyne in Hampshire built for Henry VIII's Lord Chamberlain, William, 1st Lord Sandys, and Hampton Court for Cardinal Wolsey; and also in the reign of her successor, James I (1603–25). Houses were both built and extended; and there was also much landscaping. Lacock Abbey was converted into a house by William Sharington, who had been granted it in 1539. Knole in Kent was greatly enlarged in the 1600s by Thomas Sackville, 1st Earl of Dorset, who made money both as Lord Treasurer, and by the sale of timber both for charcoal to fuel the important Wealden iron industry, and to house and ship builders.

Aside from building in the countryside, there was also much construction in towns. Population growth was concentrated there, a dynamic that provided opportunities and posed serious problems. London expanded greatly, easily retaining its status as the largest city in the British Isles. Its population grew from about 50,000 in 1500 – approximately 4 per cent of the English population – to 500,000 in 1700, nearly 10 per cent. London retained its role as the centre of government and the law, and grew more important as a home of consumption and as the commercial entrepôt between England and the wider world. Profits from trade and government helped bridge the gap between the city as a centre of production and as a centre of consumption.

London money financed economic expansion elsewhere in England. It also led to new building. In 1552 William Clifton, a wealthy London merchant, bought Barrington

Lacock Abbey, Wiltshire, acquired by William Sharington, a courtier of Henry VIII who used his position as Vice-Treasurer of the mint in Bristol, to which he was appointed in 1546, in order to mount a massive fraud that included clipping coins and making false copies of the books of the mint. Arrested in 1549, Sharington was able to regain favour and in 1552 was Sheriff of Wiltshire.

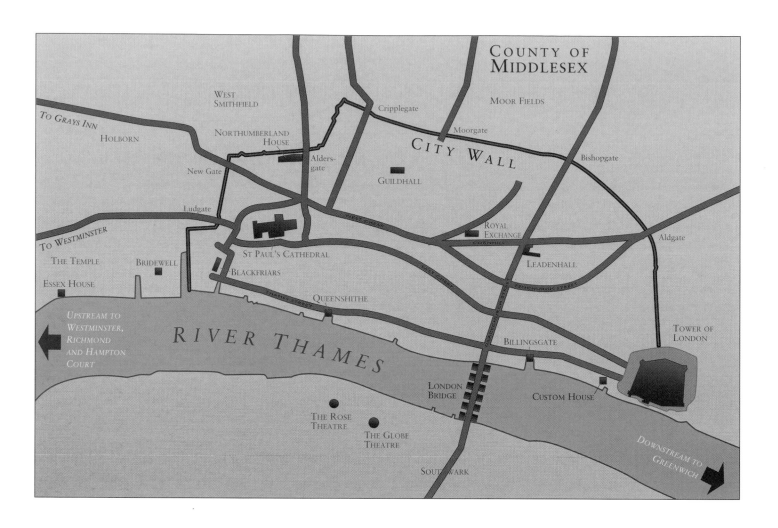

Map labels: COUNTY OF MIDDLESEX; WEST SMITHFIELD; CRIPPLEGATE; MOOR FIELDS; TO GRAYS INN; HOLBORN; NORTHUMBERLAND HOUSE; MOORGATE; CITY WALL; BISHOPGATE; ALDERS-GATE; NEW GATE; GUILDHALL; LUDGATE; ROYAL EXCHANGE; ALDGATE; TO WESTMINSTER; THE TEMPLE; BRIDEWELL; ST PAUL'S CATHEDRAL; CORNHILL; LEADENHALL; ESSEX HOUSE; BLACKFRIARS; QUEENSHITHE; THAMES STREET; UPSTREAM TO WESTMINSTER, RICHMOND AND HAMPTON COURT; RIVER THAMES; BILLINGSGATE; TOWER OF LONDON; LONDON BRIDGE; CUSTOM HOUSE; THE ROSE THEATRE; THE GLOBE THEATRE; DOWNSTREAM TO GREENWICH; SOUTHWARK

Court, a moated medieval house in Somerset, and commissioned a new house on the Elizabethan E-plan. Mercantile and industrial money flowed into country estates from other town and cities too. Outside Keighley, James Murgatroyd, a wealthy Yorkshire clothier, bought the estate of East Riddlesden in the 1630s and built the Hall. In 1642 George Baillie, son of an Edinburgh burgess, gained the estate of Whiteside on which Mellerstain was to be built by his eighteenth-century descendants; he had already purchased the estate of Jerviswood in 1636.

Cities such as Bristol, Newcastle, Norwich, York and Exeter also grew rapidly. Norwich, with a population of 15,000 people, was England's second city in 1550. It had 20,000 people by 1700. Edinburgh then had about 30,000–35,000 inhabitants and Bristol, which benefited from a shift of trade to the Atlantic seaboard, 20,000. At the outset of the period, there was a disproportionately high number of large towns in the southern half of England. This was particularly so in East Anglia and the south-west, the south-east missing out in large part because of the inhibiting effect of London on the growth of nearby towns, and because it had less industry than the other two regions. The presence of so many towns in the south impacted on not only the economic but also the political importance of the area because it was largely responsible for the high number of parliamentary boroughs there.

Thereafter, some towns enjoyed rapid growth, while others, such as Coventry and Leicester, were affected by declining industries. Some ports, such as Boston, struggled to compete as others, such as King's Lynn and Topsham, rose. In addition to being the focus for trade, consumption and services, towns were centres of government, lay and ecclesiastical.

Urban buildings from the sixteenth century survive in some quantity, but their numbers were greatly lessened by subsequent rebuilding, especially in the nineteenth century, and by German air raids during the Second World War. The latter, for example, were particularly devastating to Tudor buildings in Exeter and Plymouth, although the timber-framed Elizabethan House on New Street in Plymouth is a fine surviving example. Other good examples are the Greyfriars in Worcester, the Elizabethan House Museum in Great Yarmouth, and the Tudor Merchant's House in Tenby, Grantham House, King John's Hunting Lodge (in fact a merchant's house of about 1500) in Axbridge, and, although it was not completed until 1620, Gladstone's Land in Edinburgh. Buildings from the late seventeenth century, a period of major urban building, survive in larger quantities, in part, because of the greater use of incombustible brick.

Urban expansion was a product of the role of towns as centres of manufacturing, trade, government and leisure. Yet all four were also pursued in the countryside, just as there was much market gardening within town walls, as well as orchards and pastures,

Ancient City map of Bristol and its Suburbs, coloured and sold by Robert Walton, 1671. The interpenetration of land and water emerges clearly. Bristol was a major port. It had also been an important fortress city in the First English Civil War, but had been stormed successfully by the Royalists in 1643. The gated nature of the entrances to the city is clear.

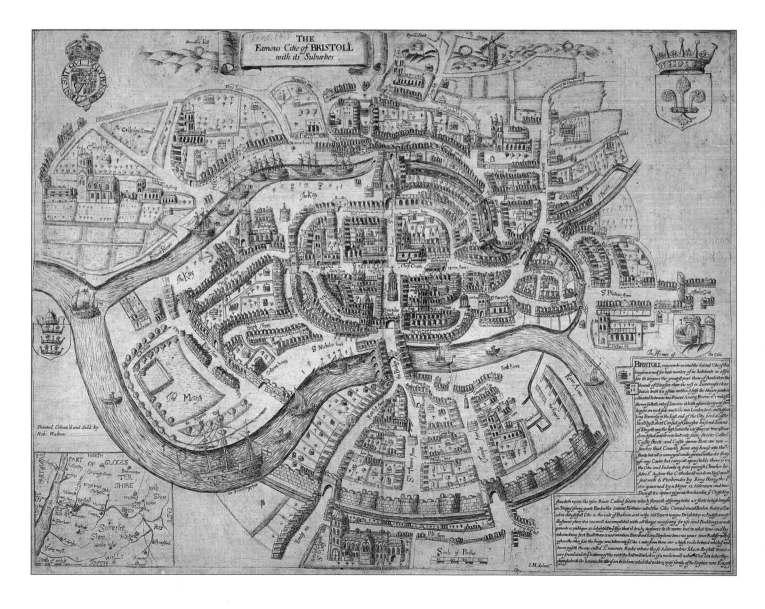

Ic it plefe ony man fpirituel or temporel to bye ony
pyes of two and thre comemoracios of falifburi vfe
enpryntid after the forme of this prefet lettre whiche
ben wel and truly correct, late hym come to weftmo-
nefter in to the almonefrye at the reed pale and he fhal
haue them good chepe . · .·

Supplico ftet cedula ·

*Advertisement printed by William
Caxton for his* Sarum Ordinal,
c. 1478.

*The wool hall, Lavenham (left).
Constructed in the early sixteenth
century it was one of many secular
and sacred buildings in the village
financed by the burgeoning wool
industry. In the 1470s Suffolk produced more cloth than any other
county. Lavenham was at the height
of its prosperity in the 1520s and
supported numerous clothiers.*

the latter particularly for milk which could not be
refrigerated, treated or preserved. With the
exception of London, cities were small and the
countryside was always nearby. In 1523
Worcester ranked sixteenth in England's towns
by population, but the population was only
about 4,000, and in 1646 only about 6,000. The
next biggest town in Worcestershire, Evesham,
had only about 1,400 people in the mid-sixteenth
century, the size of a modern village. This was
also true of the largest Welsh towns, Brecon and
Carmarthen.

Rural justices of the peace, generally the local
gentry, were responsible for much of the government of the country and the
enforcement of law – often without much regard for justice; but to disregard the law
would get them into serious trouble, either with the Assizes or with the Privy Council.
Rural fairs were important to trade, their episodic character a reminder of the rhythm
of seasonal activity that framed life. Much industry was also located in the
countryside, in part because of the importance of water power provided by fast
flowing rivers and tapped by the water wheels in mills. The first copper smelter near
Neath in South Wales, built by the Mines Royal in about 1584, depended on the
power of the Aberdulais Falls; the copper came from Cornwall, an aspect of the
maritime economy of the Bristol Channel. Evidence of Tudor copper and tin mining
can still be seen at St Just in Cornwall. Alum for use in the cloth industry was mined in
North Yorkshire and the Peak Alum Works at Ravenscar reveal the history of this
early industrial site.

The processing of rural products – grain, meat, wool, wood, hides, hops – was
central to industry throughout Britain. The woollen cloth industry brought particular
prosperity to East Anglia, producing the resources that went into constructing churches
and secular buildings in towns such as Long Melford and Lavenham in Suffolk, and
establishing elaborate churches in even the smallest villages, such as nearby Clare. The
timber-framed Guildhall of Corpus Christi in Lavenham dates from about 1528–9.
Paycocke's, a merchant's house in Coggeshall,
Essex, dating from about 1500, testifies to the
wealth of the town's lace industry.

The cost and difficulty of transport encouraged
the production of goods near to the markets for
which they were destined, a situation facilitated
by the absence of mass production. Thus, rural
Britain was dotted with brewhouses, such as the
Church House in Widecombe, and mills, such as
the Dunham Massey Sawmill near Manchester,
originally used for grinding corn, Houghton Mill
near Huntingdon, the Pitstone Windmill near
Tring, the White Mill near Wimborne, and the
Nether Alderley Mill in Cheshire. Although not
built until 1743, the City Mill in Winchester was
on the site of earlier corn mills on the River

Itchen. The products of mills and the rural economy were sold at market halls, such as that at Chipping Camden built in 1627.

Building reflected affluence and expenditure, as with the insertion of chimney stacks in many houses. Elizabethan England was a society that had more possessions than its predecessors. The world of 'things' increased. The results can be seen in the fittings of Tudor houses, both halls and kitchens. The textiles at Hardwick Hall are the finest and most complete example. The average home had fewer objects than a modern house, in large part because of the combination of low average incomes and an absence of mass production, but more objects survive from the sixteenth century than from the fifteenth, and other evidence, such as probate inventories, legal records and literary references, also suggest a marked trend towards possessing more. Increasing material consumption also invited denunciation by moralists and was seen as the cause of what was regarded as a major rise in crime.

The world of things had important cultural consequences. Craftsmanship flourished in the manufacture of many goods. The increase in the number of musical instruments, such as lutes, probably ensured that instrumental music came to play a more prominent role, especially in genteel society. Songs were set to music which it must be assumed people could readily play.

Books were an important part of this new world. The first one printed in England was published by William Caxton in 1474 and Scotland gained its first printing press in 1507. Early beginnings in printing were less important than sustained growth in the production and consumption of books and other printed material, a situation that contrasted greatly with that in, for example, the Turkish (Ottoman) empire. The

availability of books helped to encourage literacy, while printing became commercially attractive because of the strong demand for books building up in the fifteenth century. Printing was most important for its collective functions, especially the use of the Bible and Prayer Book in church before 1650, but it also offered the possibility of a more private and individual culture than that provided by the conspicuous consumption and display of public ceremonial. An example of an early library is that of Henry, 9th Earl of Northumberland at Petworth. Printing had important religious and political dimensions, especially with the publication of the Bible in English, and also energised cultural production. All forms of literature could be made readily available through print. Poetry, drama and sermons, for example, could be more easily disseminated.

The development of drama was one of the highpoints of the age. In Scotland, theatre developed, with works by Sir David Lindsay and others, but it was essentially in a court setting. In England, in contrast, public patronage and the exigencies and opportunities of the commercial marketplace were important. The Theatre, the first purpose-built public playhouse in England, was opened in London

Henry Peacham in a performance of Shakespeare's Titus Andronicus, *c. 1595. The plot of this revenge play testified to the imaginative sway of the classical world and the fascination of contemporary audiences with 'blood plays'.*

in 1576 and the Globe Theatre in 1599. The Lord Chamberlain's Men, a theatrical company in which William Shakespeare had a stake, produced plays at both theatres. The property-buying Shakespeare was himself one of the newly affluent.

As yet, the impact of popular literacy and the print revolution upon oral culture was limited. Most people could neither read nor afford books, and this was especially true of the rural majority of the population in England, Scotland and Wales. Yet there were also important changes. The publication of the vernacular Bible helped to validate both books and the use of English, rather than Latin, and the use of print for the growing number of official notices made writing more authoritative, but written sources were themselves authoritative before printing, even among those who could not write. The shift from memory to written record had given writing its authority, and it was well established by the end of the twelfth century.

Printing made writing more available in a standard form: people in London and Newcastle could read the same book (i.e. identical copies), creating a shared and repeatable culture that manuscripts could not generate. Print thus lent itself to the demands of a state that from the 1530s was legislating actively for lay and ecclesiastical matters.

The importance of education as a means to approach, understand and mediate the world of print encouraged a set of values in which learning played a greater role. Yet this was also socially divisive, for access to learning, old and new, developed within the framework and in terms of existing social structures and practices. Education, the world of print, the impact of government, and the role of London, all encouraged the gentry increasingly to view politics and society in national terms. In contrast, although about 80 per cent of London craftsmen were literate by the 1600s, there was scant opportunity for the poor to impact on the world of print. Most did not write and possibilities for publication were remote. Women enjoyed fewer opportunities than men for formal education, but most men also lacked formal education. The poor depended on charity for what little teaching was available. The vicar of the Yorkshire rural parish of Brandesburton reported to a diocesan visitation in 1764: 'Mrs Frances Barker of York left the interest of £100 to this parish towards the maintenance of a schoolmaster, who should teach 8 poor children to read and write *gratis*, till a convenient purchase could be made with the principal. This sum is now laid out in lands at Sutton. Besides these poor children there are about 30 taught from this and the neighbouring villages in reading, writing and arithmetic by Thomas Ryley. Care is taken to instruct them in the Christian religion according to the Church of England and to bring them to church', but for every child who acquired some education there were many others who received none.

Thus printing and books exacerbated social divisions, and gave an extra dimension to the flow of orders, ideas and models down the social hierarchy. The inability of the poor to express themselves was accentuated. Printing and books emphasised the dependence of the poor and illiterate on the literate.

Surveying and maps were one aspect of this social stratification of knowledge. Surveying was seen as a tool of landlord control and landlord-directed change, and maps as a means of recording this information. Sir William Cordell commissioned a survey of his manor of Long Melford in 1580. It hangs in Melford Hall, every field named. In *The Surveyors Dialogue* (1607) by John Norden (1548–1626), Surveyor to the Duchy of Cornwall, the surveyor offered an inclusive view of economic change: 'Surveys are necessarie and profitable both for Lord and Tennant', only to meet with the farmer's claim 'oftentimes you are the cause that men lose their land'. The surveyor's view – 'the faulty are afraid to be seene . . . the innocent need not feare to be looked into' – would have convinced few. The idea of 'the estimated acre' (the folk equivalent of surveying) remained legitimate into the eighteenth century, and was usually the preserve of the old men of the parish who could remember older apportionments of land. This difference underlined the tension between oral (plebeian) and literate (elite) traditions under the pressure of economic change, especially in the century 1550–1650. Norden's work included estate plans in more than twenty counties, for instance a manuscript atlas showing the Suffolk estates of Sir Michael Stanhope, as well as maps of several counties. Another surveyor, Edward Worsop, noted: 'The common people for the most part are in great feare when surveie is made of their land'.

ECONOMIC CHANGE

Alongside any emphasis on elements of continuity, it is also important to draw attention to signs of economic change. This was both quantitative (increased production) and qualitative (new methods and routes). Both were important in the sixteenth and seventeenth centuries. A more integrated economy was the most important development, the response to the increasingly insistent market economy, to the demands of a growing population and urban markets, to the availability of and

> ### FULLING MILLS IN DEVON AND CORNWALL 1500–1800
>
> *Industry was widely dispersed. The concentrations that were to be seen in the age of factories were far less apparent in the early modern period. This reflected a number of factors, including the costs and difficulties of transport, the importance of processing agricultural products, and the role of water power in many mills.*

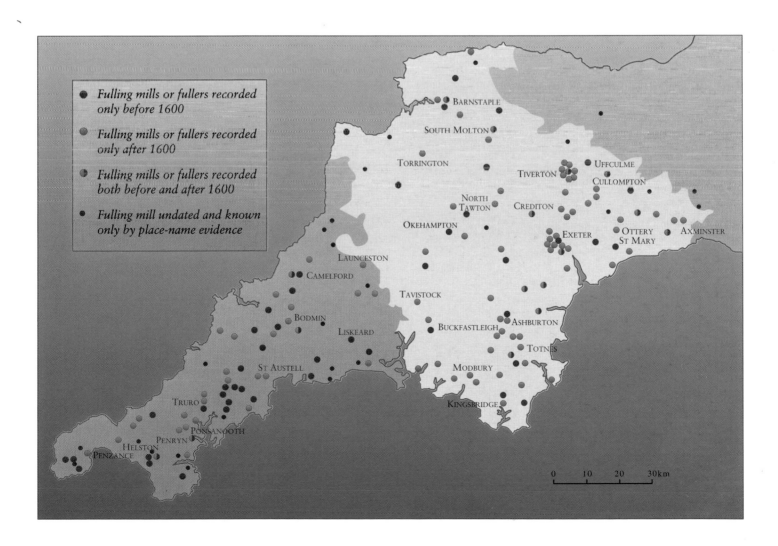

- Fulling mills or fullers recorded only before 1600
- Fulling mills or fullers recorded only after 1600
- Fulling mills or fullers recorded both before and after 1600
- Fulling mill undated and known only by place-name evidence

demand for investment income, and to the absence of internal tariffs. The spread of the market economy, the wide extent of capital accumulation, and, to a certain extent, the rise of 'new men' led to far more litigation, an increase that reached its peak in 1580–1640, when the average rate of law suits has been estimated as over one initiated for every household each year. This litigation focused on debts and contracts, aspects of the vast expansion of credit that was so necessary for the growing economy.

Trade increasingly linked distant areas. North-eastern coal was shipped from Newcastle to London, and Welsh cattle and sheep were driven to the same market. The amount of coal shipped from the Tyne rose to 400,000 tons by 1625 and to over 600,000 in 1730–1. Seventy per cent of this coal went to London in 1682, and King's Lynn and Great Yarmouth, the ports for East Anglia, took half of the rest. When the Scots invaded England in 1644, one of their objectives was to secure coal supplies for their parliamentary allies in London. Newcastle also made glass for national markets, producing about 40 per cent of all that made in England in the seventeenth century. Bristol was another major producer of glass, and also produced much refined sugar. Coal was the main fuel in sugar refining, brewing, salt-boiling and brick making by 1700.

Coal production in Lancashire, Wales and central Scotland also rose. In Culross, Fife, Sir George Bruce was granted the lease of collieries previously owned by the Cistercian abbey. He overcame problems with drainage and ventilation, thanks partly to the 'Egyptian Wheel', which was turned by horses and operated thirty-six buckets on a chain to drain the mine, the depth at which coal could be worked increased from 30 to

Collier brig discharging her cargo of coal into lighters near Limehouse, by Robert Dodd (1748–1816), a leading marine painter whose depictions of actions at sea and of tempests were particularly popular. The coal trade along the east coast, taking coal south from the Tyne, especially to London, was a central artery of British economic life.

240 feet. The new technology enabled Bruce to develop coal production in the area and workings were extended under the Firth of Forth. Some of Sir George's wealth was spent in building a house later known as Culross Palace. He also built a jetty so that coal could be more rapidly shipped.

Much Lancastrian coal was exported through Liverpool and Wigan to Ireland, especially to Dublin, an important aspect of the extent to which the Irish Sea operated as an economic zone. Sea routes were important, for the overland transport of bulky goods remained expensive. This benefited the sale, and thus production, of products that it was especially easy to move by sea, such as fish. The catching and export of Cornish pilchards rose from the 1650s, and 'pilchard ports', such as Port Isaac and Penwith, had fish cellars.

As national markets developed, so the relative importance of local consumption declined and regional variations in prices became less pronounced. These developments were important both when the economy expanded in the sixteenth century, and during its subsequent difficulties in the seventeenth century, for markets were then keenly sought. The first shipload of Cheshire cheese reached London in 1650. By 1664 more than fourteen cheese ships were sailing from the north-west, and by the 1680s over fifty. Return cargoes helped to transform the regional economy, both in the north-west and elsewhere. Cheese also came to London from Somerset via Bristol.

Sales to national markets brought money and, in some cases, workers into areas that produced these products, and increased local demand, especially for food. The development of coal and lead mining in County Durham in the sixteenth and seventeenth centuries led to a rise in population, from about 35,000 in 1550 to about 70,000 in 1700, and the enclosure of land so that it could be more easily farmed and adapted to new agricultural methods. By the end of the century, most of the lowland east of the county was enclosed. There was also much enclosure in south-west England, Yorkshire and South Wales. Increased sales of Cheshire cheese drove land prices up in Cheshire and led to the creation of new businesses. The Bristol market was supplied with butter and meat from South Wales, cheese from Cheshire and Somerset, milk, eggs and poultry from the West Country, and, by the close of the eighteenth century, potatoes from south Gloucestershire.

Landlords and merchants sought new ways to make money. Searching for coal, William Stanley, 6th Earl of Derby ordered surveys on his Lancastrian property at Knowsley Park in 1602, and Sir Richard Molyneux followed suit nearby in 1610. The earls of Powis benefited greatly from the discovery of a lead mine at Llangynog in north Montgomeryshire in 1692: in 1725–45 it produced a profit of £140,000. Cutting down woods – a traditional form of exploiting resources – gathered pace, in order to provide new land for farming, fuel for industry and timber for construction. This was especially true in southern England and Wales, and less so in Scotland. Wood from the Weald was used for charcoal for the local iron industry and a local ironmaster was probably responsible for the Jacobean house at Bateman's. The wealth of the Wealden iron industry also led to the development of fine villages, such as Chiddingstone. New Forest trees were cut down for warships, their Derbyshire counterparts for pit props for coal mines. From 1750, Henry, 1st Earl of Powis, benefited from the expansion of the naval market for the oak trees on his estates. Meanwhile, the drainage of marshy areas, especially parts of the Fens, coastal Sussex, and around the Thames estuary, in the seventeenth century, provided more land for cultivation.

THE MAIN NAVIGABLE RIVERS OF ENGLAND AND WALES, SHOWING
NAVIGATION IMPROVEMENTS UP TO 1727

*Much of England was within reach of a navigable river, but prior to the canals there were
no links across the Midlands, the south of England or the Pennines.*

Qualitative changes were limited. Most industrial processes and agricultural methods did not alter, and the developments that did occur were modest compared to those in the eighteenth century. Nevertheless, floating water meadows (water meadows with a moving cover of water provided by channels) were developed from the early seventeenth century to increase the yield of meadowland. (Floating water meadows have been revived by the National Trust in the valley of the Windrush on the Sherborne estate in Gloucestershire.) There was also a greater use of fertilizers, especially lime, new rotations, and new crops (or crops new to particular regions), such as turnips, clover and lucerne. Duck decoys, such as that at Boarstall in Buckinghamshire, introduced from Holland by Charles II were a new way to obtain winter food. In industry, water-powered blast furnaces, from 1494, and slitting mills, from the 1620s, made it easier to work iron. Sixteenth-century hammerponds (man-made, spring-fed ponds that provided water-power for hammering wrought iron) can still be seen in the Weald, including at Ludshott and Shottermill.

The canals that created new links, greatly easing the transport of bulky goods, especially coal, were not dug until the second half of the eighteenth century. There were, however, earlier efforts to improve rivers for barge transport. The stretch of the Thames below Oxford became navigable again for barges in 1635, following the construction of the poundlocks. The Wey was one of the first rivers to be made navigable. This 15.5 mile waterway, opened to barges in 1653, linked Guildford to Weybridge on the Thames, and thus to London. Major improvements followed, although, in most cases, not until after the growth in political stability following the consolidation of William III's position in the early 1690s. The Aire and Calder navigation to Leeds and Halifax in 1699–1700 was an important step. The Stour was made navigable to Sudbury in 1705, the Avon between Bath and Bristol was improved by 1727, the Mersey to Manchester by 1734, and the Douglas to Wigan by 1742.

The Newark lock on the River Wey filling with water. A 15.5 mile length of the Wey opened to barge traffic in 1635. It linked Guildford to Weybridge on the Thames and thus to London.

Another qualitative change stemmed from the steam engine. The first one was developed by Thomas Savery in 1695 and improved by Thomas Newcomen, with his Steam-Atmospheric Engine of 1712. This pumped water out of Cornish tin mines and coal mines. The first Newcomen steam engine in the Cumbrian coalfield was completed in 1717, and there were at least five in Ayrshire, another coal-mining area, by 1750.

Alongside growth, there was also great diversity and a sense of the mutability of achievement. The latter, in part, reflected a mentality of cyclical development, not steady growth. Daniel Defoe noted, in his *A Tour through the whole island of Great Britain* (1724–6), a book whose publication reflected widespread interest in the nature of the country, that:

The fate of things gives a new face to things, produces changes in low life, and innumerable incidents; plants and supplants families, raises and sinks towns, removes manufactures and trades; great towns decay and small towns rise; new towns, new palaces, new seats are built every day; great rivers and good harbours dry up, and grow useless; again new ports are opened, brooks are made rivers, small rivers navigable, ports and harbours are made where none were before, and the like.

MAPS AND MAPPING, 1400–1700

Thanks to printing and European exploration, European mapping changed radically from the late fifteenth century. There had been, however, an interesting earlier cartographic tradition, in which the English had been especially important. The great *mappae mundi* (world maps) of the thirteenth and early fourteenth centuries produced in the English or closely related north French traditions – the Ebstorf, Vercelli, Hereford, Duchy of Cornwall maps – sought to order the entire known world. There were also maps of Britain, notably the Matthew Paris and Gough maps, and the production of estate maps.

Maps were first printed in Europe in the 1470s. As a result of new techniques, they could be more speedily produced and widely distributed. Consequently, most mapmakers had more, and more recent, maps to refer to when they were producing their own. Printing facilitated the exchange of information, the processes of copying and revision that were so important for mapmaking. The introduction of printed maps spread the idea of using maps and plans among the public at large: the first to be printed in England appeared in 1535 and illustrated the Exodus route of the Bible. Printing led to an emphasis on the commercial aspect of mapmaking and a public world of maps, and thus to a new dynamic for the production of maps and the propagation of mapping.

There was also a revolution in the kind of map that was produced. Earlier maps were generally itinerary or picture maps, and were not drawn to a consistent scale. There was

Norfolk, by Christopher Saxton, 1574. This may have been the first of the Saxton county maps to be printed. A wealthy county, Norfolk was the most agriculturally advanced part of the country, although the heaths of the south-west and fenland of the west were less prosperous. In Norwich it also had a leading centre of the cloth trade.

considerable stylization in the depiction of physical features, for example coastlines, in medieval maps, as the mapmakers were primarily concerned with recording their existence, rather than their accurate shape. Although partly a matter of contemporary conceptual standards, the nature of the available information was also important. In contrast, the trend in fifteenth- to seventeenth-century maps was to emphasise the need for precision in the portrayal of the crucial physical outlines – coastlines and rivers. In the 1540s, scale was introduced to topographic maps, and, by the end of the century, maps drawn to scale were well established. New techniques in drafting and presentation were discovered and adopted. The increasing use of the compass in mapmaking from the late fifteenth century was reflected in a growing tendency to draw local maps with north at the top. Triangulation was introduced, the plane table and the theodolite invented, and there was a more consistent and sophisticated use of uniform conventional symbols in place of pictures on maps, for example to signify towns.

Maps came to play a greater role in a number of fields. One was used in the negotiations that led to the Anglo-French Treaty of Ardres of 1546, although the discussions were not without serious difficulties. Before the treaty, William, Lord Paget, and a French emissary went with several guides to examine the source of a proposed boundary stream and fell into a serious dispute over which of five springs it was. Within Britain, estate maps supplemented or replaced written surveys. A group of cartographers, including William Lambarde (1536–1601) and John Norden, produced maps that helped to consolidate the visual image of counties. Based on surveys by Christopher Saxton, that led to the engraving of thirty-four county maps, the first printed atlas of the counties of England and Wales was published in 1579. Saxton's large general map of England and Wales was printed in 1583. Like the atlas, it bore the royal arms. Such maps were an aspect of majesty, a proclamation of the extent of the state, and of its unity in and under the crown. Saxton's maps were copied with few, if any, changes for two centuries. Meanwhile, in 1573 Humphrey Llwyd, an MP and a noted antiquarian, produced the first map of Wales to reflect a considerable degree of accuracy. More generally, the concept and use of maps spread.

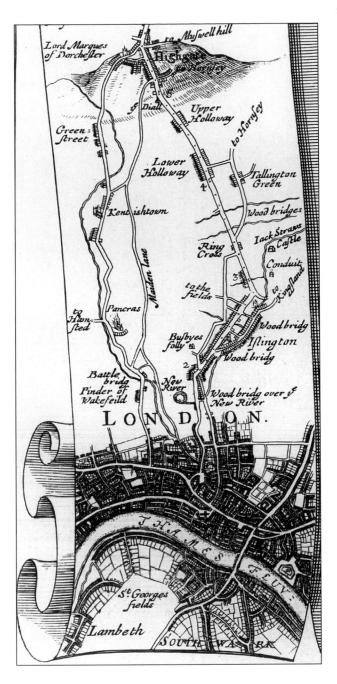

John Ogilby's map of routes through Islington and Highgate, from his Britannia *(1675). His strip maps used a scale of one inch to one (statute) mile. This map is a reminder of how much of Middlesex was still countryside.*

Land surveyors developed appropriate conventions in the way they recorded information so that estate maps from different areas could be compared. The estate map of Cotehele that probably dates from the 1550s lacks a sense of scale, and is, in part, diagrammatic. In contrast, the maps of Cotehele produced in 1731 and 1784 were more reliable as to scale and distance. This was also true of the estate map of 1699 for Baddesley Clinton, the Stourton map of 1725, that can be contrasted with the 1785 plan of the grounds at Stourhead to indicate what Henry Hoare achieved, and George Ingham's 1764 survey map of Kedleston. Charles, 2nd Earl of Radnor, owner of Lanhydrock, commissioned Joel Gascoyne's *Land Atlas* of 1694–9, a masterpiece of the estate surveyor's work. It depicts over 40,000 acres of his Cornish estates in colour on

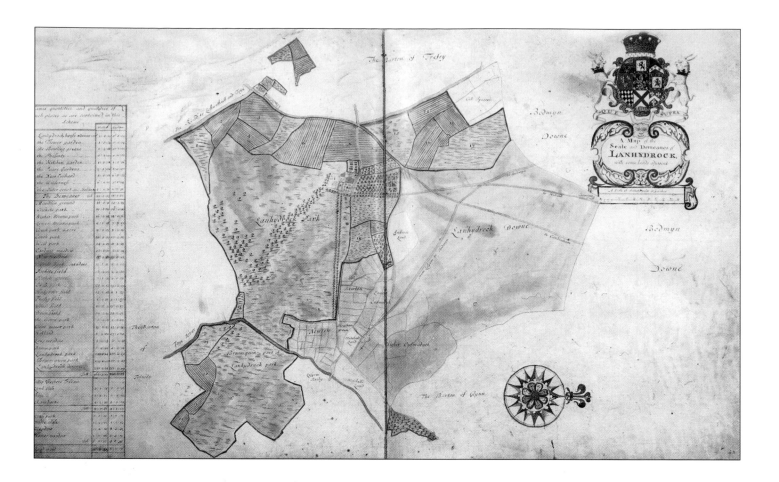

The Lanhydrock estate from Joel Gascoyne's estate atlas for the Robartes family, 1694–9. Gascoyne also produced a nine-sheet Map of the County of Cornwall newly Surveyed *(1699) on a scale of about one inch to one mile.*

258 parchment maps. For the county, Richard Carew of Antony wrote a topographical *Survey of Cornwall* (1602). Gascoyne also produced the Stowe Atlas for the Grenville family. The quality of the mapping was superior to that at the beginning of the century, for example William Senior's 1610 map of the estate at Hardwick.

Although the Land Surveyors' Club, the forerunner of the Institute of Chartered Surveyors, was not founded until 1834, guides to surveying appeared much earlier, including William Leybourne's *The Compleat Surveyor* in 1685. In *The Duty of a Steward to his Land* (1727), Edward Laurence claimed, 'As a steward should know the Quantity and Quality of every parcel of land occupied by the several tenants, so likewise he should have a map of the whole drawn out in the most perfect method; which may show . . . the true figure of every parcel . . . so nearly that he may detect any tenant from alienating the least parcel of any land from his lord'.

Aside from specific improvements in mapping techniques and concepts, which by the late seventeenth century were pretty well developed, maps were increasingly used for general reference beyond the *ad hoc* circumstances, political, estate or otherwise, of their inception. In 1675 John Ogilby brought out *Britannia, Volume the First*, the initial part of an intended multi-volume road atlas. (The other volumes never appeared.) Maps also became more predictable as mapping conventions developed. Improvements in cartography led to increasing awareness of distinctive approaches and changes in the art, and criticism of the efforts of predecessors, as in *The Construction of Maps and Globes* (London, 1717), which has been attributed to John Green.

THREE

The First Two Tudors

Henry VII (1485–1509) is generally overshadowed by his second son, Henry VIII (1509–47), a larger-than-life character who had a succession of six wives and is also famous for breaking with the Catholic church. Yet the father's achievements were crucial. Henry VII established the Tudor dynasty, brought an end to civil war, and re-created both royal authority and the practice of firm government. He also made England a more significant power, with the result that his elder son, Arthur, was able to secure an important bride – Catherine of Aragon, a Spanish princess: neither Edward IV nor Richard III had married so well, although their sister Margaret became the wife of the Duke of Burgundy. Arthur predeceased his father. His younger brother, Henry VIII, married his widowed sister-in-law soon after his accession.

The reassertion of royal power in Henry VII's reign was more than a matter of the destruction of the Yorkists or a simple reaction against the protracted disorder of the Wars of the Roses. Far from relying simply upon 'new men', as was at one time suggested, Henry VII understood the need to work with the nobility, to win their cooperation, and to ensure that they looked to him for support, patronage and profit; the process reached its apogee with, and was greatly helped by, Henry VIII's dispersal of the monastic estates in the 1530s. Henry VII was more cautious in his distribution of wealth and power than Edward IV had been. The strongest magnate, Henry Percy, 4th Earl of Northumberland, was killed in unclear circumstances in 1489, probably while trying to impose order during a tax rising in Yorkshire. Other nobles were kept accountable with bonds – enforced payments that were forfeit if their behaviour became unacceptable.

Yet, Henry felt able to rely on some nobles, including his uncle, Jasper Tudor, Duke of Bedford in the Welsh Marches, his stepfather, Thomas Stanley, 1st Earl of Derby, in Lancashire, and John De Vere, 13th Earl of Oxford, in East Anglia. Royal estates and positions were entrusted to the care of local landowners. The stewardship of Marlborough and Devizes, for example, was jointly exercised by a series of Wiltshire landowners: after Sir Roger

Richmond Palace in the time of Henry VII, sketch by Anthony van Wynegaerde. Much favoured by Edward III, who died there, and restored by Henry V, the palace was rebuilt, extended and given the name Richmond by Henry VII, a monarch also known for the chapel he built at Westminster Abbey. Palaces along the Thames were popular with the Tudors. Elizabeth I died in Richmond Palace in 1603, but it fell into decay during the Civil Wars.

Tocotes, appointed in 1485, came Richard Beauchamp, Lord St Amand (1492); then Anthony St Amand and Edward Dudley together in 1508; Sir Edward Baynton in 1526; and Sir William Herbert in 1544 or 1545. Henry reappointed many of Edward IV's JPs who had been dismissed by Richard III.

There were still serious problems of government control under Henry VII. The Cornish, who rose in May 1497 in opposition to taxes to pay for war against Scotland, were joined by some of the lesser gentry, and were able to march across southern England without opposition. At Wells, James, Lord Audley joined the rebels, but Henry gathered an army at London and defeated the Cornishmen at Blackheath on 17 June. Perkin Warbeck (see p. 26) landed in Cornwall in September, and advanced, intending to topple Henry. Exeter, however, resisted attack, Warbeck's army dispersed, and Warbeck was captured.

Success in dealing with the nobility helped in the improvement of government effectiveness under Henry VII, although it is important not to exaggerate the extent of change. Law and order were enhanced, the private armed forces of nobles limited, and government finances improved, so that Henry left a modest fortune on his death. The role of the royal justice can be traced in the history of individual properties. For example, in 1500 the Abbot of Ramsey, who owned Houghton Mill, built a barrage on the Ouse to ensure water for his mill. The flooding this produced prompted the villagers to seize the floodgates violently. But the dispute was settled in the royal courts with a decision that all floodgates should be opened when the river was in spate. Unlike Edward IV in 1469, Henry did not face a successful rebellion. Furthermore, neither his death, nor the succession of his heir caused a political crisis. Nevertheless, the Tudor hold on power was still fragile at the close of the reign, and royal patronage was not always sufficient in building up loyalty.

In his early years as king, Henry VIII took a prominent role in the highly competitive international relations of the period. War with France led Henry, who saw himself as a chivalric figure, to campaign in person in 1513 and 1523, winning the battle of the Spurs (a minor clash) in 1513. In 1520, at a meeting that became known as the Field of the Cloth of Gold, Henry showed his competitive instincts in a meeting near Calais with Francis I of France; Francis beat Henry in a wrestling match, while the English nobles prided themselves on not speaking French.

The war with France had more of an impact on Scotland. In 1513, James IV of Scotland invaded England in support of his ally France; he had with him 26,000 men, the largest army that had hitherto marched south. English troops, numbering 20,000 under the Earl of Surrey, blocked the advance at Flodden, and the more mobile English billmen (soldiers carrying a bill, which was shorter and more flexible than a pike) defeated the opposing pikemen. James IV was among the casualties. He left an heir, James V, born the previous year. Initially, young James was under the control of his stepfather, Archibald Douglas, 6th Earl of Angus, but in 1515 John Stuart, 4th Duke of Albany, gained the regency and forced James's mother, Margaret, to hand the king over. Angus regained power in 1525, but, only three years later, James used a hunt from Falkland Palace as a cover to escape his regent. Angus's castle at Tantallon was besieged by royal forces under James V and Angus fled to England. Aristocratic risings were crushed as James established his power.

Over the border the money for war with France was raised by Henry's leading minister, Thomas Wolsey, the able and greedy son of an Ipswich butcher who became Archbishop of York, a Cardinal and Lord Chancellor. Thomas Becket had been Chancellor and an Archbishop, but Wolsey was no Becket. Financial demands lessened the popularity of Henry's policies. In 1525 the attempt to levy an 'Amicable Grant' led to serious riots and the abandonment of the tax. Wolsey was disliked by the nobles who saw him as an upstart depriving them of political power.

Henry's position was challenged by the succession. His wife, Catherine of

The gatehouse at Falkland Palace. From here the young James V used the cover of a hunting expedition to escape from the regent, Archibald Douglas, 6th Earl of Angus. He subsequently established his own authority in Scotland.

Henry VIII, a pose of power. Henry enjoyed splendour and demanded obedience. The first king of England to be addressed as 'Majesty', Henry did not tolerate disagreement.

Aragon, had borne five children, but only a daughter, Mary, survived. In England, unlike France, rule by a woman was legal, but Henry I's daughter, Matilda, had failed to establish herself as queen in the 1130s. The succession and then marriage of any female ruler was bound to be a vexed issue in a society that assumed male dominance. Henry was trying to end his marriage with Catherine in favour of a woman who might provide him with a son even before he fell in love with Anne Boleyn. He sought its annulment on the grounds that the Pope lacked the power to dispense with the biblical injunction against marrying a brother's widow, as Henry had done. His sister Margaret had successfully gained a divorce from her second husband, the Earl of Angus, in 1525. Catherine, however, was also the aunt of the Holy Roman Emperor Charles V, the most powerful ruler in Italy, and the papacy proved unyielding.

Henry's mounting anger led in 1529 to the fall of Wolsey, who had failed to obtain an annulment; and subsequently to the rejection of papal jurisdiction over the English church. The Act of Restraint of Appeals [to Rome] of 1533, was the first claim of imperial status for the realm. England was proclaimed jurisdictionally self-sufficient and the sovereignty of law made in Parliament was established by Henry. In 1534, by the Act of Supremacy, Henry became the 'Supreme Head' of the English church .

The previous year, an English court had granted Henry an annulment, and before 1533 was out he both married Anne Boleyn and had a daughter, Elizabeth, later Elizabeth I, by her. The Act of Succession of 1534 bastardised Mary and put the children of Henry's marriage to Anne first in the succession.

Opposition to either the break with Rome or Henry's new wife was treated harshly. The most prominent opponent, Sir Thomas More, who had actively pursued Protestants as heretics, resigned as Lord Chancellor in 1532 in protest at Henry's divorce, was imprisoned for refusing to swear the oaths demanded under the Act of Succession, and beheaded for treason in 1535 after a manipulated trial. John Fisher, Bishop of Rochester, was also beheaded for refusing to accept Henry as head of the church. The Treason Act of 1534 extended treason to the denial of royal supremacy and gave additional weight to what was (from the crown's point of view) a favourable use of judicial discretion by reducing the authority of juries in such cases.

Henry's breach with papal authority increasingly interacted with the Protestant Reformation which had begun with Martin Luther's challenge to the papacy in Germany in 1517. At that point, Catholicism was the sole permitted form of worship in Britain. The tiny Jewish minority had been expelled from England under Edward I. The Lollard heresy, that, in large part, sprang from the teachings of John Wycliffe in the fourteenth century, had had lasting impact: it continued and melted into early Protestantism in London, but the numbers involved were very few.

Although, prior to the Reformation, hostility to the wealth and privileges of the clergy was widespread, this was not new, nor incompatible with the extensive popular devotion of the period. There was much church building and renovation in the late fifteenth and early sixteenth centuries, for example in Suffolk and south-west England. St Michael's, Honiton, was greatly enlarged from 1478. Carlisle Cathedral, a monastic foundation, gained splendid choir stalls in the mid-fifteenth century; Rochester, another monastic foundation, a Perpendicular-style Lady Chapel in 1490. At Rock in Worcestershire, the tower and the south aisle were added to the church in 1510. Ashleworth in Gloucestershire reflects the continued vitality of the church: the manor belonged to a wealthy monastery, St Augustine's, Bristol, and a largely fifteenth-century parish church was joined in about 1500 by a large 126 foot stone-tiled tithe barn. Marmaduke Huby, Abbot of Fountains Abbey 1495–1526, built a tall perpendicular tower and raised the number of monks at his religious house.

Christian devotion was also firmly grounded in communal experience and identity in the localities, with a 'sacred landscape' of sites attracting local observance. Local shrines and particular saints, such as Brannoc, whose miracles included the useful resurrection of a cow, continued to enjoy much support and to sustain a sense of community. Shrines continued to attract bequests. There is evidence that the religious orders were less important than in the past and some less successful monasteries and priories were suppressed in the 1520s, but religious houses still played a major role in the spiritual life of the population and were important in local economies. The donations of pilgrims worshipping at the shrine of the Holy Blood at Hailes Abbey paid for attractive cloisters constructed in the fifteenth century. Nunneries acted as centres

Anne Boleyn (c. 1507–36), 1533, by an unknown artist. Daughter of a courtier and with a post in the household of Henry VIII's first wife, Anne was the sister of Henry's mistress Mary. In 1532, Anne became Henry's lover and in 1533, after she became pregnant, his second wife. The birth of Princess Elizabeth was followed by two miscarriages, and in 1536 Anne was accused of adultery and executed to make way for Jane Seymour.

A later image of Henry VIII trampling papal authority and turning to Protestantism. Shakespeare's Henry VIII *(1613) presented Archbishop Cranmer (to the left of the king) as an honest replacement for Cardinal Wolsey. Elizabeth's christening is the triumphant conclusion to the play. The Globe burned down at the premiere when a cannon fired in the stage action set the thatch alight.*

for distributing alms and provided education for children. Monasteries and nunneries were grounded in their localities through the important role of local recruitment. Religious vitality was also shown in local culture. Mystery plays developed in the period – the York ones were written down in the 1460s or 1470s, those of Towneley/Wakefield in the 1520s, and the Chester and Coventry plays were reworked in the 1530s.

Henry VIII himself was doctrinally conservative. In 1521 he wrote *Assertio Septem Sacramentorum* against Luther, his book earning him the title 'Defender of the Faith' from Pope Leo X. In fact, there were few Protestants in England until Henry's break with Rome weakened traditional authority and encouraged their spread. In the 1530s the growing influence of Protestantism in circles close to Henry had an effect on policy, but, personally, Henry was no Protestant and he did not wish to see any abandonment of the Catholic faith. The church under Henry is better described as Henrician than Protestant but he had certainly moved away from the organisational structures of the Catholic church. His contemporary James IV (1488–1513) made annual pilgrimages to Whithorn, Tain and other Scottish shrines, while James V (1513–42) made frequent journeys to Our Lady of Loretto near Musselburgh. Henry was willing to see the English counterparts of these shrines desecrated.

The production of an official English Bible and the dissolution of the monasteries were the major developments of the 1530s, each resulting from, but less reversible than, Henry's matrimonial peregrinations. The first complete translation of the Bible to be printed in English, that by Miles Coverdale, was dedicated to Henry in 1535. Henry argued that the 'word of God' supported the idea of royal supremacy, and this encouraged the translation of the Bible. An official English Bible was produced (1537), and every parish church was instructed to purchase a copy (1538), a marked extension of the authority of print and a testimony to the effectiveness of the publishing industry. A Welsh New Testament, commissioned by Elizabeth I, was to follow in 1567. Bishop William Morgan's translation of the whole Bible into Welsh appeared in 1588 with a dedication to Elizabeth. He grew up at Tŷ Mawr in Gwynedd, although the sixteenth-century farmhouse there postdates him.

The great pilgrimage shrines in England were destroyed from 1535 onwards, producing much loot for Henry. Monasticism, one of the most prominent symbols of the old ecclesiastical order and an important aspect of the international character of the church, was attacked by Protestants as an anachronistic abuse, and, more potently and significantly, destroyed by the government between 1536 and 1540. The 1536 Act dissolving the smaller monasteries with annual incomes of less than £200, and transferring their property to the crown, was followed by the dissolution of the rest. Chantry chapels followed in 1545 and 1547.

Monks were driven from their monasteries, the buildings looted of valuables, and the often extensive estates sold. Formerly flourishing complexes were turned into ruins. Many, such as Fountains Abbey, Hailes Abbey, Mount Grace Priory, Cartmel Priory, and St Michael's Church on Glastonbury Tor, part of Glastonbury Abbey, can be visited today, potent witnesses to the devastation and greed of the period. Yet more than devastation and greed were involved. Established beliefs were also attacked. The royal commissioners who dissolved Hailes Abbey in 1538 removed the Holy Blood that had been authenticated by the Patriarch of Jerusalem and declared it 'honey clarified and coloured with saffron'. The Rood of Grace at Boxley Abbey was also denounced as a fraud.

The fifteenth-century tower is all that remains of St Michael's Church on Glastonbury Tor, part of Glastonbury Abbey, Somerset, one of the many flourishing monastic houses ruined at the Dissolution.

Many monasteries, such as Mottisfont Abbey, served as the basis for new estates and buildings, often literally so, as stone and other building materials were reused. Some of the 12,000 tonnes of stone used by the Cecils to cover the large façade of Burghley House came from monastic buildings in Stamford. The Priory of St Mary at Merton, London, was demolished and used to build Henry's new palace at Nonsuch. The Elizabethan house that replaced Buckland Abbey incorporated the ruins of the abbey church. Fountains Hall was partly built with stone from the abbey. Lacock Abbey became a country house that incorporated much of the abbey. Some of the stone from the Abbey of Kirkwood was used for Newark Park, which was built by Sir Nicholas Poyntz, Groom of the Bedchamber to Henry VIII, on abbey land. Anglesey Abbey was built in 1600 on the site of an Augustinian priory, and another priory became Canons Ashby House, the home of the Drydens. Rice Mansel purchased Margam Abbey in 1540 and it became the principal seat of the Mansels; their former seat, Oxwich Castle, in turn,

became less important. Some of the surviving reworkings, such as Priory Cottages in Abingdon, are less splendid. Bourne Mill was built by Sir Thomas Lucas as a fishing lodge in 1591 from the ruins of the Abbey of St John in Colchester. Brownsea Island in Poole harbour, seized from Cerne Abbey, was fortified against France by the crown.

Monastic estates served as the basis for the landed position of those whom Henry VIII favoured, and the transfer of assets to the social elite and to rising individuals helped to keep both loyal. Established families, such as the Gages in Sussex, received church lands, in their case property from Battle Abbey. Lanhydrock, a manor of the Priory of St Petroc, was bought by the Glynns of Glynn, the adjoining estate. The Luttrells of Dunster Castle obtained Dunster Priory. New men also obtained land. William, 1st Lord Paget, rose from a humble background to become one of Henry VIII's leading diplomats. His landed position was based on former church lands, including those of the Benedictine abbey at Burton in Staffordshire. He established a presence in the county, building Beaudesert, a large house which was pulled down in the 1930s.

There were also rapid changes in ownership, as initial grantees sold their new gains or had them confiscated, particularly during the turmoil of Edward VI's reign. In 1551 the future Mary I (1553–8) condemned the Privy Council, claiming with a degree of accuracy 'my father made the most part of you almost from nothing'. Important sites

Ruins of thirteenth-century Hailes Abbey, Gloucestershire. This Cistercian abbey, a celebrated pilgrimage site, became yet another silent mark of Henry VIII's plundering.

The Great Barn at Buckland Abbey. The fifteenth-century arch-braced roof protected the harvest from the estate of the Cistercian abbey. The floor was cobbled until the 1950s and the abbey watermill was originally near the west porch. The Elizabethan house that replaced Buckland Abbey incorporated the ruins of the abbey church.

within towns were also freed for development by the Dissolution. In London, Austin Friars went to the Lord Treasurer, Sir William Paulet. Monastic patronage over church livings was also taken over by the laity. In some cases monastic churches were purchased by parishes, as in Tewkesbury, and this gave communities an increased ability to control much of their religious life.

The destruction of the monasteries was a major break with the past, a shattering of popular devotion and institutional continuity that helped make it harder to think of an unchanging religious system. Henry's reluctance to support theological or liturgical change, and the lack of much national enthusiasm, helped limit the progress of Protestantism, but his destructiveness had undermined the Catholic Church and thus hit traditional patterns of faith. The ending of Purgatory and the consequent prayers for the dead destroyed the links between the communities of the living and the dead. The loss of the monasteries brought much disruption, including, in many localities, the breakdown of poor and medical relief. Nevertheless, though in the short term monastic charity was ended, before long Protestant-influenced patterns of charitable giving developed. Instead of bequests going to masses for the dead and chantry priests, they were now more

Henry VIII and Parliament in 1523. In order to finance war with France, Parliament was pushed into voting a four-year subsidy, an unpopular step. Parliament's role expanded with the Reformation legislation of the 1530s.

frequently left for parish charities, educational provision and almshouses.

For a society that disliked change and had little confidence in the future, the ending of monasticism and the destruction of the monasteries were very disturbing. They led to unfounded rumours about what Henry might do next – including the report that he would tax the sacraments – and in 1536 prompted major risings in Lincolnshire and Yorkshire, the latter known as the Pilgrimage of Grace. Neither, however, was as much of a challenge to Henry as the baronial rebellion of 1460 had been for Henry VI, because neither rising set out to overthrow the king. An emphasis on the need to remove allegedly evil ministers, especially Thomas Cromwell, the feared son of a Putney alehouse-keeper, and to reverse unpopular religious policies, particularly the dissolution of the monasteries, was vitiated by protestations of loyalty to the king and a willingness to accept his misleading promises of pardon and concessions. This was just as well for Henry, as the government's initial military response to the risings had been unimpressive. As a result, a truce was conceded in late October and a pardon in December, the latter a serious humiliation for Henry. Once the rebels had dispersed, however, there was a retribution and the pace of monastic dissolution accelerated.

The Wakefield Plot, a conspiracy in the West Riding of Yorkshire in 1541, indicated that tensions continued. Henry was also determined to remove aristocrats he suspected, especially if they were descendants of the house of York, like the De La Poles. Charges of treason led to the execution of Edmund De La Pole, Earl of Suffolk in 1513, Edward Stafford, 3rd Duke of Buckingham in 1521, Henry Courtenay, the Marquess of Exeter in 1539, and the aged Margaret, Countess of Salisbury in 1541; while in 1537, on the death of the 6th Earl, Henry gained the Percy family's earldom of Northumberland.

Henry's lack of religious constancy continued to owe much to his changing desires. Anne Boleyn's failure to produce a son endangered her position, and she was brought down by factional hostility. After her execution in 1536, on the trumped-up charge of adultery, Henry made no attempt to reconcile himself with the papacy, even though Catherine was also dead. He married the innocuous Jane Seymour, but she died in 1537, after giving birth to the future Edward VI (1547–53). The speedy rejection by Henry of his fourth wife, the unattractive Anne of Cleves, in 1540 was linked to the fall and execution of Thomas Cromwell, who had supported the marriage. As part of the move towards a more conservative religious solution, Henry also supported the reinstatement of key Catholic doctrines in the Act of Six Articles of 1539 and had three Protestants burned for heresy in 1540. He then married the Catholic Catherine Howard, a member of the powerful conservative Howard faction, headed by the Duke of Norfolk, but she was executed for adultery in 1542. Henry's sixth wife, the

Protestant widow, Catherine Parr, survived him. At the end of his reign, Henry, although faithful to many aspects of Catholicism, disgraced the Howards and executed Norfolk's heir, the Earl of Surrey, an accomplished poet and general.

The succession was left to Edward, and power to Jane Seymour's brother, Edward, Earl of Hertford, who became Protector and Duke of Somerset. Expensive wars with France and Scotland in the 1540s, including an unsuccessful invasion of France in 1544, ensured that Edward was also left a squandered legacy. Much had also been spent on a system of fortifications along the south coast designed to protect against French invasion; several of the positions survive, including Camber, Deal and Walmer Castles. Lindisfarne Castle off the north-east coast of England was constructed on the site of a ruined fort of the 1540s built against the French. Tax demands to pay for wars and defence pressed hard on the economy.

Such an account presents England very much as a unit, and that, indeed, was what it was as far as Henry's aspirations were concerned. Parliament was used to assert royal control over ecclesiastical jurisdiction. The preamble to the Act of Restraint of Appeals of 1533 declared: 'this realm of England is an empire, and so hath been accepted in the world, governed by one supreme head and king having the dignity and royal estate of the imperial crown of the same'. By the Acts of Union this unitary approach was extended to Wales, where 'Marcher' lordships had left extensive governmental and jurisdictional powers over much of the principality with lords who wielded them as an aspect of their inheritance: although many had been absorbed into the crown with the duchies of Lancaster and York, the earldom of March, and the Neville lands. The Acts of 1536–43 assimilated all Wales into the English governmental system, and gave parliamentary representation and English law to the whole of the principality. The lordships were reorganised into shires.

More generally, within England and Wales, concern over uniformity and the determination to enforce change led to new claims for royal authority, the extension of royal power, the reorganisation of existing governmental practices, and the creation of new administrative agencies. In 1536 Henry resumed the special powers of the English palatinates. As a consequence of the royal supremacy, all religious questions became political, and thus it was necessary, in a period of religious flux, to extend the scope of governmental surveillance, manifested in reports on events around the country.

Deal Castle, Kent, seen from the south, built as part of a chain of defences constructed during the 1540s to defend England in the event of French invasion. There was no invasion although a sizeable French force intervened in Scotland. The vulnerability of fortified positions was demonstrated when Calais fell to the French in 1558. England was really protected by the Channel, the navy and greater French interest in the Low Countries and Italy.

MID-SIXTEENTH-
CENTURY REBELLIONS

*The Tudor state faced
widespread rebellion and
opposition in mid-
century, but it never
cohered to mount a
decisive challenge. This
was a reflection of the
disparate nature of
opposition, and the
authority enjoyed by the
monarch.*

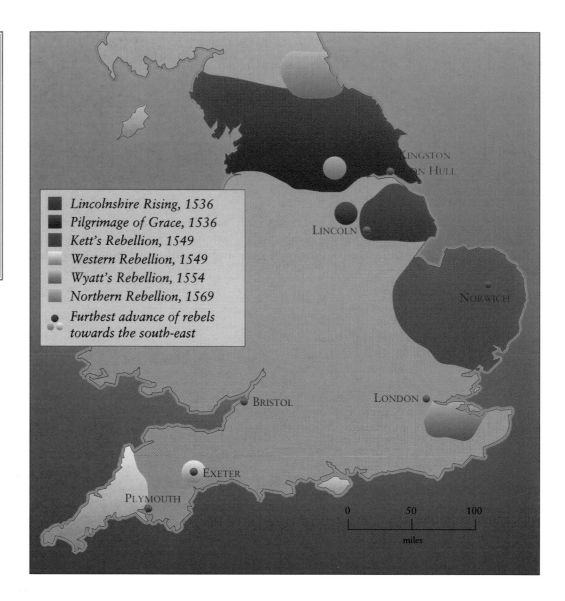

- Lincolnshire Rising, 1536
- Pilgrimage of Grace, 1536
- Kett's Rebellion, 1549
- Western Rebellion, 1549
- Wyatt's Rebellion, 1554
- Northern Rebellion, 1569
- *Furthest advance of rebels towards the south-east*

Concern with the political and religious views of individuals was an aspect of the process by which the Tudor realm was re-created, less as a feudal polity dependent on relations between monarch and lords, and more as a state in which all were answerable to the sovereign.

The dissolution of the monasteries was accomplished by national commissioners and led to the display of royal power throughout the country. In Carlisle, as far distant from London as any city in the kingdom, the Sub-Prior of the Augustinian Priory, Sir Richard Howthwaite, was executed in 1538 for involvement in the Pilgrimage of Grace, and on 9 January 1540 the royal Commissioners appeared, accompanied by cavalry and spearmen. The Prior duly surrendered the Priory and all its possessions. In 1541 the last Prior, Lancelot Salkeld, became the first Dean of the Cathedral Church of St Mary, Carlisle – a measure of continuity – but only under royal supervision. The Priory possessions that Henry had not taken reverted to the Dean and Chapter. The same process was followed at Durham.

In the first major redrawing of the diocesan boundary for centuries, six new sees were created: Bristol, Chester, Gloucester, Oxford, Peterborough and Westminster.

This greatly altered the ecclesiastical geography of England. For example, the far-flung see of Lincoln was divided. At a more detailed level, until the creation of the diocese of Gloucester in 1541, Gloucestershire east of the Severn was part of the diocese of Worcester. Henry himself bullied bishops into handing over what he wanted. As part of the general seizure of church lands Thomas Cranmer, Archbishop of Canterbury, was forced to hand over the Kent palace and estate of Knole. He also had to transfer Wimbledon and Mortlake to Thomas Cromwell. Cromwell also gained Lewes Priory.

Uniformity in aspiration did not amount to similarity in practice. Under both Henry and his successors, the pace of religious change and the effectiveness of royal control varied. This variation had an important geographical component, with Catholicism surviving better, for example, in Lancashire and Sussex than in East Anglia and Kent. Due to Kent's proximity to the coast, it had been exposed to Anabaptist refugees from Germany and the Netherlands. But Sussex remained Catholic partly because of the influence of the powerful Howards at Arundel. Other factors were also at stake. There were also religious differences by age, sex and social group, not that there was any uniformity of devotion within individual categories. Henry acted against both Protestants and Catholics, and the progress of state Reformation in Britain was always such that there were these two 'fronts'. Combined with the divided nature of Protestantism, each front created different tensions, but, under Henry and Edward VI, the crucial divide was between the government and Catholic opponents of state-enforced change.

The key geographical dimension was of opposition that was at a distance from London – in Yorkshire in 1536 and in Cornwall in 1549. These distant areas appear more conservative, although there were many supporters of traditional Catholicism in and near London. This conservatism was more than a matter of religious sentiment, important as it was: in addition, habits of local autonomy clashed with the ability of the Tudor state to enforce national policies.

This was also the case in Scotland, where there was the additional complication of foreign pressure. James V (1512–42, r. 1513–42) also resisted Protestantism, which came into east coast ports from Germany and, later, Geneva, seeking in the parliament of 1541 to protect Catholicism, although he favoured a measure of reform. Allied to France, the Scots' traditional ally against England, in 1542 James faced attack from Henry VIII who sought to cover his rear before a projected invasion of France. A Scottish counter-invasion was crushed at the battle of Solway Moss in 1542, and James died soon after, leaving the succession to his new born daughter, Mary, Queen of Scots. When Henry died in 1547, both England and Scotland faced a volatile situation – both were headed by weak, young monarchs.

Knole, Bourchier's Tower, looking west across the Stone Court. This great inner gatehouse takes its name from Thomas Bourchier, Archbishop of Canterbury, who bought the manor of Knole in 1456 and then began work on a palace. When he died in 1486, he left Knole to the see of Canterbury. In 1538 Henry VIII obliged Thomas Cranmer to part with the house. Elizabeth I gave it to her favourite Robert Dudley in 1561.

*The wedding portrait of Henry
VIII's sister Mary Tudor, widow of
Louis XII of France, and Charles
Brandon, Duke of Suffolk. They
married in 1515. Suffolk was the
favourite of Henry VIII and acted
for him as general (against the
Pilgrimage of Grace, 1536, and
France, 1544) and as courtier and
official. An astute player of court
politics, Suffolk benefited from
Wolsey's fall.*

This was especially threatening because, in both England and Scotland, assertive monarchs, such as Henry VIII and James V, had governed as much by establishing and backing supporters in particular localities, as by relying on legislative edicts for the entire realm. Thus, after the 1536 rising had revealed the weakness of his position in Lincolnshire, Henry VIII established his friend and brother-in-law, Charles Brandon, 1st Duke of Suffolk (*c.* 1484–1545), in the county. Brandon then cemented his position by building up an affinity (a private following). The Presidencies of the Councils of the North and the Marches were given to nobles, and they dominated the new lord lieutenancies: twenty-four of the thirty serving in 1569 were nobles. The first of Oxfordshire, appointed in 1543, was the same Charles Brandon who had helped impose Henrican authority in Lincolnshire. Although theoretically restricted by law, retaining (building up armed clientele) by nobles continued, occasionally leading to serious problems in the localities. Henry kept control of such aristocrats through their attendance at court, through taking the court itself travelling, through shared participation in military activities and the hunt, and through patronage. Such processes of government appeared suddenly tenuous when it became clear that the new monarch would not control the situation personally, as would be the case during the minority of Henry's son and successor, Edward VI.

FOUR

The Later Tudors,
1547–1603

Henry VIII had kept his grip on the domestic situation, helped by his clear right to the throne, his unwillingness to turn too obviously to either religious option, and by the selective use of terror. The situation for the crown was less favourable under his successors. The Tudor state had relied hitherto on adult male rulers and the last minority had been that of Edward V in 1483. The accession of the young Edward VI created problems, although nothing to match those that had affected Edward V.

In the late fifteenth century, however, English and Scottish politics had not been complicated by religious disputes. In the mid-sixteenth century, these disputes helped to demonise opponents and made it harder to ensure cooperation and consensus. During Edward VI's reign England was open to the influence of continental Protestantism, and there was a surge of Protestant activity, including publishing. Leading continental Protestants were given posts at Oxford and Cambridge, German Martin Bucer becoming Professor of Divinity at Cambridge. Edward's uncle, the Protector, Edward Seymour, Duke of Somerset, allied with Thomas Cranmer, Archbishop of Canterbury (1533–56), introduced Protestant worship in 1549 with the Uniformity Act and the Book of Common Prayer. Due to Edward's minority, the Council had assumed the royal supremacy, and Acts of Parliament played a major role in this shift. The Uniformity Acts of 1549 and 1552 provided a statutory, institutional character to the royal supremacy. Old service books were burned. Hostile clerics, such as Dean Salkeld of Carlisle, resigned. But equally, Protestant radicals, who went further than the pace of government change, were punished: accused of heresy, Joan Boucher, 'Joan of Kent', was burned in 1550.

Hostility to religious change played a major role in the widespread uprisings in south-west England in 1549. The local gentry failed to suppress the revolts which began in Cornwall; the Justices of the Peace there were especially passive. John, Lord Russell, who had been made Henry VIII's principal agent in the West Country after the execution of the Marquess of Exeter for treason in 1539, was unpopular with the gentry and ineffective in preventing rebellion. The resistance of the city of Exeter to rebel siege was more important. Professional troops from outside the region had to be used to suppress the rising. The rebels were defeated at Fenny Bridges near Honiton on 28 July, the siege of Exeter was raised on 6 August, and the rebellion finished by the

Wadham College, Oxford. Important posts at both Oxford and Cambridge universities were awarded to leading Protestant theologians from the continent in the mid-sixteenth century.

end of August. Slaughter in battle and in execution claimed a high proportion of those involved.

The rising that year in Norfolk was very different. It focused not on religious changes, but on opposition to landlords, especially their enclosure of common lands and their high rents, and to oppressive local governments. Led by Robert Kett, the rebels seized Norwich, but they were crushed by professional troops at the battle of Dussindale nearby. The ability of rebels, who rarely had firearms, to resist professionals was lessened by the effectiveness of the firearms used by the latter. In 1549 there was also disorder in Hampshire, Kent, Leicestershire, Oxfordshire, Rutland and Sussex. Whatever the habits of obedience that had been encouraged under Henry VIII, their impact proved limited at the first crisis.

The risings of 1549 destabilised Somerset's government, and raised the stakes in the factionalised politics of the period. His aristocratic opponents blamed the risings on Somerset's opposition to enclosures, and the disruptive consequences of the expectations for change that he was alleged to have inspired with his support for reformist idealism, particularly John Hales's enclosure commission. By embracing these concerns, Somerset in turn increased the number of the opponents.

After Somerset was overthrown as Protector by the Council in October 1549, John Dudley, Earl of Warwick, one of the Council leaders, who had risen through service to Henry VIII, became its Lord President (1550–3) and Duke of Northumberland in 1551. He was representative of general

Looking towards the Lady Chapel, built from 1224 onwards, Worcester Cathedral. The statue of the Virgin that once stood in the chapel was destroyed on the orders of Bishop Latimer during the Henrician Reformation.

aristocratic views on economic regulation and social policy – in other words not interested in either. Concern about the possibility of fresh popular risings further helped ensure aristocratic support for Northumberland, but his pro-Protestant religious policy angered many peers. Having allied with conservative councillors to remove Somerset, Northumberland kept them from power. Somerset, an alternative focus of loyalty, was executed on fabricated charges in 1552.

Northumberland was ambitious and able, but his basis of support rested on control of Edward. Widely distrusted, Northumberland further lessened his popularity by actively backing Protestantism, an action that may have owed something to his sense of Edward's personal convictions. The Second Prayer Book of 1552 rejected Catholic doctrine and practice, including the bodily presence of Christ in the Eucharist. It was more clearly Protestant than the First Prayer Book, let alone than the more conservative religious solutions of Henry VIII. In addition, religious paintings were whitewashed, rood screens destroyed, stone altars replaced, church vestments removed, stained glass and statues smashed. The traditional liturgy, which had brought comfort for generations, disappeared. The 1547–8 accounts of the churchwardens of Bishops Stortford show them selling by weight a cross, chalices, a pyx, censers, an incense boat and broken altar vessels. More were sold in about 1550 and altars were removed. There was local resentment – rood screens were focal points of collective pious activity. In Worcester Cathedral, the statue of the Virgin Mary that had stood in the Lady Chapel was ruined on the orders of Bishop Latimer.

Had Edward VI lived as long as any of the other Tudor monarchs, then Northumberland would have been in a better position to consolidate his position and enforce Protestantism. However, Edward's deteriorating health led Northumberland to try to act as a queen-maker. The unmarried Edward was persuaded to exclude his half-sisters, Mary and Elizabeth, from the succession, claiming that they were illegitimate, although Mary was next in line under the Succession Act of 1543 and by Henry VIII's will. Lady Jane Grey, grand-daughter of Henry VII through his second daughter, was declared next in line. She was married to Lord Guildford Dudley, one of Northumberland's sons, and, when Edward died in July 1553, was proclaimed queen.

The determined Mary, in turn, proclaimed herself queen at Norwich and began raising troops. This could have been the first stage in a bitter and lengthy civil war. Northumberland set out from London to defeat her. His support, however, was far more fragile than that of Edward IV's father, Richard, Duke of York, had been a century earlier in the 1450s. Although backed by the Council, Northumberland lacked any real dynastic legitimacy and he stretched the bounds of the acceptable. Yet, had Mary been seized, as Northumberland had planned, or defeated and slain, then Northumberland might well have been able to preside over a new political system, especially if Elizabeth had been imprisoned. It was not to be. Support fell away from the unpopular Northumberland. He lacked the position of Richard III in 1483. The county elites, London, and the Council rallied to Mary, and, without a battle, the Duke was arrested and, eventually, executed.

Mary Tudor was a convinced Catholic, who was determined to return England to the Catholic fold. A parliamentary statute declared her power identical to that of a male ruler. She persuaded Parliament to repeal Edward's religious legislation and her father's Act of Supremacy. She restored papal authority and Catholic practice, although a papal dispensation from Julius III allowed the retention of the former church lands by those who now held them. The Pope had no choice: their return would have alienated most of the propertied and the powerful, such as the Gages who were active supporters of the Queen. Mary determined to marry her younger first cousin, Philip II of Spain, the leading unmarried Catholic prince, and thus, she hoped, ensure a Catholic succession. This unpopular plan helped squander the support she had received in 1553 and provoked risings that were encouraged by the envoys from France and Venice, opponents of Philip. A minor rising occurred in Devon in favour of Elizabeth and Edward Courtenay. (The latter was the great-grandson of Edward IV, via Edward's youngest daughter, and therefore a Yorkist candidate for the crown.) There was also a minor revolt in the West Midlands – on behalf of Lady Jane. These risings reflected the number of possible claimants to the throne, and the continued danger of a new civil war over the succession. Both were swiftly put down.

The major rising of the reign was led by Sir Thomas Wyatt and began in Kent, although there was also backing in Hampshire, Surrey and Sussex. Unlike with the Peasants Revolt in 1381 and Cade's Rebellion in 1450 (see p. 21),

Mary I, 1516–58, Queen of England from 1553, by Giacomo Antonio Moro. Mary was badly affected by the annulment of her parents' marriage. In the shadows for the rest of Henry VIII's reign and that of Edward VI, Mary was frequently unwell, and from 1549 was under pressure for continuing to hear the Mass. Her mission to restore England to Catholicism fell victim to her inability to have a child.

London stayed firm with the government, the rebels' advance was blocked at Southwark Bridge, and Wyatt was defeated. The crisis led to swift punishment, including the execution of Lady Jane Grey, her husband, her father, and Wyatt. Elizabeth was implicated in Wyatt's rising, but Mary preferred to detain rather than execute her.

Mary then married Philip, and pressed on the re-Catholicisation of England and Wales with widespread popular support. Rood screens were rebuilt, old service books and church vestments brought back from hiding – many had to be literally dug up. In Bishops Stortford in 1554–5 a mass-book, a manual and processioner, a pyx, a holy-water stoup, altar clothes, a new rood, incense, and an incense boat were all bought at parish expense. In distant Carlisle, Salkeld returned as Dean.

Re-Catholicisation was reinforced by the punishment of those deemed heretics. On 4 February 1555 the first victim was burned at Smithfield. Others followed across the country, including initially at Coventry, Hadleigh and Gloucester. London, Kent and Sussex had a disproportionately high number of martyrs, being geographically nearest to continental Protestantism.

Mary, however, did not give birth to her hoped for heir and her reign became increasingly unhappy after war was declared on France in June 1557. This was both costly and unsuccessful. In January 1558 the French took Calais, the last English possession in France.

Mary is chiefly remembered as a persecutor. Nearly 300 Protestants were burnt at the stake during her reign, including leaders such as Hooper, Cranmer, Latimer and Ridley, and others fled. One refugee, John Foxe published in 1563 his *Acts and Monuments of the Church*, popularly known as the *Book of Martyrs*. This oft-reprinted martyrology was extremely influential in propagating an image of Catholic cruelty and Protestant bravery that was to sustain a strong anti-Catholic tradition. The Scottish Protestant cleric John Knox more bluntly called Mary 'that wicked Jezebel of England'.

Religious reaction to the Marian regime had a political counterpart. In place of the service nobility favoured under Henry VIII and Edward VI, the older noble families whom Henry had turned against – the Howard dukes of Norfolk and Percy earls of Northumberland – were restored to favour, and this was also true of Edward Courtenay until he was implicated in the Wyatt rising and sent to the Tower in 1554. The earldom of Northumberland was restored to Thomas Percy, the 7th Earl in 1557. Nevertheless, Mary maintained the role of Parliament and was obliged to rely on inherited councillors and administrators whom she did not trust. Most of those who could have been punished for heresy or sedition escaped penalty because Mary needed her father's trusted servants.

The reign of the sickly Mary was brief and her chances of success limited by the absence of an heir in spite of two phantom pregnancies. Counter-Reformation Catholicism thus appeared to have little chance in England and Wales. The following century, however, was to show, in European countries, such as Bohemia, that, if political circumstances were favourable, Catholicism could be re-established and Protestantism driven underground.

The reigns of Edward VI and Mary were troubled in core areas of England, and also, albeit less conspicuously so, on the Celtic margins. The Henrician state had a precarious basis in the latter, and there were problems in mid-century. Under Mary, Lewis Owen, Sheriff of Merioneth, was ambushed and killed – a response by yeomen to an assertor of royal power, who was especially unpopular due to his undistinguished background and attempt to benefit his family. Such episodes, however, were overshadowed by the crises of 1549 and 1553 in southern England.

The Tower of London seen from the south-east. Edward Courtenay was one of many implicated in risings and plots during the mid-sixteenth century; he was imprisoned here in 1554. The Tower remained important as both a prison and a fortress.

More distant areas were to receive more governmental attention later in the century.

The situation in mid-century Scotland was even more troubled than that in England. Somerset had continued English intervention, in order to establish English influence and to block the French by betrothing Edward to the infant Mary, Queen of Scots. This, it was hoped, would unite Britain, but Somerset's policy did not win Scottish support. In September 1547 he invaded and defeated a larger Scottish force at Pinkie. The Scottish army, at least 25,000 strong, and composed principally of pikemen, was badly battered by English archers and cannon, some fired from nearby warships, with over 6,000 killed compared to 800 English casualties. Somerset exploited the victory by taking a large number of positions where he established English garrisons, but this policy did not make English rule popular, proved ruinously expensive, and had to be abandoned in 1549 in the face of French intervention. Domestic instability in England also made it harder to sustain intervention in Scotland. Sir John Luttrell of Dunster Castle, who had been put in command of the fort at Broughty Craig, had to be ransomed after the position fell.

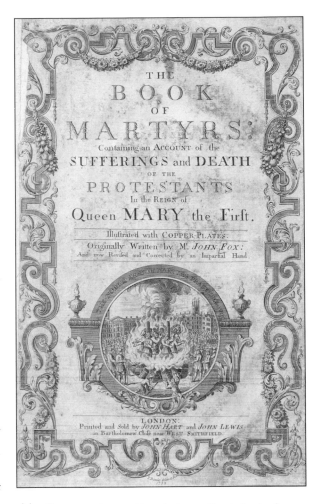

Mary, Queen of Scots, was sent to France in 1548, and in 1558 married Francis, the heir to the French throne. The following year, he became the first and last king of both France and Scotland. These strong pro-French Catholic links, which reflected the regency of James V's widow, Mary of Guise, were unwelcome, especially to Protestants, and in the 1550s the Lords of the Congregation formed a Protestant league. The crisis came to a head in 1560 when Mary of Guise died, the French troops were expelled, and a parliament dominated by Protestants abolished papal authority and the Mass, and introduced Protestant theology.

Mary Tudor was succeeded in 1558 by her Protestant half-sister, Elizabeth (d. 1603). The dying queen maintained the order of succession, although she greatly disliked Elizabeth. Elizabeth's lengthy reign, which lasted until 1603, allowed for the consolidation of a relatively conservative Protestant church settlement, and also contrasted both with the chaos of the preceding two reigns and with the disturbed situation in contemporary France, where the lengthy civil Wars of Religion were soon to begin. Personality was important. Like her grandfather, Henry VII, Elizabeth was a skilful manipulator, not a zealot. In religion, she sought to avoid extremes and would have preferred a settlement closer to that of her father: Henrician Catholicism without Pope or monks. She was, nevertheless, a Protestant in the last analysis. Mary's ministers and favourites were mostly dismissed, and the domestic political situation led Elizabeth in a more Protestant direction, but the Protestant settlement she introduced, with new Acts of Supremacy and Uniformity, was more conservative than that of Northumberland. Salkeld was able to continue as Dean of Carlisle. Elizabeth also sought to prevent further change and this led to disputes with the more radical Protestants, the Puritans.

Her preference for stability was a matter of more than personality and prudence. There was also need for it. Over the previous three decades there had been a lack of continuity in personnel, institutions and policy. Westminster Abbey, for example, a Benedictine foundation, surrendered to Henry VIII in 1540, and was re-established as a cathedral for the new diocese of Westminster, one of Henry's six new sees. Ten years

Frontispiece to Foxe's Book of Martyrs *from one of the many later editions. A Protestant cleric who went into exile under Mary, John Foxe provided an account of England as a kingdom that had been in the forefront of the advance towards the Christian faith. This claim for a separate religious identity encouraged the sense of the English as a chosen people.*

later, when the diocese was abolished, the abbey became a second cathedral for London, only for its monastic status to be restored in 1556. In 1560 Elizabeth refounded the abbey as a collegiate church enjoying exemption from episcopal control, but, more importantly, this arrangement was then maintained.

Despite Elizabeth's caution, there was no turning back to Catholicism, and with time this had a greater impact – those who had lived in an unchallenged world of Catholicism died, and an increasing percentage of the population had been educated in a Protestant Christianity. This was also true of the clergy. With time, a better-educated

A Tumultuous Age

The political shifts of the Tudor age can frequently best be followed by their impact on individuals. The most prominent are well known, but they were not alone in having an impact on their age, nor in registering its tumultuous passage. Those of influence left not only the famous houses of the period, such as Hampton Court, but also less prominent buildings. Sutton House in Hackney was built in 1535 when Hackney was still a village outside London. It remains a Tudor house, with oak-panelled rooms and carved fireplaces, and the peacefulness of the property gives no hint of the life of its builder, Sir Ralph Sadleir (1507–87). Sadleir's career was an instance of the openness of the Tudor system to talent. His father was a senior member of the household of a noble, and Sadleir had to make his way in the world. He was helped by a good education and by the patronage of Thomas Cromwell. Cromwell introduced Sadleir to royal favour and he became a Gentleman of the King's Privy Chamber, before being sent on three diplomatic missions to James V. Success led to Sadleir being knighted and becoming one of the two principal Secretaries of State. Sent to Scotland to further Henry's interests after the death of James V in 1542, Sadleir was nearly shot and had to be escorted back to England. In 1547 he was part of Somerset's invasion force and displayed great bravery against the Scottish pikemen at Pinkie.

During Mary's reign, the Protestant Sadleir retired from politics, but, with Elizabeth's reign, he returned to office as a protégé of Cecil. In 1559 he was appointed Warden of the East and Middle Marches in succession to the Earl of Northumberland, a marked extension of royal authority, and in 1560 he negotiated an alliance with the Scots and reported critically on the loyalty of the Percys. The flight of Mary, Queen of Scots, brought Sadleir fresh tasks. In 1568 he was one of the three commissioners instructed to investigate her case. He subsequently had to arrest Thomas Howard, the Duke of Norfolk, and to accompany the expedition sent to suppress the Northern Rising. In 1580–1 Sadleir was appointed the guardian of Mary, in 1586 was one of the judges at her trial at Fotheringhay, and in 1587 he was sent on a mission to Scotland to explain to James VI why his mother had been beheaded. Although never a leading politician, Sadleir was an important second-rank figure, and his life testified to the impact of politics, religion and succession on those who served the crown.

The Armada window, Sutton House. The only sixteenth-century window remaining in the house, it is believed to have been made from timbers from a ship that sailed in the Spanish Armada of 1588.

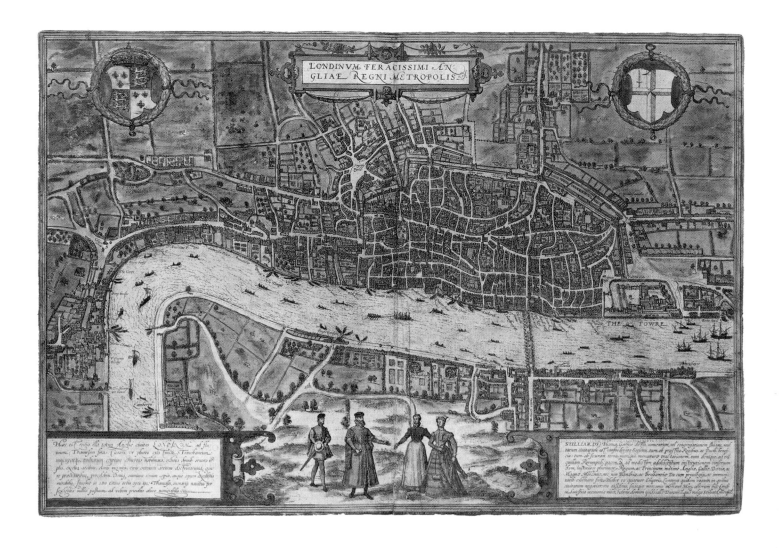

and more committed Protestant parochial clergy developed. Furthermore, traditional Catholic ways of looking at the world faded out or were brought to a close. The mystery plays came to an end. The last recorded performances at York, Coventry and Chester were in 1569, 1571 and 1575 respectively, and attempts to revive performances at York in 1579 and Chester in 1591 were abortive. Some public rituals were brought to a close, but were replaced with others like the queen's accession day. In Tewkesbury, however, plays were still being performed inside the church in 1600, and as late as 1576 the chalice had not been replaced with a communion cup.

Elizabeth was more cautious than Mary, Queen of Scots, who returned to Scotland in 1561 as a young widow. Mary could not accept the religious changes introduced by the Edinburgh Parliament, but lacked the political ability to reverse them and to build up a strong body of support in the complex and bitter world of Scottish baronial factionalism. The Lords of the Congregation thwarted her, while Mary's marital problems increased her unpopularity. Her second marriage to her cousin, Lord Darnley, was unsuccessful, and in 1566 he played a role in the murder of her favourite, David Rizzio. Mary possibly then conspired with the brutal James, Earl of Bothwell, who in 1567 murdered Darnley and married her. The Protestant Lords forced Mary to abdicate in 1567 in favour of James VI, her infant son by Darnley. The Protestant

Braun and Hogenberg's Londinium Feracissimi Angliae Regni Metropolis *(1572) from* Civitatis Orbis Terrarum, *Volume I (1612–18). Rapidly growing in the Tudor period, London posed problems of political management but the Tudors did not face the breakdown of control that was to confront Charles I.*

Elizabeth I proceeding to Westminster on the day before her coronation, 14 January 1559. The queen is accompanied by Lord Ambrose Dudley and Lord Giles Paulet and followed by her Master of Horse, Lord Robert Dudley. The Dudley brothers were sons of the Duke of Northumberland executed after Mary's accession. Robert Dudley became Elizabeth's favourite. He was rumoured to be responsible for the suspicious death of his first wife Amy Robsart. Her death did not clear the way for marriage to Elizabeth.

Reformed church was officially recognised. Mary escaped in 1568, but was defeated at Langside and fled to England.

Elizabeth had now become the most experienced politician in her kingdom, anxious to preserve the royal prerogative, but knowing when to yield without appearing weak. She had favourites, especially Northumberland's son, Robert Dudley, Earl of Leicester, but did not give them power, and she never married. The contrast with her half-sister Mary Tudor rested on more than the longevity of Elizabeth's reign. Claiming that she was an exceptional woman because chosen by God as his instrument, Elizabeth was pragmatic and generally more successful in coping with, indeed exploiting, divisions among her advisers than Mary had been. She presented herself as 'mere English' and sought to cultivate relations directly with the gentry.

Elizabeth's personality and ability were important because she now faced a series of crises, mostly arising from the threatening international situation. The combination of the Catholic Counter-Reformation, the power of Philip II's Spain, particularly thanks to the civil wars in France, the issue of the English succession, and the fate of Scotland and Ireland, ensured that it was impossible to cut England off from her neighbours.

Elizabeth's Protestant settlement aroused Catholic concern, and this at a time of growing energy in the Catholic effort to drive back Protestantism. Some clerics who refused to accept Elizabeth's settlement established seminaries on the continent, most prominently at Douai, to train missionaries to reconvert England. This encouraged government action against Catholics, especially priests. Catholic houses from the period such as Baddesley Clinton and Coughton Court in Warwickshire, Oxburgh Hall in Norfolk, Benthall Hall in Shropshire, Moseley Old Hall in Staffordshire, and Speke Hall in Liverpool, contain priest-holes: hiding places. During the period when Catholics were being hunted down nine men stood motionless with their feet in water for four hours in the priest-hole at Baddesley Clinton in 1591. After he converted to Catholicism in 1580, Sir Thomas Tresham spent much of the remainder of his life in prison or under house arrest, was heavily fined, and was unable to complete his lodge at Lyveden New Bield. His son was imprisoned for complicity in the Gunpowder Plot of 1605.

The situation became volatile in 1568 when the Catholic Mary, Queen of Scots, fled to England where she was next in line in the succession. Mary's presence acted as a focus for discontent and she was imprisoned. In 1569 a court conspiracy to replace Elizabeth's leading minister, William Cecil, and to marry Thomas, Duke of Norfolk, a leading religious conservative, to Mary, and to acknowledge her as heir to the throne, was thwarted.

Nevertheless, in November 1569 the fall out from the conspiracy triggered the last major provincial rising in Tudor England, the Northern Rising. This was led by Thomas Percy, 7th Earl of Northumberland, and Charles Neville, 9th Earl of Westmorland, whose local positions were endangered by a lack of royal favour: the relationship between power in the localities and royal patronage was the crucial factor in noble power. There was a strong interaction of political and religious hostility to the government in the rising, not least resentment at the way Elizabeth was using loyal

Protestants attached to the York-based Council of the North to undermine the independent power of native magnate families. In addition, the Bishop, Dean and Chapter of Durham were all propagating Protestantism. The disclosure of the court conspiracy led Elizabeth to order the two earls to London, but they refused this dangerous command and gathered their men to resist any attempt to compel them. The Earls of Northumberland and Westmorland marked the beginning of the rising by occupying Durham Cathedral on 14 November and celebrating mass. Catholic worship was subsequently restored in many churches. In County Durham only Sir George Bowes, Constable of Barnard Castle, a royal lordship, backed Elizabeth. The Earls' revolt was a powerful defiance of royal power by a rising led, unlike those hitherto in the century, from the top of the social hierarchy. Furthermore, unlike the risings in 1536 and 1549, there was in Mary a clear monarchical alternative to the sovereign: she was the granddaughter of Henry VII through his elder daughter Margaret, who had married James V. The threat from the Earls was diminished by the absence of foreign military support, especially from Spain and Scotland, and by their inability to reach and release Mary when they marched south on 15 November. Having turned back south of Knaresborough on 24 November, the Earls besieged Barnard Castle and it surrendered. They subsequently disbanded their forces and fled when a strong royal army advanced.

Northumberland was handed over by the Scots in 1572 and beheaded at York. The titles and honours of the house of Neville, the family of the Earl of Westmorland, who fled overseas and died in the Netherlands in 1601, were extinguished. Raby Castle, the seat of the Nevilles, was forfeited to the crown. The Percy stronghold of Warkworth was systematically pillaged of timber and fittings. This was scarcely a new policy – previous rebellious northern earls had been killed – but it represented a major change in the political geography of the country. Thereafter, there was not a serious 'northern' problem (within northern England) for the security of governments based in southern England, as there had been for most of the previous 600 years, going back to Northumbrian opposition to the expansion of the Old English house of Wessex in the tenth century. This change was to be consolidated in 1603 with the personal union of England and Scotland when James VI of Scotland became James I of England. The union greatly lessened the possibilities of local magnates playing the two states off against each other. Religion, instead, became more important to the political geography of both England and Scotland.

Retribution after the rising reflected the social politics of Tudor England and demonstrated that Elizabeth had learnt the lesson of the causes of the revolt. Propertied rebels were treated lightly. None of the nineteen leaders from County Durham attainted by Act of Parliament was executed. Eleven went into exile, but eight were pardoned. The

A view of the north-east corner of Baddesley Clinton, Warwickshire. The moated courtyard house was built for the Brome family in the fifteenth century. During the period of Elizabeth I's reign when Catholics were being hunted down, nine men stood motionless in the priest-hole here for four hours.

Coughton Court, Warwickshire. The gatehouse dates from 1530 and the half-timbered courtyard is Elizabethan. Sir Nicholas Throckmorton of Coughton Court was imprisoned for his part in the 1582 plot against Elizabeth that bears his and his nephew's name.

Earl of Northumberland's punishment did not destroy the Percys, for his brother, Sir Henry Percy, had served Elizabeth, and became 8th Earl, and many other families were able to save their estates through such divided loyalties. The instructions for the court martial that tried most of the rebels were that those with freehold, copyhold or estates of substance were to be spared execution. Instead, it was the poor who were punished: different contemporary lists give 228, 305 and 313 as the number of those hanged. Many others had to buy pardons, while the homes and villages of the rebels were plundered.

The failure of the Northern Rising was one of the major stages in the political unification of England, for it marked the end of any viable prospect of regional autonomy centred on a different political and/or religious agenda. This was important because the north was more religiously conservative than the south. Even in 1569 the rebellion had been intended to ensure a change in the policy of the central government. Thereafter, politics centred far more on nationwide attempts to influence the centre, rather than local efforts to defy it.

The Northern Rising was followed by an escalation in tension between Elizabeth's government and Catholic Europe. In 1570 the Pope excommunicated and deposed Elizabeth. This eased the path for a number of unsuccessful conspiracies designed to replace Elizabeth with Mary, Queen of Scots, notably the Ridolfi (1571–2), Throckmorton (1582–3), and Babington (1586) plots. In 1579 the Pope launched an unsuccessful invasion of Ireland. The government responded firmly, in England as well as Ireland. Norfolk was beheaded in 1572 for conspiring with Mary, Queen of Scots, and for his role in the Ridolfi Plot. Catholics were purged from the Lieutenancy and the commissions of the peace, arrested and fined. Francis Throckmorton was racked into confessing to the plot of his name and executed in 1584 while Henry, 8th Earl of Northumberland, was imprisoned; he died, apparently a suicide, in the Tower in 1585. (He had been sent to the Tower in 1571 for negotiating with Mary, Queen of Scots, and was sent again in 1582 and 1584 – on both occasions because of his involvement in plotting.) The cautious Elizabeth was reluctant to try Mary, a fellow ruler and a relative, but in 1586 the interception of her letters revealed that she had agreed to Elizabeth's assassination in the Babington plot. As a result, Mary was convicted of treason, a questionable charge as she owed Elizabeth no allegiance – and beheaded at Fotheringhay Castle in 1587.

Two years earlier, English military support for Dutch Protestant rebels against Philip II and English raids on Spanish trade and colonies, especially those by Sir Francis Drake, had led to war between the two powers. This conflict was most famous for the Armada of 1588, a Spanish attempt to send a major fleet up the Channel in order to cover an invasion of England from the Spanish Netherlands (modern Belgium) by the effective Spanish Army of Flanders, under the Duke of Parma. On 28 May the Armada of 130 ships and 19,000 troops left Lisbon, under the Duke of Medina-Sidonia. Storm damage necessitated refitting

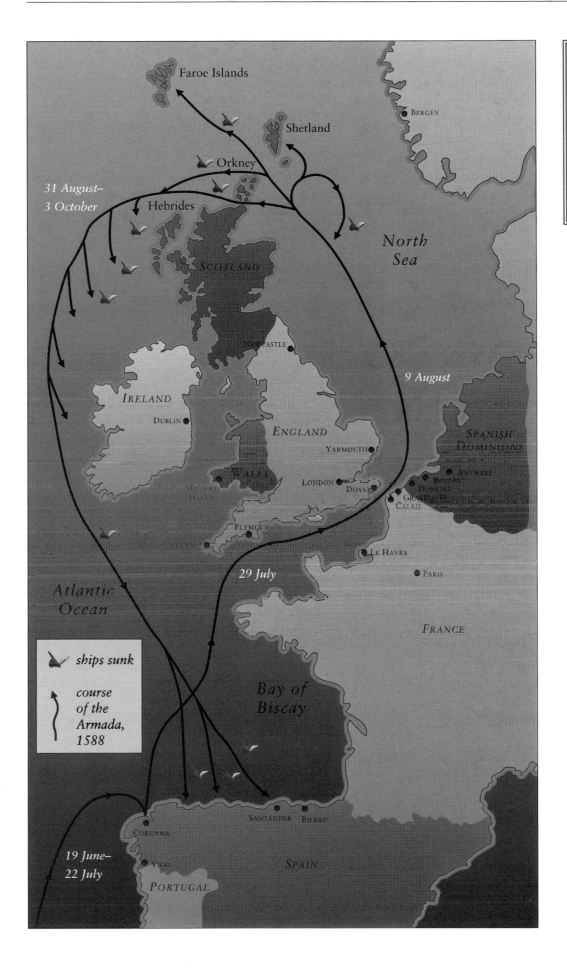

Faroe Islands

BERGEN

Shetland

Orkney

North
Sea

31 August–
3 October

Hebrides

SCOTLAND

NEWCASTLE

9 August

IRELAND

DUBLIN

ENGLAND

YARMOUTH

SPANISH
DOMINIONS

WALES

ANTWERP

LONDON

BRUGES

MILFORD
HAVEN

DOVER

DUNKIRK
GRAVELINES
CALAIS

PLYMOUTH

LE HAVRE

PARIS

Atlantic
Ocean

29 July

FRANCE

ships sunk

course
of the
Armada,
1588

Bay of
Biscay

SANTANDER

BILBAO

CORUNNA

19 June–
22 July

VIGO

SPAIN

PORTUGAL

ROUTE OF THE
SPANISH ARMADA,
1588

The Armada was a serious
challenge to Elizabethan
England. It brought the
country, briefly, into the
front line of the European
Wars of Religion.

Compton Castle, Devon. From here John Gilbert aimed to protect Torbay against the Armada.

in Corunna, and it was July before the slow-moving fleet appeared off The Lizard in Cornwall. The Spanish warships then headed for Calais, maintaining a tight formation to protect their more vulnerable vessels, while harried by long-range English gunnery. This did scant damage, and, during nine days of engagements, the Spanish retained their formation. The English fleet, with the advantage of superior sailing qualities and compact four-wheeled gun-carriages, which permitted a high rate of fire (many of the Spanish guns were on cumbersome carriages designed for use on land), suffered even slighter damage, and was most endangered by a shortage of ammunition. When the naval commander Medina-Sidonia anchored off Calais, he found that Parma had been able to assemble the transport vessels necessary to embark his army for England, but that they could not come out until after the English and Dutch squadrons had been defeated.

Instead, the Spanish formation was disrupted by an English night attack using fireships, and the English fleet then inflicted considerable damage in a running battle off Gravelines. A strong south-westerly wind drove the Armada into the North Sea. With no clear tactical objective after Parma's failed embarkation, the Spanish commanders ordered a return to Spain via the hazardous north-about route around the British Isles. A succession of violent and unseasonal storms lashed the fleet as it passed north of Scotland and down the west coast of Ireland; ship after ship was smashed or driven ashore, and only a remnant of the fleet reached Spain.

Elizabeth's reported speech to the troops assembled at Tilbury to repel the invasion is well known. She stressed both her own dedication to, and her identification with, England, and her remarks were not idle ones: four years earlier, the other leading Protestant champion and opponent of Philip II, William of Orange, had been assassinated:

> I am come amongst you . . . not for my recreation and disport, but being resolved, in the midst and heat of battle, to live or die amongst you all, and to lay down for my God and my kingdom and for my people, my honour and my blood, even in the dust. I know I have the body of a weak and feeble woman, but I have the heart and stomach of a king, and of a king of England too, and think foul scorn that Parma, or Spain, or any prince of Europe should dare to invade the borders of my realm.

Had the army of Flanders landed, the situation might have been less happy. The English defences were inadequate: poor fortifications, insufficient and mostly poorly trained troops, inadequate supplies. Warning beacons such as that on Cley Hill could only do so much. Efforts were made to improve the defences along the south coast – John Gilbert from Compton Castle sought to protect Torbay, while cannon were mounted on the walls of Corfe Castle – but defensive coverage was patchy. It is scarcely surprising that Providence was identified with a victory that owed much to the problems of the Spanish navy, luck, and winds favourable to the English, as well as to the heroism and fighting quality of their navy. This luck fuelled the development of a providential sanction to English Protestantism, which was confirmed in 1688 by the 'Protestant Wind' that helped another William of Orange, later William III. What to us shows the tenuous survival of Elizabeth's regime, to contemporaries displayed the unassailable nature of divine approval.

The failure of the Armada was not the end of the struggle; indeed it was really only the first major Spanish attack. War continued until 1604 and alongside successes, such as Drake's attack on Corunna in 1589 and the defeat of the Spanish invasion force in Ireland at Kinsale in 1601, there were failures. The Spanish navy and empire proved more resilient than had been hoped, mounting fresh armadas in 1596 and 1597 (only

Corfe Castle, Dorset. Cannon directed at the Spanish Armada were mounted on its walls.

The Armada portrait of Elizabeth I by George Gower. War with Spain fostered national consciousness, popular allegiance to Protestantism grew, and new national days of celebration recalling England's recent Protestant history became popular. Church bells were rung every 17 November to celebrate the accession of Elizabeth.

for those to be dispersed by storms) and using convoy systems and improved fortifications to see off English attacks in the Caribbean. The English were greatly helped by Spain's military commitment in the Low Countries and France, which diverted most of the Catholic power's strength.

But the war did have a major impact on England. Spanish support for the opposition made the English conquest of Ireland more difficult, although in 1603 the rebellion begun in 1594 by Hugh O'Neill, Earl of Tyrone, ended with his surrender. The cost of war with Spain and in Ireland created major political problems, helping to ensure that, from 1585, Elizabeth's rule was more troubled. Inflation and a lack of crown revenue created a difficult situation. Elizabeth preferred to cut public expenditure rather than reform the revenue system. Demands for additional taxation and attempts to raise funds by unpopular expedients – especially forced loans, ship money, and the sale of monopolies to manufacture or sell certain goods – led to bitter criticism in the parliaments of 1597 and 1601. Tax demands were especially unwelcome because of harvest failures and related social tensions. Monopolies were a very different kind of grant to crown lands: they entailed economic control and profiteering, were politically risky, and were national rather than local in their impact.

Henry VIII's use of Parliament to legitimate his dynastic and constitutional objectives had increased the frequency and role. Despite Henry VIII's wishes, and largely due to the minority of Edward VI that followed, parliamentary management became a more important issue. In his *De Republica Anglorum* (1565), Sir Thomas Smith noted:

The most high and absolute power of the realm of England consisteth in the parliament . . . The parliament abrogateth old laws, maketh new, giveth order for

The siege of Enniskillen Castle by government forces in February 1594 at the start of the Nine Years' War in Ireland. In 1541, Henry VIII had assumed the title of 'king of Ireland' and claimed the headship of the Irish Church. Ireland, however, rejected the Reformation and thus diverged from the general model of British development.

things past and for things hereafter to be followed, changeth rights and possessions of private men, legitimateth bastards, establisheth forms of religion, altereth weights and measures, giveth forms of succession to the crown . . . And the consent of the parliament is taken to be every mans consent.

In short, the source of sovereign authority was the crown in Parliament. In the 1580s, William Lambarde noted the 'stacks of statutes' that the justices of peace were told to implement. Churchwardens were also expected to do more. The greater role of JPs encouraged a stronger, public focus for localism in the courts of quarter sessions and the gentry, as JPs came to have a greater contact with the expectations and demands of central government.

This was an important aspect of the social politics of the period, for the rise of a more numerous and independent gentry was a crucial development of the century. This rise reflected the difficulties experienced by the peerage and its failure to be the prime beneficiary of the socio-political changes of the period. The creation of stronger links with the gentry was one of the major achievements of the Tudors. It contrasted markedly with the situation in France where politics was organised far more in terms of aristocratic clientage systems and the crown had fewer links with those who were below the apex of these systems.

The use of the gentry as the basis of local government ensured that state policy bore the imprint of local power. This posed problems in the event of differences between ruler and gentry, in particular if the ruler sought to interfere with local autonomy, but these differences did not become serious until the reign of Charles I. In the meanwhile, the system worked reasonably well in England and Wales. The gentry proved less disruptive in national politics than many aristocrats had been in the fifteenth century. Furthermore, increased use of the gentry helped to consolidate a sense of county community, although this varied across England and Wales for there was no typical county.

Puritanism was a source of tension, leading to serious parliamentary clashes. This was particularly so in 1587, when Puritan MPs tried unsuccessfully to legislate for a Presbyterian church settlement, a move bitterly opposed by Elizabeth who wished to continue church government by bishops. After John Whitgift became Archbishop of Canterbury in 1583, the Queen's wish to impose uniformity on dissident clergy in the national church was implemented. Whitgift's humble origins and anti-Puritan tendencies were not popular with his fellow Privy Councillors.

Elizabeth also found it difficult to create a stable and effective central government after the ministers who had served her so long – William Cecil, Lord Burghley; Robert Dudley, Earl of Leicester, and Sir Francis Walsingham – died. In 1601, Elizabeth's arrogant favourite, Robert Devereux, 2nd Earl of Essex, unsuccessfully attempted to stage a coup in order to seize Elizabeth and destroy his rival, the chief minister, Burghley's son, Sir Robert Cecil. Essex sought more power for the nobility and remarked 'to serve as a servant and a slave I know not'. He was supported by seven other peers, but failed totally and was beheaded. The episode challenged political assumptions and the mystique of monarchy. Elizabeth herself became less adept and tolerant in her last years than she had been earlier in the reign. She emphasised authority and showed herself unable to accept disagreement, prefiguring the situation under James I and Charles I.

Nevertheless, there was nothing to match the crisis atmosphere of the mid-sixteenth century, either in domestic politics, the religious situation, social disorder, the succession, or Anglo-Scottish relations. The war against Spain was more successful than those against France and Scotland had been. Irish opposition was overcome. Serious economic problems led to a national poor law, not to a major rebellion. In another index of stability, England was less prepared for civil conflict than most countries. There had been an extensive abandonment of castles, in some cases from the 1470s, and far more actively during the Tudor period. Dunstanburgh Castle was already much ruined in 1538 and Dunster Castle in 1542, as a consequence of a lack of maintenance for decades. In 1597 a survey found that Melbourne Castle, a Duchy of Lancaster possession in Derbyshire, was being used as a pound for trespassing cattle. The castle itself was demolished for stone in the 1610s by its new owner, the Earl of Huntingdon. Warkworth Castle was neglected and when James I visited it in 1617 he found sheep and goats in most of the rooms. Bramber Castle, formerly a Sussex stronghold of the Howards, was in ruins.

The Elizabethan period did not end on a triumphant note. There were problems aplenty, and the government had a stop-gap feel to it, but, as ever, it is necessary to place these problems in context. Britain had not experienced sustained civil war comparable to that in France, nor a financial crisis similar to that in Spain, and the Stuart succession was inaugurated in 1603 without a civil war. These were no mean achievements.

The remains of the west wall of the keep, Bramber Castle, Sussex. By the early seventeenth century the former stronghold of the Howard family was in ruins.

FIVE

Britain and the Wider World

Buckland Abbey, the Devon home of Sir Francis Drake, contains in the Drake Gallery two sixteenth-century flags bearing the royal arms, perhaps flown on board *The Golden Hind* at Deptford when Drake was knighted in April 1581. This honour reflected his profitable, plundering circumnavigation of the globe in 1577–80, the first by an English sea captain. This voyage was not an isolated episode, but, instead, an early example of a major expansion in English overseas activity. To discuss this first in the section of the book devoted to the seventeenth century may appear surprising. Generally, the political struggles of the period take precedence, especially the Civil War. Yet, Britain's interaction with the wider world was arguably the most important feature of its history. It was in the seventeenth century that the English established a presence in India and the West Indies and, more significantly, became the leading colonial power on the eastern seaboard of North America. The notion of an oceanic and colonial destiny became well established and England, by the end of the century, was the leading naval power in the world. Trans-oceanic trade became more important. The sea came to play a greater role in the collective imagination, a process that culminated in 1740 with the maritime theme of James Thomson's ode *Rule Britannia*:

> Rule Britannia, rule the waves,
> Britons never will be slaves.

Britain had done poorly from the first burst of European trans-oceanic activity at the cusp of the fifteenth and sixteenth centuries. Despite discovering the fishing wealth of Newfoundland waters, John Cabot's voyages were very much on the margins of profitable activity. Not only did English expeditions fail to discover the direct route to Asia that they sought through a north-west passage to the north of America, or a north-east passage north of Asia, they also missed out on the compensation of American bullion that Cortes and Pizzarro had seized for Spain. In addition, English commercial penetration of the Indian Ocean only began after the Portuguese were well established there, while the development of trade with Muscovy and Turkey did not produce profits to match those with more distant markets. Thus, the crowns of England and, to

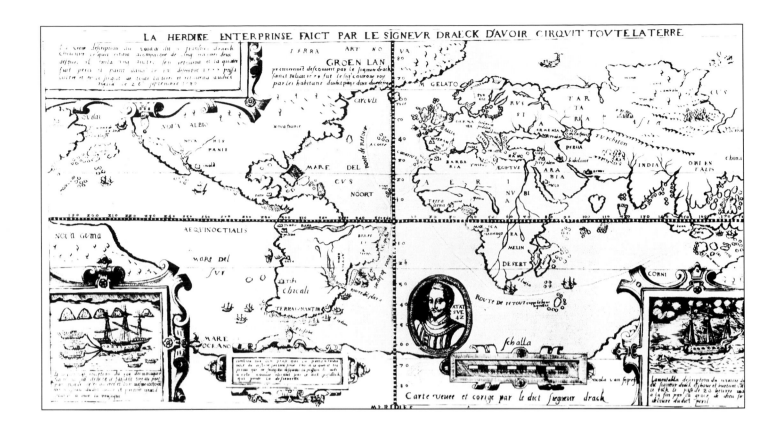

a greater extent, Scotland failed to gain an infusion of trans-oceanic wealth, especially American bullion, except, in the English case, vicariously through attacks on Spanish settlements and trade.

Nevertheless, from the 1550s, the focus on continental adventures declined and long-distance seafaring was encouraged by the crown. There was a growing awareness of the nature and opportunities of the wider world. The Drake Cup at Buckland was engraved with a version of Mercator's world map of 1587, and in about 1596 London audiences heard of Shakespeare's Antonio, the merchant of Venice: 'He hath an argosy bound to Tripolis, another to the Indies . . . he hath a third at Mexico, a fourth for England'. Geography offered a new ideal of science as a tool for understanding and controlling nature, and this potential made the subject popular. Service of the state encouraged an interest in mathematical geography, while descriptive geography encouraged readers to regard the world as a source of wondrous tales and new goods, thus creating attitudes that encouraged the exploitation of foreign peoples. There was a close relationship between the study of geography and the development of ideas of English power and imperial growth, and such a relationship was especially pronounced at the court of James I's eldest son, Prince Henry. At least thirty-seven men who were connected with his circle had an interest in some aspect of geography.

Privateering attacks on the Spanish New World had become important from the 1560s. Santo Domingo was sacked in 1584 and Puerto Rico in 1598. Yet such attacks yielded only transient gains and were increasingly thwarted by the strength of Spain's imperial defences. The development of trade routes was more important, as was the beginning of settlement in North America. In 1600 an East India Company was founded to trade by sea with south and south-east Asia and the East Indies, principally in order to

World Map detailing the expeditions and global circumnavigation of Sir Francis Drake, 1577–80. Drake was long a lodestar of English heroism. Under Drake's Flag (1883) was one of George Alfred Henty's popular adventure stories for boys. On his circumnavigation, the second in history, Drake claimed California for Elizabeth I.

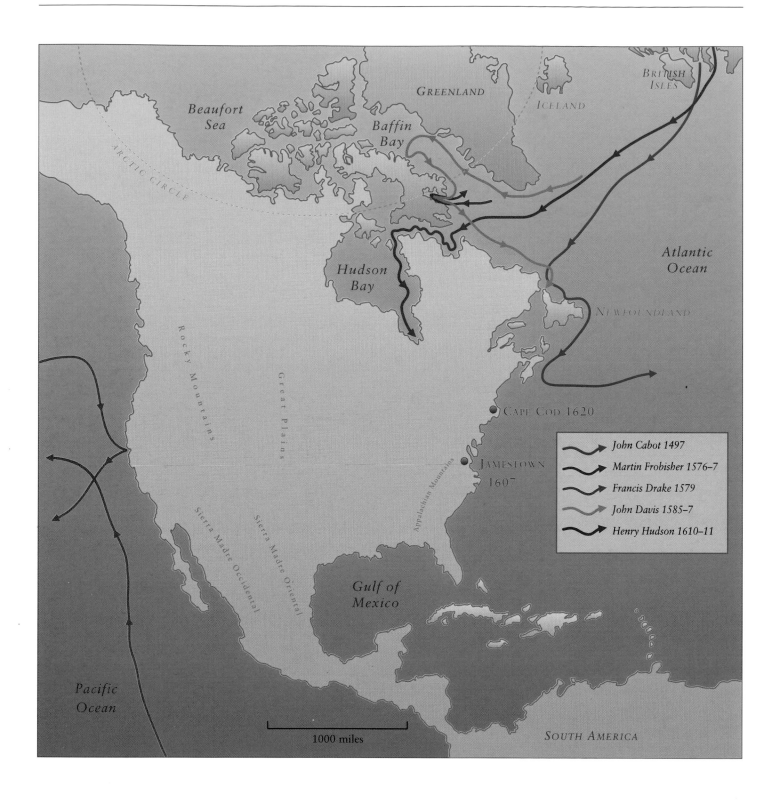

Beaufort
Sea

GREENLAND

ICELAND

BRITISH
ISLES

ARCTIC CIRCLE

Baffin
Bay

Atlantic
Ocean

Hudson
Bay

NEWFOUNDLAND

Rocky Mountains

Great Plains

Appalachian Mountains

CAPE COD 1620

Sierra Madre Occidental

Sierra Madre Oriental

JAMESTOWN
1607

	John Cabot 1497
	Martin Frobisher 1576–7
	Francis Drake 1579
	John Davis 1585–7
	Henry Hudson 1610–11

Gulf of
Mexico

Pacific
Ocean

1000 miles

SOUTH AMERICA

EXPLORATION OF
NORTH AMERICA

*English exploration
focused on the north
Atlantic coastline of
North America.*

obtain spices. It was eventually to form the basis of Britain's Indian empire. The company was a chartered monopoly trading body that spread the considerable risks of long-distance trade among a number of investors and drew on the wealthy mercantile world of London. Both joint stock companies and the privateering war with Spain were perfect examples of the 'partnership' approach to government that was more generally seen with the growth in the role of the gentry. They also created precedents for the huge developments of the later seventeenth century. In the early seventeenth century, the crown moved away from the Elizabethan interest in distant waters, but, by that time, the maritime community had developed a momentum of its own; the East India Company and the North American colonies owed relatively little to the crown.

North America initially seemed a far less profitable prospect than the East Indies, but attempts were made to establish English claims. On his circumnavigation, although he missed the entrance to San Francisco harbour, Drake claimed 'Nova Albion' – the Californian coast – for Elizabeth. Humphrey Gilbert claimed Newfoundland for the queen in 1583. An attempt was made to establish a colony on the eastern seaboard, called Virginia in honour of the unmarried sovereign. In 1585 108 colonists were landed on Roanoke Island off the coast of what is now North Carolina, but they found it difficult to feed themselves and were taken off the following year. A second attempt was made in 1588, but when a relief ship arrived in 1590 it found the village deserted: disease, starvation or natives may have wiped out the colonists. It was not until a base was established by the Virginia Company at Jamestown in the Chesapeake in 1607 that

Virginia, showing in the upper left a picture of Chief Powhatan by John Smith, 1624. The Atlantic is to the south. The map shows how bays and rivers aided English penetration.

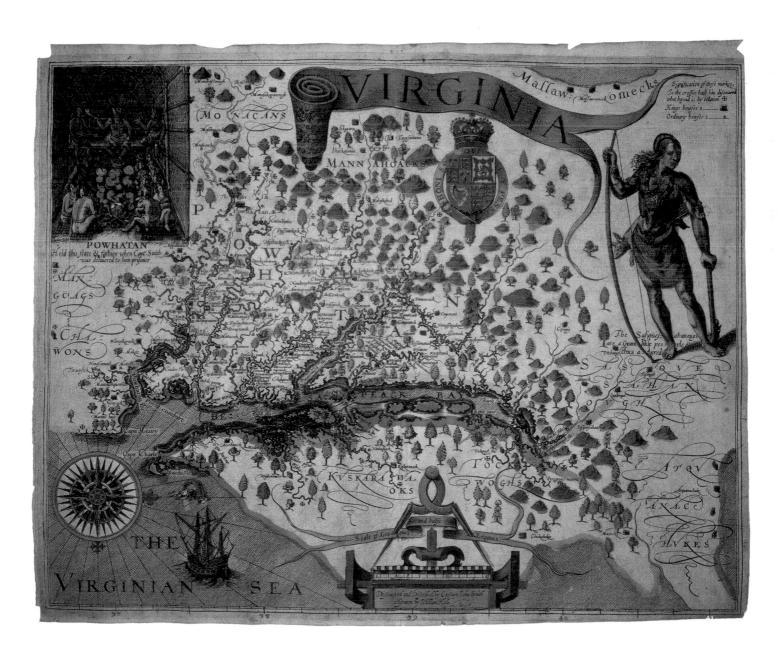

a permanent colony was founded. Despite heavy initial losses, largely due to the impact of disease in an unfamiliar environment, the colony expanded and Indian resistance was overcome. Then in 1620 the *Mayflower* made a landfall at Cape Cod, and the development of a colony in New England began.

The English were not the only European presence on the eastern seaboard. The Spaniards were established in Florida, and the French in the St Lawrence valley and Acadia (now Nova Scotia). The Dutch were in the Hudson valley, the Swedes in the Delaware valley. Yet by 1674 the English were the sole European power between Acadia and Florida, and in 1713 and 1763 respectively these were ceded to Britain. Having overrun New Sweden, the Dutch, were, in turn, defeated in the Second and Third Anglo-Dutch Wars. Captured a second time in 1674, New Amsterdam became New York. Government support for colonies was crucial in the Dutch wars: both Oliver Cromwell and Charles II saw England as a maritime and commercial power, dependent upon its seamen and its merchants for success in a competitive world.

The English were also successful, although only after some difficulty, against the native population. In the Pequot War of 1637 the overwhelming superiority of the English in firearms brought them victory in the Connecticut River valley. The spread of firearms among the native population lessened this advantage, and the rising in New England of 1675–6 – 'King Philip's War' – was suppressed with considerable difficulty. The English also benefited from extensive migration to their North American colonies and from their local numerical superiority. About 7,900 of the 11,600 native Americans living in Southern New England on the eve of King Philip's War, died through battle, disease or exposure, or were removed for sale as slaves or became permanent refugees. This, in turn, created fresh opportunities for English expansion and settlement.

During the second half of the seventeenth century new colonies were founded – notably Carolina and Pennsylvania – and the pace of migration was such that, by 1700, the population was considerably greater than that in French North America. This was important both in terms of the potential for local military resources, especially militia, and because it helped ensure that British North America was an increasingly important part of the British economy – both as a source of vital raw materials and as a market.

These processes continued in the eighteenth century. The navy grew in size and administrative sophistication. Existing colonies expanded. Georgia was founded as a new colony and saw off Spanish attack in the War of Jenkins' Ear (1739–48). New settlements included Baltimore (1729) and Savannah (1733). There was also expansion to the north. In the War of the Spanish Succession (1702–13), Nova Scotia was captured for Britain and the British position in Hudson Bay and Newfoundland was accepted by France.

Where it resisted, the native population, took heavy blows. The Tuscaroras responded to the advance of Carolina settlers by mounting raids in 1711, but were defeated two years later. Provoked by exploitation by Carolina merchants and landowners, the Yamasee of the Lower Savannah River attacked South Carolina in 1715, raiding to within 12 miles of Charleston. The initial response was unsuccessful, but the Carolinians benefited from growing divisions among their opponents and the Yamasee were pushed back. Defeat had a crucial demographic impact on the natives. The number of Tuscaroras fell from 5,000 to 2,500. Many took refuge with the Iroquois and those that remained were grouped by the colonists in a reservation that by 1760 contained only about 300 people. From 1715 most of the Yamasee were killed or enslaved by the

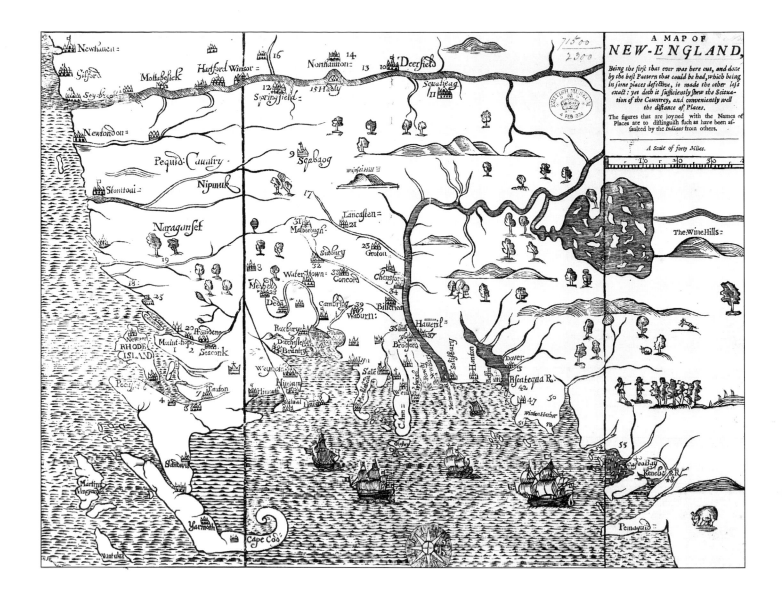

A MAP OF NEW-ENGLAND,

Being the first that ever was here cut, and done by the best Pattern that could be had, which being in some places defective, it made the other less exact: yet doth it sufficiently shew the Scituation of the Countrey, and conveniently well the distance of Places.

The figures that are joyned with the Names of Places are to distinguish such as have been assaulted by the Indians from others.

A Scale of forty Miles.

colonial militia. Such measures helped to expand the British world. In places there was successful resistance. Guerrilla warfare by the Western Abenaki in the 1720s kept settlers out of what was to be Vermont. Cherokee resistance in 1760–1 and Pontiac's War west of the Appalachians in 1763–4 restricted the settlers' advance, but none of these struggles impinged on the central positions of British North America. The settlers were there to stay. As the colonial population rose, so the direct impact on Britain increased.

Island colonies were also established. Bermuda (1613) was followed by West Indian colonies: St Kitts (1624), Barbados (1627) and Nevis (1628). The biggest acquisition, Jamaica, did not follow until 1655, but, by the end of the century, a plantation economy was well developed. It produced sugar for Britain and other European markets, providing the prime source of re-exports; and was worked by slaves brought from West Africa. British coastal bases there included Accra (1672).

The combination of North America and the West Indies led to a major expansion in British trade, an expansion that can be better charted thanks to the marked improvement in the collection of statistics during this period. The office of Inspector General of Imports and Exports was established in 1696, as was the Board of Trade and Plantations. William Blaythwayt of Dyrham Park was a Commissioner of the

New England, the Atlantic at the bottom. The placenames reflect the expropriation of native land and the role of English settlement. New England was the term first used in 1614 by Captain John Smith when he described the coastline north of the Hudson. His Description of New England *(1616) popularised the idea.*

Sail boats on the Thames by the Tower of London, by Samuel Scott, 1753. London's seventeenth-century townscape is visible in the background with both the Monument and St Paul's Cathedral. Scott, famous for his shore and river scenes, was called the English Canaletto.

Board in 1696–1706, and American materials, especially woods, were used in building his house.

New statistics made it easier for contemporaries to assess the importance of trade. Average journey times across the Atlantic fell, the number of crossings increased, and the shipping seasons were extended. Average annual exports to North America rose from £0.7 million in 1701–5 to over £2 million in 1786–90, a period of low inflation. English shipping tonnage rose from 340,000 in 1686 to 421,000 in 1751. Imports of tobacco through Liverpool rose from 1.49 million pounds in 1689–96 to 2.86 million pounds in 1703–12. The number of Glasgow's ships rose from 30 in the late 1680s to 70 by the 1730s.

These increases were accompanied by changes in the economic geography of Britain itself. The initial impact of trans-oceanic trade and fishing had been concentrated in the West Country, especially Bristol, but also the ports of north Devon – Bideford and Barnstaple – and south Devon, especially Dartmouth. Well over 200 ships were employed in the Newfoundland cod fishery in the early seventeenth century, and in the eighteenth century, Dartmouth, Exeter and Poole dominated this industry. In the same period, trans-oceanic trade was increasingly handled not only by Bristol and London, but also by Glasgow, Liverpool, Whitehaven and Lancaster.

Many of these changes were still very much in the future in the seventeenth century. This was also true of the emergence of the British in India. Although Madras, Bombay and Calcutta were all English bases before the end of the seventeenth century, the East India Company did not become an important territorial power in India until after Robert Clive's victory over the far larger forces of the Nawab of Bengal at Plassey in 1757. Yet it is important to recall these developments when discussing the struggles within Britain in the seventeenth century, and to consider how far the course of the latter helped make possible Britain's emergence as a world power.

SIX

James VI & I

Compared to the drama of the reigns of Elizabeth I and Charles I, the intervening one appears to lack excitement. It is best known for the Gunpowder Plot of 1605, the discovery of which is still celebrated every year on Guy Fawkes Night, 5 November. Yet the years of James's reign were important. They witnessed both the establishment of permanent colonies in North America and the highpoint of the English stage. In addition to Shakespeare, Francis Beaumont, Thomas Dekker, John Fletcher, Ben Jonson, Philip Massinger, Thomas Middleton, William Rowley and John Webster were all producing plays for the London stage.

James VI and I, 1566–1625, king of Scotland from 1567 and of England from 1603, the first of the Stuart kings.

These were also important years for architecture. The Banqueting Hall in Whitehall was built by Inigo Jones, Surveyor of the King's Works, 1619–22. Jones was initially known as a designer of court masques, but his most significant achievement was the introduction of a classical architectural style to England where Renaissance influence had until then been fairly superficial. The Banqueting House was intended to be the nucleus of a massive new palace at Whitehall. Fearful of assassination, James had disliked the colonnade in the previous hall on the site.

The ceiling of the Banqueting Hall, commissioned by Charles I and painted in the early 1630s by Rubens, displayed the apotheosis of James. He is seen being escorted to heaven and depicted as the heir of Arthur and the monarch of universal peace. Charles was presented by Rubens as God's representative on earth. Also, James's statue was inserted in the gatehouse tower of the Bodleian Library at Oxford, with a testimony to his interest in learning and peace.

In addition, James's reign left a series of splendid stately houses, new-built or embellished. All apparently testified to the success of the period. Examples include Audley End, Blickling Hall,

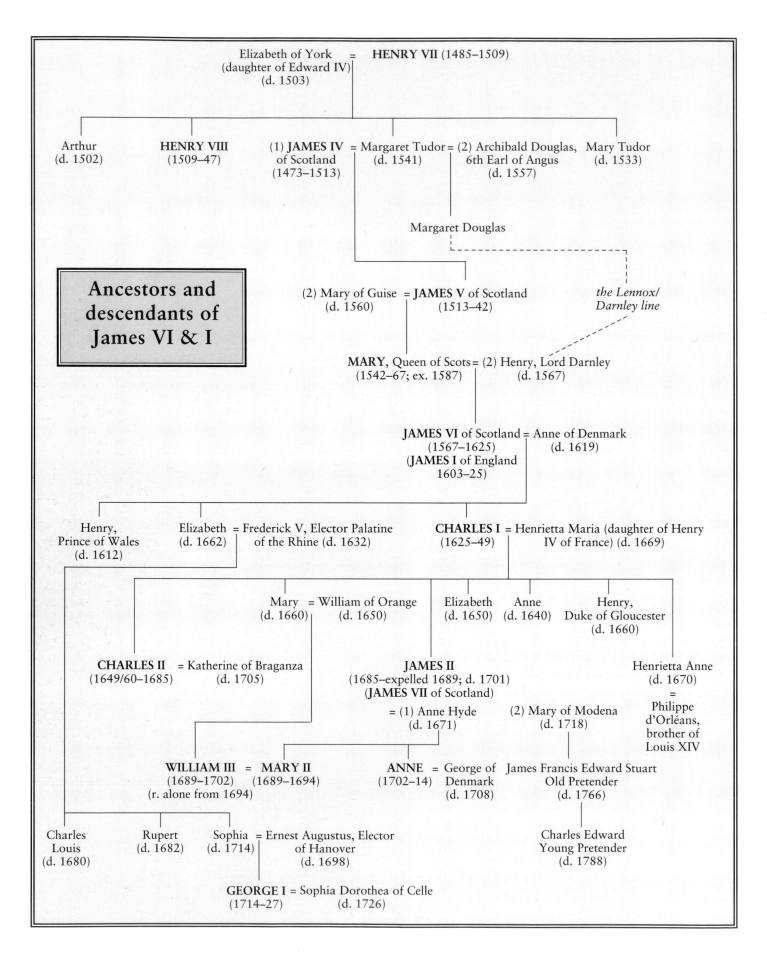

Ancestors and descendants of James VI & I

Elizabeth of York = HENRY VII (1485–1509)
(daughter of Edward IV)
(d. 1503)

Arthur (d. 1502)

HENRY VIII (1509–47)

(1) JAMES IV = Margaret Tudor = (2) Archibald Douglas, Mary Tudor
of Scotland (d. 1541) 6th Earl of Angus (d. 1533)
(1473–1513) (d. 1557)

Margaret Douglas

(2) Mary of Guise = JAMES V of Scotland   the Lennox/
(d. 1560) (1513–42)   Darnley line

MARY, Queen of Scots = (2) Henry, Lord Darnley
(1542–67; ex. 1587) (d. 1567)

JAMES VI of Scotland = Anne of Denmark
(1567–1625) (d. 1619)
(JAMES I of England
1603–25)

Henry, Elizabeth = Frederick V, Elector Palatine   CHARLES I = Henrietta Maria (daughter of Henry
Prince of Wales (d. 1662) of the Rhine (d. 1632)   (1625–49) IV of France) (d. 1669)
(d. 1612)

Mary = William of Orange   Elizabeth   Anne   Henry,
(d. 1660) (d. 1650)   (d. 1650) (d. 1640) Duke of Gloucester
                                                  (d. 1660)

CHARLES II = Katherine of Braganza   JAMES II   Henrietta Anne
(1649/60–1685) (d. 1705)   (1685–expelled 1689; d. 1701) (d. 1670)
                                      (JAMES VII of Scotland)   =
                                      = (1) Anne Hyde (2) Mary of Modena Philippe
                                        (d. 1671)   (d. 1718)   d'Orléans,
                                                                          brother of
                                                                          Louis XIV

WILLIAM III = MARY II   ANNE = George of James Francis Edward Stuart
(1689–1702) (1689–1694) (1702–14) Denmark Old Pretender
(r. alone from 1694)   (d. 1708) (d. 1766)

Charles   Rupert   Sophia = Ernest Augustus, Elector   Charles Edward
Louis   (d. 1682) (d. 1714) of Hanover   Young Pretender
(d. 1680)   (d. 1698)   (d. 1788)

GEORGE I = Sophia Dorothea of Celle
(1714–27) (d. 1726)

Chastleton House, Knole, and the original Ham House. This was also true of Scotland. Alexander Irvine, 9th Laird of Drum, was responsible for the Jacobean mansion that in 1619 joined the earlier fortified tower house at Drum. The shift from keep to stately home was symptomatic of an apparently more peaceful society. Town walls and castles fell into ruin. John Speed described Northampton Castle in 1610: 'gaping chinks do daily threaten the downfall of her walls'.

There was indeed much cause for contentment. This may appear a surprising remark given the civil war that was to follow in the next reign, or indeed given the problems of James's reign, including serious difficulties with Parliament. With the exception of the acrimonious, and short, Addled Parliament of 1614, James ruled without the two Houses between 1610 and 1621. The 1621 session saw serious trouble over foreign policy. There were disputes over church government, the expansion of the peerage angered many existing aristocrats, and rural tensions led to serious disturbances.

Yet it is necessary not to be dominated by hindsight, and to note that, in many respects, James's reign was relatively successful. He avoided both any equivalent to the slide into civil war that was to occur in 1638–42 and any crises similar to those in contemporary France or the Austrian Habsburg dominions. The Treaty of London with Spain of 1604 was scarcely glorious and it was to be criticised by many who were opposed to any settlement with Spain. Nevertheless, peace helped lessen domestic financial burdens and was necessary since Spain was shedding itself of other foes by negotiating settlements with France (1598) and the Dutch (1609). James was careful thereafter to avoid war until persuaded into an unsuccessful conflict with Spain in 1624. Crucially, he refused to take part in the Thirty Years' War (1618–48), on behalf of the Protestant powers, even though they included his son-in-law, the Elector Palatine, and, from 1621, the Dutch. The problems his son Charles experienced as a result of war with France and Spain underline the wisdom of James's neutrality.

There was religious tension, but no overt conflict in Britain. A small group of Catholics put gunpowder in the cellars under Parliament, planning to blow it up when James I opened the session on 5 November 1605, and hoping that the destruction of the royal family and the Protestant elite would ignite rebellion. Conspirators gathered at a number of Catholic houses, including Coughton Court. The attempt to warn a Catholic peer, William Parker, 4th Baron Monteagle, to be absent, led, however, to the exposure of the plot. Guy Fawkes was tortured to force him to reveal the names of his co-conspirators and then executed. A number of

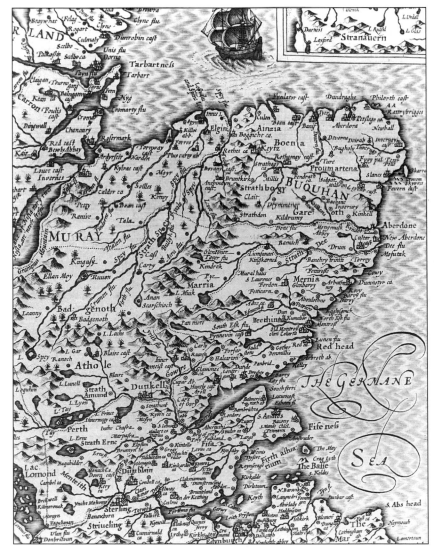

Lothian, Fife and the Highlands, from John Speed's map of Scotland. Speed was an assiduous cartographer whose maps were published as an atlas, the Theatre of the Empire of Great Britain *(1611). Speed was quick to see the commercial value of maps. He printed town maps as insets on his county maps. The* Theatre *was reissued in fourteen editions up to 1770.*

conspirators, including Robert Catesby and Thomas Percy, died resisting arrest. Henry Percy, 9th Earl of Northumberland, was sent to the Tower and held there until 1621, although his crime was Catholicism, rather than conspiracy.

Yet the plot was not followed by any attempt to extirpate Catholicism, nor did Catholic survivalism pose serious political problems. In general, religious tension diminished under James, although it remained an important source of future difficulties. At the Hampton Court Conference of 1604, James helped to lessen differences by allowing theologians of various Protestant views to participate. James, himself, supported moderate church reform: he had strong views on religious observance, and on behaviour on Sundays.

Serious episodes of organised defiance of royal authority in England were less common than in many other countries, including Scotland. There were particular problems on the borders of Highland estates, to where landless men were driven. In the 1630s, Sir William Forbes of Craigievar in Aberdeenshire and his kinsmen at Corse suffered greatly from a band of Highland raiders led by Gilderoy. In 1636, twelve of the band, including the leader, were captured and hanged, and their heads displayed as a warning. England was less disturbed.

Another success important to British political geography was the changing relationship between England, Ireland and Scotland. This was not a case of the end of frontiers, for both Scotland and Ireland remained states in their own right. Despite James' hopes for a 'union of love', or at least a measure of administrative and economic union, between England and Scotland, the union remained essentially personal. There was fear in England about the legal and constitutional implications, and the Westminster Parliament rejected a parliamentary or legal bond. Scotland was governed by the Scottish Privy Council, but the absentee kingship proved relatively successful. The Presbyterians were persuaded to accept a modified episcopal (bishops) system. Whereas the personal union between Sweden and Poland broke down, that between Scotland and England continued until destroyed by Charles I's policies.

Windsor in the reign of James I, by an anonymous artist. Windsor had long been a fortress, but it was becoming a palace. The estate was very popular with monarchs who enjoyed hunting.

James went south to claim his new crown in 1603 and stayed there, except for one visit. He was, therefore, less exposed than his predecessors on the Scottish throne to the impact of quarrels between Scottish barons or their defiance of royal authority. James's succession to the English throne was followed by a firm campaign of repression against the border reivers or moss-troopers who dominated the Anglo-Scottish border lands. Many were killed and one of the most persistently troublesome clans, the Grahams, were forcibly transplanted to Ireland in 1606. The government of the English frontier regions also changed, becoming more like that of ordinary shires. The Wardenships of the Marches ceased and James sold Dunstanburgh Castle in 1604.

Catholic Ireland had been conquered by 1603. For the first time, the English controlled the entire island. This conquest brought a measure of unity, and, thereafter, Ireland was to be contested as a unit. Conquest was followed by a major extension of the policy of 'plantation': the expropriation of land in favour of Protestant landowners, and, in part, its settlement by English and Scottish settlers. This was particularly the case with Ulster. Resulting discontents over land, religion and political status were to lead to rebellion in 1641, but, during James's reign, from the perspective of London, the Irish situation seemed more promising.

Hand coloured map of Cornwall from the third edition of Theatre of the Empire of Great Britain *by John Speed (1627). Speed also published a* History of Great Britaine *dedicated to James I, a testimony to growing interest in British history. The second edition, published in 1623, was reprinted in 1625 and 1627, a third followed in 1632.*

95

James himself was perceptive, conciliatory, clever, complex and self-indulgent. Far from being a warrior king, like his contemporaries, his brother-in-law, Christian IV of Denmark, and Gustavus Adolphus of Sweden, James was best served by peace. This enabled him to pursue his interest in controversy that led to a series of writings, most famously against tobacco and witches, and in support of the divine right of kings, but also the Directions to Preachers of 1622.

In spite of a love-match with Anne of Denmark and fathering three children, the bisexual James was also keen on a series of pretty young men. This had serious political implications because of his willingness to promote them to the aristocracy and at court. One favourite, Robert Carr, Earl of Somerset, and his wife were found guilty of poisoning Sir Thomas Overbury in the Tower of London in 1613 but were reprieved by James and comfortably confined at Greys Court. Overbury knew too much about the seamy side of court intrigues. Another favourite, George Villiers, became Duke of Buckingham and the key advisor of James's heir, Charles. Unpopular, greedy and intolerant of disagreement, Buckingham was impeached in 1626 and murdered in 1628.

The royal court was a major centre of patronage, and a cultural intermediary between Britain and the continent. Under James, it was also corrupt and sleazy, which hardly contributed to the prestige of monarchy, although his bounty to courtiers eased political differences at the top. Other mores and styles were also on offer, and in some cases they were dramatically different to the life at court. In 1621 a play written by Jasper Garnett, a local schoolmaster, and put on in Kendal Castle included some biting social satire. Hell was declared to contain 'Land lordes and puritanes and Sherriffe Bailiffes and other sortes of people whom they would have made odious'. The author defended himself when his case came before Star Chamber after he was accused of making subversive comments: 'What was then acted was a representation of ravens feeding of poore sheepe in Hell which ravens were compared to greedy landlords and the sheep to their poore tenantes . . . but the same was not intended against any of the County of Westmorland than against other counties and all in general.'

The play's criticism of 'false landlordes' could be presented as supportive to the social hierarchy, but its values were different from those of masques at court. At the other end of the spectrum, with its distinctively sober and pious lifestyle, Puritanism could be similarly satirised, as with the hypocritical zealot Zeal-of-the-Land Busy in Ben Jonson's *Bartholomew Fair* (1614), and 'we of the separation' in his *The Alchemist* (1610), but it proposed a set of values against which the royal court seemed corrupt. Little Moreton Hall, with its biblical texts decorating the chapel and the parlour frieze depicting the story of Susannah and the Elders, was a world away from James's tastes. A less overt challenge to the style of the court was that of James's eldest son, Prince Henry: he offered the muscular kingship that James conspicuously lacked, but predeceased his father in 1612. As with Henry VII's offspring, the way was left clear for succession by the second son, in this case the man who was to become Charles I (1625–49), a withdrawn and rigid individual who lacked the flexibility and intelligence necessary to avoid the problems that stemmed from the partisan and divisive policies he supported.

SEVEN

The British Civil Wars

The mid-seventeenth century witnessed the greatest crisis in British society. Britons fought against and killed other Britons as never before. These conflicts are often known as the English Civil Wars. But to call them English is wrong and misleading – a higher percentage of the Irish population died. The wars were about the control of the three kingdoms (Scotland, Ireland England – the last including Wales).

Not only were there civil wars in England/Wales, Scotland and Ireland, but these were interconnected. In 1644, 25 per cent of serving troops were out of theatre – for example, there were 4,000 Irish troops in England and 6,000 in Scotland. And the war was a major struggle. More than half the total number of battles ever fought on English soil involving more than 5,000 men were fought between 1642 and 1651. Out of an English male population of about 1.5 million, over 80,000 died in combat and another 100,000 of other causes arising from the war, principally disease. Bitter civil conflict was not new and more men may have fought at Towton (1461) in the Wars of the Roses than in any of the battles of the Civil War, but the sustained level of hostilities, the Britain-wide scale of the conflict, and the vicious politicisation of popular attitudes were unprecedented.

The war was vicious. After the Battle of Hopton Heath (19 March 1643), Sir John Gell, the Parliamentary Governor of Derby, paraded the naked corpse of Spencer Compton, 2nd Earl of Northampton, round the town. Few prisoners were taken by any side in Ireland: in 1649 when Cromwell's men stormed Drogheda, the garrison of about 2,500 was slaughtered, the few who received quarter being sent to work on

Charles I, 1600–49, king of England, Scotland and Ireland from 1625. He lacked the character and talents required to be a successful monarch.

the sugar plantations in Barbados. Largely as a result of subsequent famine, plague and emigration, the conquest of Ireland in 1649–52 led to the loss of about 40 per cent of the Irish population, and was followed by widespread expropriation of Catholic land.

The conflicts reflected Charles I's failure to run a multiple monarchy, indeed any monarchy, effectively. His inheritance was a promising one and Britain crucially was not involved in the Thirty Years' War currently being fought on the continent. However, Charles, who came to the throne in 1625, lacked common sense, flexibility and pragmatism, was devious and untrustworthy, and his belief in order and in the dignity of kingship led him to take an unsympathetic attitude to disagreement. After encountering severe problems with Parliament over his financial expedients, especially the forced loan of 1626, Charles dispensed with it in 1629 and launched his 'Personal Rule'.

Charles was isolated from the wider political world, and the informal channels of royal authority did not work well. There was tension over his novel financial demands, especially the extension of Ship Money, the levy paid by coastal areas in support of the navy that Charles decided to extend to inland areas in 1635, but most did not follow John Hampden in refusing to pay. Monopolies remained a grievance, and fines, for example for not taking up knighthood if a wealthy landowner or for encroaching on royal forests, made enemies. Thomas Wentworth, 1st Earl of Strafford, aroused much unease as President of the Council in the North, 1628–32, and, more particularly, Lord Deputy of Ireland, 1632–9. His policy of 'thorough' government in Ireland, by which he meant disregard of private interests and emphasis on royal power, was seen as tyrannical.

The toleration of Catholics at court – where the Catholic French queen, Henrietta Maria, was a prominent figure – was very unpopular; so was the Arminian tendency within the Church of England associated with William Laud, whom Charles made Archbishop of Canterbury in 1633. Arminianism was an anti-Calvinist doctrine that attacked the Calvinist views prevalent both in the Church of England and among its Puritan critics until the 1610s. Arminianism became influential in the church in the 1620s, especially when Richard Neile, Bishop of Durham, became principal church adviser to James I, and was even more so under Charles I, who was greatly influenced by Laud. Calvinists were denied favour, and Arminian clerics gained preferment. The preaching of Calvinist doctrine was limited, as Laud sought to enforce uniformity on a church that had been diverse in many respects for decades. He was unwilling to permit Puritan clerics to comply with his regulations occasionally, and insisted that parish churches should match the more regulated practice of cathedrals. This authoritarianism compounded the offensive nature of Laudian ceremonial and doctrine – not least its stress on the sacraments and church services that emphasised the cleric, not the congregation.

Arminianism was seen as crypto-Catholic and thus conducive to tyranny by its critics, and Charles could be harsh towards critics. He saw difference as subversive, and equated Puritanism with Calvinism and the two with opposition to due authority. His political thought and manner were divisive. Prerogative courts under royal control, especially Star Chamber and High Commission, gave out savage penalties. Most people, however, were reluctant to enter into rebellion, and it was a tribute to Charles's political incompetence that he transformed dissent into political disaster. In Exeter, for example, the rival Parliamentary and Royalist camps that emerged in the 1640s were continuations of the divisions of the 1620s and 1630s when the Puritan Mayor, Ignatius Jurdain, had split the City Council. Yet before the 1640s there had been no fighting.

The outbreak of civil war in England reflected a spiral of concern arising from Charles's mishandling of crises in Scotland (1638) and Ireland (1641). In Scotland,

Edinburgh Castle, captured by the rebellious Scottish National Covenanters under Alexander Leslie in 1639.

Charles proved a poor political manager. His commitment to religious change – towards a stronger episcopacy and a new liturgy – and his aggressive treatment of Scottish views led to a hostile national response. Instead of compromising with the 1638 National Covenant (an agreement to resist ecclesiastical innovations unless they were appointed by the General Assembly), Charles tried to suppress the Scots in the Bishops' Wars (1639–40). This was the start of the Civil Wars, and it was symptomatic of the whole period of conflict: Charles mishandled the situation and lost, religion played a major role in the war, and it involved different parts of the British Isles, each of which were themselves divided.

The first Bishops' War was essentially a matter of inconsequential border manoeuvres. The supporters of the National Covenant, or Covenanters, under Alexander Leslie captured Aberdeen and Edinburgh Castle without loss in 1639, and went on to deploy a large army to block an invading force under Charles I, which encamped near Berwick. Neither side wanted a confrontation, and a treaty was signed in June 1639. The English army had been poorly prepared, its logistics wrecked by inadequate finance. When fighting resumed in 1640 the Scots successfully invaded Northumberland and Durham, capturing Newcastle on 30 August.

To help deal with the crisis, in April 1640 Charles summoned Parliament in England, the first to meet since 1629. However, the 'Short Parliament' refused to vote supply until grievances had been redressed. The impatient Charles dissolved it after only three weeks, infuriating many MPs. This did not solve the problem, and concern about

Close-up view of the barrel-vaulted plaster ceiling in the Gallery at Lanhydrock, depicting a scene from Noah's Ark. Religious themes and scenes were not restricted to ecclesiastical buildings. The ceiling was commissioned by John, 2nd Baron Robartes of Truro, leader of the Parliamentarians in Cornwall.

Charles's views was increased by the Canons of 1640, church laws passed by the convocation of clergy that stated the legitimacy of Laudian views.

Threatened with bankruptcy as a result of the Scottish invasion, the king had to summon what became the Long Parliament in November 1640. The period of 'Personal Rule' had generated a series of grievances and much fear about his intentions, ensuring that the elections were more contested than hitherto, and that there were many county petitions. The traditional political skills of compromise, inclusion and conciliation appeared no longer possible. Previously loyal gentry turned against the king, making it difficult to settle or ease serious disputes over politics and religion. In an angry and desperate attempt to rebuild the political system, Parliament turned on Charles's ministers and policies. Prerogative courts were abolished, Strafford attainted, and a bill passed providing for Parliaments every three years. Charles conceded some points and allowed Parliament to proceed against Strafford, but he responded firmly to attacks on church government.

In an atmosphere of mounting crisis, the need to raise an army to deal with a major Catholic rising in Ireland in November 1641 polarised the situation. Who was to control this army? A debate over the issue exacerbated tensions over parliamentary pressure for a change in church government. Charles resorted to violence, invading Parliament on 4 January 1642 in order to seize the 'Five Members', his leading opponents, but they had already fled by river to the City of London, a centre of hostility to Charles, especially after Royalist supporters were overthrown in the election to the Common Council. As both sides prepared for war, Charles left London in order to raise funds, a fatal step.

The resulting move towards war found the south and east of England, the navy, and many of the large towns backing Parliament, while Charles enjoyed greatest support in Wales, and rural parts of north and west England. Towns such as Blackburn, Bolton, Exeter, Gloucester, Hull, Manchester, and Plymouth supported Parliament, while their hinterlands backed Charles. Each side had support in every region and social group. There were, for example, parliamentary supporters in Cornwall and in Worcestershire, both predominantly Royalist counties. Nevertheless, although it is dangerous to adopt a crude socio-economic or geographical determinism, parliamentary support can be identified as being strongest in the most economically advanced regions. Yet, the relationship between religious and political differences, and socio-economic groups was complex – and the latter always tended to be divided. Thus, the Derbyshire lead miners were split between supporters of Parliament and of the king, as were economic interests in London.

Belief was important. Charles I received much support because he was the focus for powerful feelings of honour, loyalty and duty. Religion was a crucial factor. Many Parliamentary supporters were vehement in their hostility to Catholicism in Charles's circle. The Puritanism of much of Northamptonshire was crucial in its support for

quick

Parliament: it was also very important in Buckinghamshire. John, 2nd Baron Robartes of Truro, the leader of the Parliamentarians in Cornwall, a devout Presbyterian, had the ceiling of the Gallery at Lanhydrock ornamented with scenes from the Old Testament. Personal clashes also played a role, as with the rivalry between Edward Phelips of Montacute, a Royalist, and John, Lord Poulett, in Somerset. Divisions created long before the 1640s could also be important. In Leicestershire rivalry between the Greys of Groby and the Hastings of Loughborough had been strong for a century. The Puritan Lord Grey of Groby became commander of the Midland Association for the Parliamentarians, and Sir Henry Hastings was commander of the Royalist garrison at Ashby de la Zouch. Individual families, such as the Carews of Antony, were torn apart ideologically.

Fighting in England started in Manchester in July 1642, and Charles raised his standard at Nottingham on 22 August. There was a widespread desire to remain neutral, for example in Cheshire, Lancashire, Leicester and East Yorkshire, but the pressure of war wrecked such hopes, and the conflict spread. Both sides tried to raise the Trained Bands (militia). Initial moves by the combatants rapidly defined zones of control. Thus, William Cavendish, 1st Earl of Newcastle, speedily established the royal cause throughout Durham and Northumberland, including Newcastle, before moving into Yorkshire. On 11 January 1642, Charles I appointed the Earl of Newcastle Governor of Hull, but, at the same time, Parliament appointed a wealthy East Riding landowner, Sir John Hotham, Governor. The Hothams secured Hull, but in March 1642 Charles stationed a garrison in nearby York. Hotham was forced to show his hand on 23 April when he refused Charles entry to Hull on the grounds it would be compromising the town's security. Charles declared him a traitor.

Further south, William Seymour, Marquess of Hertford, Charles's Commissioner of Assay and Lieutenant-General for the western counties, tried to rally Somerset for Charles, but found Wellington, Taunton and Dunster held for Parliament. He was driven from Wells and eventually forced to withdraw from Cardiff. Parliament appointed Baron Robartes Lord Lieutenant of Cornwall, an act of defiance of royal authority, and he raised a regiment. The Parliamentarians also established their position in south-east England, gaining strategic points such as Dover and Portsmouth. Proximity to London was important in determining this region's loyalty. East Anglia was another region that rapidly declared for Parliament.

In the first major battle of the war, Charles narrowly defeated the main Parliamentarian army under Robert Devereux, 3rd Earl of Essex, at Edgehill (23 October), but he failed to follow up by driving decisively on London. Banbury and Broughton Castles in Oxfordshire, the latter the house of the Parliamentarian Lord Saye and Sele, were captured, but the Royalist impetus was not maintained. Advancing on London, Charles captured Brentford on 12 November, but was checked at Turnham Green the next day: he failed

Robert Devereux, 3rd Earl of Essex. Son of Elizabeth I's executed courtier, and Parliamentarian commander-in-chief 1642–5, he checked Charles I at Turnham Green in 1642 and relieved Gloucester in 1643, but failed to win any victories.

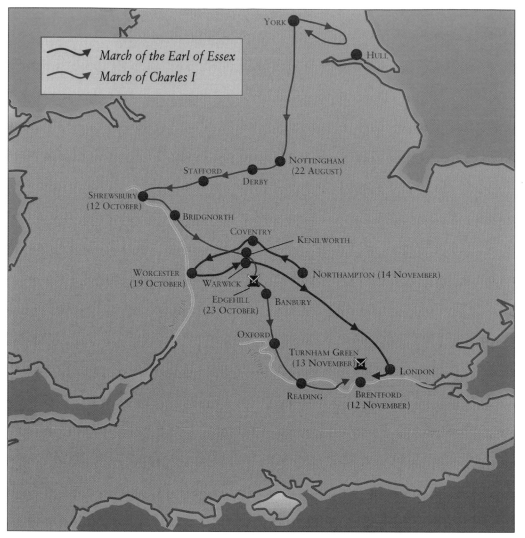

March of the Earl of Essex
March of Charles I

YORK

HULL

NOTTINGHAM (22 AUGUST)
STAFFORD
DERBY
SHREWSBURY (12 OCTOBER)
BRIDGNORTH
COVENTRY
KENILWORTH
WORCESTER (19 OCTOBER)
WARWICK
NORTHAMPTON (14 NOVEMBER)
EDGEHILL (23 OCTOBER)
BANBURY
OXFORD
TURNHAM GREEN (13 NOVEMBER)
LONDON
READING
BRENTFORD (12 NOVEMBER)

to press home an advantage in what were difficult circumstances, and retreated to establish his headquarters at Oxford. Charles's best chance of winning the war had passed. The Scots meanwhile sent an army to reimpose Protestant rule in Ulster.

In 1643 the Royalists overran most of western England, crushing the Parliamentarians at Stratton on 16 May and Roundway Down on 13 July. Bristol fell on 26 July to Royalist assault after a brief siege. However, the Royalist sieges of Gloucester and Hull were both unsuccessful, and the principal battle in the vital Thames valley and surrounding area – the first battle of Newbury (20 September) – was inconclusive. The Royalist cavalry outfought its opponents, but the infantry was less successful. (The Royalist dead were commemorated by the nineteenth-century Falkland Memorial.) The Royalists, in

THE EDGEHILL CAMPAIGN, 1642

The initial major battle was indecisive. Charles I narrowly won but failed to destroy the Earl of Essex's army or to exploit his success with energy and skill. Essex was able to return to London and when Charles approached the city he found himself outnumbered. Charles failed to press home the attack in what were difficult circumstances, and retreated to establish his headquarters at Oxford.

fact, had many successes in 1643, but did not challenge the Parliamentary heartland. The 11 mile long defence system rapidly constructed for London – an earthen bank and ditch with a series of forts and batteries – was never tested in action, but was a testimony to the resources available for the Parliamentary cause.

As well as the major battles, there were also many small-scale actions that were important locally, for the Civil War was both a national conflict and a series of local wars. At Winceby on 11 October 1643, for example, a minor cavalry engagement won by Oliver Cromwell was crucial to the course of the conflict in Lincolnshire and led the Parliamentarians to capture Lincoln. The war in south-west Wales swayed to and fro but had only a limited relationship with the struggle elsewhere. Military units had a sense of locality, and many were reluctant to travel far from home. In 1645 the Northern Horse was allowed to return from Oxford to Yorkshire after threatening mutiny. But the Royalist Yorkshire Trained Bands moved into the Midlands in 1643, and James, 7th Earl of Derby, had to send his best regiments from Lancashire to the main Royalist field army at Oxford that March.

Generally, local engagements reflected and affected the geography of the Civil War, which in turn led to the establishment of garrisons. In towns, like Parliamentarian Northampton and Royalist Worcester, surviving medieval walls were supplemented by new fortifications. Castle walls were similarly improved, for example in Northamptonshire at Rockingham Castle. Hartlebury Castle and Dudley Castle were major Royalist sites in Worcestershire, Dunster Castle, after its capture in 1643, in Somerset. Castles provided good bases for garrisons, and many were brought back into habitation and use. Warkworth Castle in Northumberland, for example, was garrisoned. From Northampton, the Parliamentarians competed for control of the south-west of the county with Royalists from Banbury Castle, which had been refortified and established as a garrison to protect the Royalist capital at Oxford. The Parliamentarian garrison in Leicester and its Royalist counterparts in the stately homes of Ashby de la Zouch and Belvoir Castle brought much devastation to Leicestershire. Similarly, the Royalist position in Worcestershire was challenged from Gloucester, leading to advances as far as Worcester in 1643 and to the capture of Evesham in May 1645. The Parliamentary garrison in Warwick Castle dominated the county.

Control over bridges, such as those at Upton-upon-Severn, Pershore and Tadcaster, was very important in local campaigning. The bridge over the Avon at Stratford was broken by the Parliamentarians in December 1645 in order to cut communications between Oxford and the West Country. Derbyshire was a linchpin of the parliamentary cause in the Midlands, and, therefore, the goal of Royalist attacks from Yorkshire and the Midlands. Control of Derbyshire, especially the crossings over the River Trent, would have linked these areas and helped the Royalists to apply greater pressure on the East Anglian-based Parliamentarian Eastern Association. Royalist failure in Derbyshire lessened the coordination of their field armies, and led to longer lines of communication. Thus local struggles interacted with the national, and the latter could transform the former. This was true not only of the movement of armies, but also of the institutionalisation of war. Demands on the localities from both sides became more insistent, as the cost of the conflict rose and resources available in

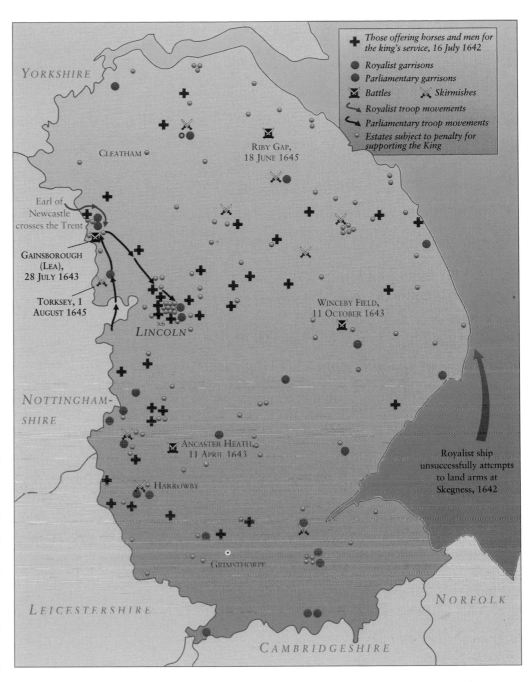

THE CIVIL WARS IN LINCOLNSHIRE

Lincolnshire saw less conflict than Yorkshire or many of the Midlands counties, but even so it was still affected by the war, not least because of the proximity of the key Royalist base at Newark.

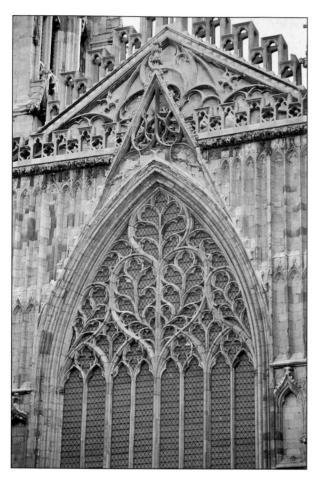

The central window of the west front, York Minster. The Parliamentarians and the Scots laid siege to the Royalist-held city on 18 April 1644. Attempts to relieve it ended on 2 July in one of the most decisive battles of the war.

the early stages were used up. Meanwhile, reliable and experienced commanders replaced local gentlemen in positions of local power. Thus Sir William Russell was succeeded as Royalist Governor of Worcester in December 1643 by Sir Gilbert Gerrard: localism was eroded, just as earlier neutralism had been ended. The arrival of field armies could lead to the capture of positions that had conferred local control. Thus, on 30 May 1645 a Royalist force of over 10,000 stormed and took Leicester. Ably defended positions, however, could resist such pressure, as Gloucester showed in 1643. Captured by the Royalists in 1643 and regained in 1644, Taunton resisted a Royalist siege in 1645, until relieved after the defeat of the Royalist field army.

In January 1644, the Scottish Covenanters entered northern England on the side of Parliament, while, on 29 March, the Parliamentarian position in southern England was stabilised when Sir William Waller defeated the Royalists under Sir Ralph Hopton at Cheriton in Hampshire. The possibility of a Royalist advance on London from that direction was now at an end. Pressure on the Royalists in Yorkshire led the now Marquess of Newcastle to move south from Durham, and the Scots followed, linking up with the Parliamentarians near York on 18 April. They then besieged York.

A Royalist attempt to relieve the city led, on 2 July 1644, to one of the two decisive battles of the war. The Scots, joined to a Parliamentarian army under Sir Thomas Fairfax and Oliver Cromwell, crushed the Royalists under Prince Rupert – Charles's nephew and son of Frederick V, Elector Palatine – and the Marquess of Newcastle on Marston Moor outside York. Both sides deployed cavalry on the flanks and infantry in the centre. The Parliamentarian/Scots army launched a surprise attack at about 7 p.m. The Royalist cavalry was successful on the allied right, but, on the allied left, Cromwell and Alexander Leslie drove their opponent's cavalry from the field. The infantry struggle in the centre ended when Cromwell's cavalry joined the assault on the Royalist foot soldiers. The allies lost about 1,500 men, the Royalists 3,000 and their cannon. York surrendered on 16 July.

The north of England had been lost for Charles I, as had any sense of Royalist invulnerability. Remaining Royalist positions in the north were now in danger. Newcastle was stormed on 20 October 1644. That year, in the Midlands, the Royalists were beaten at Nantwich (25 January), but relieved at Newark (22 March), and held off Parliamentary attack near Oxford at Cropredy Bridge (29 June). The Royalist cause was showing serious signs of strain in several counties, including Gloucestershire and Wiltshire. Morale was suffering, as were finances: receipts declined from late 1643. Royalist divisions were also growing more acute.

Nevertheless, the war was not over. The Earl of Essex advanced into Cornwall, in part in response to requests from John Robartes of Lanhydrock, only to be cut off by Charles I and defeated at Lostwithiel (2 September). Returning to Oxford, Charles fought off a larger Parliamentary army at the inconclusive second battle of Newbury (27 October); both battles revealed the incompetence of the Parliamentary generals. Charles's supporter, James Graham, 1st Marquess of Montrose, had more success in Scotland, winning a major battle at Tippermuir on 1 September: Montrose's men won a firefight and then charged successfully. Meanwhile, Charles had rejected advice that he negotiate with Parliament, advice that he again rejected in January 1645.

In England in 1645, in the second decisive battle of the war (Naseby on 14 June) the new Parliamentary force – the New Model Army – under Fairfax and Cromwell, defeated Charles, thanks, in large part, to the superior discipline of the Parliamentary cavalry. Rupert swept the cavalry on the Parliamentary left from the field, but was unable to prevent his troops from dispersing to attack the Parliamentary baggage train. Cromwell, on the right, defeated the Royalist cavalry opposite and then turned on the veteran but heavily outnumbered Royalist infantry in the centre, which succumbed to an overwhelming attack. Nearby 5,000 Royalists, out of an army of 7,600, were captured: the leading Royalist field army had been destroyed. In the words of Clarendon, the Royalist historian of the war, Naseby was where 'king and kingdom were lost'. Carlisle had successfully resisted a Scottish siege since the previous October, but it asked for terms when the news of Naseby arrived.

Parliamentarian commanders, Sir Thomas Fairfax, Lord Fairfax, Skippon, Cromwell, Essex, Warwick, Leslie, Manchester. Cromwell's rise to prominence depended on his association with the New Model Army. By 1648 the list of commanders looked very different, as death and the radicalisation of the Great Rebellion brought many changes.

Thereafter the Royalist situation was one of inexorable collapse, although, hopeful of success by Montrose and naturally stubborn, Charles refused to negotiate. Thanks to superior Parliamentary fire-power, the principal Royalist army in the west was defeated at Langport on 10 July 1645. Bristol was successfully stormed on 10–11 September, the Parliamentarians were victorious at Rowton Heath near Chester on 24 September, and, by the end of the year, the Royalists were reduced to isolated strongholds. Montrose, meanwhile, had been successful at Inverlochy (2 February), Auldearn (9 May), Alford (2 July) and Kilsyth (15 August), and had gained control, albeit often temporary, of much of Scotland, but, at Philiphaugh on 13 September, he was surprised and defeated by David Leslie. Montrose fled back to the Highlands, his prestige shattered.

The Royalist cause collapsed in 1646. Chester surrendered on 3 February, and the victorious Parliamentarians vandalised the cathedral, breaking the stained glass and damaging the organ and much else. Besieged since November 1645, Dunster Castle fell

BERWICK

NEWCASTLE
CARLISLE
DURHAM

Tyne

NORTH SEA

IRISH SEA

*Marston
Moor*

SKIPTON ☒ YORK

HULL

☒ *Preston*

☒
*Adwalton
Moor*

Mersey

LINCOLN

CHESTER

☒ *Winceby*

Dee

DERBY

NOTTINGHAM

STAFFORD

KING'S LYNN

SHREWSBURY

NORWICH

COVENTRY

☒ *Naseby*

WARWICK

HUNTINGDON

Worcester ☒

Teifi

STRATFORD

NORTHAMPTON

CAMBRIDGE

WORCESTER

Edgehill ☒ ☒ *Cropredy Bridge*

HEREFORD

Lune

GLOUCESTER

OXFORD

LONDON

CARDIFF

Lansdown
☒
BRISTOL

Roundway
☒ *Down*

READING

☒

BATH

DEVIZES

Newbury

CANTERBURY

BRISTOL
CHANNEL

DOVER

☒
Langport

WINCHESTER ☒ *Cheriton*

BRIGHTON

EXETER

☒ *Lostwithiel*

PLYMOUTH

ENGLISH
CHANNEL

0   50   100

miles

to the Parliamentarians on 22 April. On 5 May 1646 Charles gave himself up to the Scots army in England. The remaining Royalist strongholds surrendered: Worcester on 23 June, Oxford on 24 June, Pendennis Castle on 16 August 1646, Raglan Castle the same month, Harlech in February 1647.

Parliamentary victory was due in part to the support of the wealthiest regions of England and Scotland, and to the folly of Charles, but chance also played a major role, and the Parliamentarians were fortunate to be able to win before war-weariness sapped their war effort. The Royalist army in England was impressive, in Scotland Montrose was a good general, and it took a long time for the Parliamentarians to create a winning team. The New Model's equipment and fighting style were essentially similar to those of their opponents: the major difference was that they were better disciplined and supported by a more effective infrastructure and supply system. The New Model Army was a national army able to operate in national strategic terms with a unified command under Fairfax, with Cromwell as commander of the cavalry. The army was more cohesive and better cared for than other forces, and its initial success was largely due to it being paid with remarkable regularity, at least for the first two years. Promotion was by merit and Cromwell chose officers and men imbued with the same religious fervour as his own. It became a force for political and religious radicalism. The army was well equipped and under the control of Parliament, not of competing local interests. Its capability reduced the importance of Scottish intervention, which had been very important in 1644.

Oliver Cromwell, 1599–1658, English school, seventeenth century. He rose to prominence not as an MP but as a general. Tactically astute and a master of strategy, he found government of the country from 1653 far less easy. He kept order but could not find a successful balance of army and civilian aspirations.

Having won, the victors fell out. Parliament, the army leadership and the Scots clashed over church government, negotiations with Charles, and army pay arrears and control, and these disputes interacted with and exacerbated each other. Agitators or delegates appointed by regiments pressed Parliament for arrears and in August 1647 the army occupied London. The army was opposed to the creation of a Presbyterian establishment to replace that of the Church of England. Instead, there was considerable support for a degree of religious pluralism, with toleration of Independent sects. The problems of settling these difficult points were exacerbated by Scottish demands for a Presbyterian church settlement and by the increasing difficulty of trusting the imprisoned Charles to refrain from undermining any agreement.

In 1648, in the Second Civil War, the Scots invaded on behalf of Charles, who had agreed to recognise Scots Presbyterianism, and there was a series of Royalist risings, particularly in Kent and South Wales. All were crushed; especially emphatic was Cromwell's victory over the overstretched and poorly coordinated forces of invading Scots at Preston on 17 August. In contrast, while they were allied with the Parliamentarians, the Scots had been able to campaign as far south as Hereford in 1645. News of Preston led the Royalists in the south-east, who had retreated into Colchester and been besieged there, to surrender.

*The Commandery, Worcester.
Charles II's limited forces were
hemmed in by a greatly superior and
well-commanded force at Worcester
on 3 September 1651. This Tudor
building, incorporating parts of an
earlier hospital, became the Royalist
headquarters.*

*The original late fifteenth-century
door of the Commandery.*

The army showed considerable harshness in suppressing the risings. Some surrendering Royalist officers, such as Sir George Lisle and Sir Charles Lucas after the siege of Colchester, were summarily executed for having broken their parole. The army followed up the Second Civil War by purging Parliament, in order to stop it negotiating with the king (Pride's purge, 6 December 1648), trying and executing Charles for treason against the people (30 January 1649), declaring a republic, and then conquering first Ireland and then Scotland. Thanks to religious zeal, the army had not been intimidated about confronting their anointed king. It was argued that Charles had given his word of honour not to fight again, and that he had broken it when he encouraged the Second Civil War. The army leaders were determined to punish Charles as a 'Man of Blood' who had killed the Lord's people.

Sad but firm in the portrait at Antony House, painted at his trial by Edward Bower, Charles refused to plead, claiming that subjects had no right to try the king and that he stood for the liberties of the people. He was executed at the centre of royal power, outside the Banqueting Hall in Whitehall. The execution made compromise with the Royalists highly unlikely, and entrenched the ideological position of the new regime.

The character and policy of this regime was unsettled and subject to pressure. The Levellers, a radical group with much support in the army, pressed for major social and political changes, but their mutiny in the army in May 1649 was crushed by Cromwell. Radical hopes were thus dashed. Having invaded Ireland from South Wales in 1649 and stormed Drogheda and Wexford, Cromwell attacked Scotland the following year, in response to the Scottish acceptance of Charles I's eldest son, the future Charles II. He was crowned King of the Scots in 1650. This was a threat to the regime in England: the Presbyterian Scots were opposed to the support for religious Independency in England, and the majority were royalists.

Fairfax resigned rather than invade Scotland, leaving Cromwell in command. Unable to breach the Scottish fortified positions around Edinburgh, and outmanoeuvred by David Leslie, he retreated to Dunbar. Cromwell, cut off from England by a force twice the size of his own, launched a surprise attack which defeated the Scottish cavalry, while much of the infantry surrendered (3 September). Edinburgh was then captured.

The following year, Cromwell used his control of the sea to outflank the Scots at Stirling and occupy Perth, but Charles II invaded England, hoping to ignite a Royalist rebellion. Few rose to join him and he was hemmed in by a greatly superior and well-commanded force under Cromwell at Worcester (3 September): 27,000 to 15,000. Many of the militia that were mustered to defeat Charles and the Scots were now ready for service – but not at Worcester. The Royalists launched an initially successful frontal attack on Cromwell's position, but numbers and generalship told and the Royalist army was overwhelmed. Hiding in an oak tree and supporters' houses en route, including Moseley Old Hall, Charles II fled to France, leaving the Royalist cause crushed. Cromwell saw the hand of Providence in his victory, 'a crowning mercy'.

By the summer of 1652, all Scotland had fallen. It could no longer serve as an alternative model to developments in England. The Scottish Parliament and executive

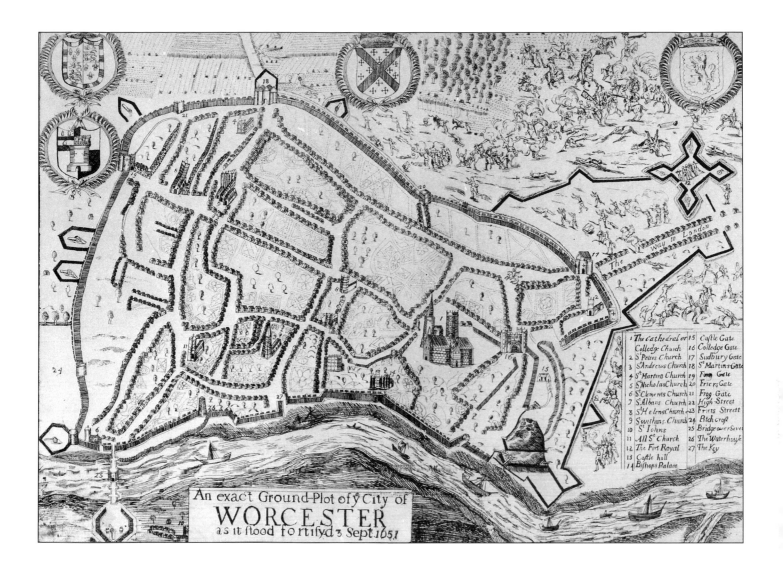

An exact Ground-Plot of y City of
WORCESTER
as it stood fortifyd 3 Sept 1651

1	The Cathedral or	15	Castle Gate
	Colledge Church	16	Colledge Gate
2	St Peters Church	17	Sudbury Gate
3	St Andrews Church	18	St Martins Gate
4	St Martins Church	19	Fore Gate
5	St Nicholas Church	20	Friers Gate
6	St Clements Church	21	Frog Gate
7	St Albans Church	22	High Street
8	St Helens Church	23	Friers Streett
9	S withins Church	24	Atch crofs
10	St Iohns	25	Bridge over Seve
11	All St Church	26	The Waterhouse
12	The Fort Royal	27	The Key
13	Castle hill		
14	Bishops Palace		

Worcester, as it was fortified in 1651. Worcester and Gloucester, major crossing points over the Severn, played an important role in the strategy of mid-seventeenth-century warfare. Control over crossing points gave armies an important degree of initiative.

council were abolished. In 1654 Scotland was asked to send members to the London Parliament, and measures were taken to adopt English law in Scotland. The power of the Scottish nobility was curtailed. The Isle of Man fell on 31 October 1651 and the Channel Isles that December.

The conquest of Scotland brought the period of conflict to an end, although Royalist conspiracies continued. One had already been uncovered in October 1649. Colonel John Saul led an unsuccessful rising in Norfolk in 1650, in 1653 William, 9th Earl of Glencairn, led a Highland rising that was brought under control the following year, and, in March 1655, John Penruddock seized Salisbury before retreating and being defeated at South Molton in Devon. The Cromwellian regime responded to Royalist conspiracies with counter-intelligence operations.

The Civil Wars left a heavy legacy that was to influence political attitudes for decades. There had been much devastation – least where there had been little fighting, such as in Kent, East Anglia, and Surrey, and conversely far more in Ulster, much of Scotland, the Severn and Thames valleys, the Midlands, and the West Riding of Yorkshire. Towns that were stormed, such as Bristol, or underwent major sieges, such as Newark, were damaged, but others, such as Portsmouth and Winchester, were also affected. The last battle of the First Civil War, at Great Torrington, Devon on 16–17

February 1646, led to the destruction of the village church and of many buildings. At an individual level, the impact of the conflict was often crippling. Drum Castle, a Royalist stronghold, was twice captured and four times garrisoned. The house and estate were both devastated. The younger son of the laird died in prison, while the laird's wife and daughter-in-law were turned out of the captured castle with nothing but 'two grey plaids and a couple of work nags'. The Royalists in Scotland, in their turn, pillaged the estate of Brodie Castle in 1645 and plundered and partly burnt the house.

In England, Royalist estates were sequestrated and their owners permitted to have them back only if they paid a fine (compounded) and agreed to take the oath, the

View of the main gatehouse of Powis Castle with towers and mullion windows with hood mouldings. The gateway was 'burst quite in pieces' by explosives during the successful Parliamentary attack in 1644.

Solemn League and Covenant, which required reform of the church – Catholics usually refused to take it. Royalist landowners faced opposition from their tenants, including a refusal to pay rents and entry fines. Individual Royalists suffered greatly. Edward Sackville, 4th Earl of Dorset, had a son captured and murdered, while Knole was occupied and the contents seized. He only regained his estates in 1650 at the cost of a heavy fine. Sir John Hotham and his elder son, Captain John, were executed in January 1645 after being found guilty of defecting from Parliament. The captain's unsuccessful plea for clemency referred to 'the cries and tears of a poor wife, helpless children and desolated family'. A posthumous child was born nine months later. Sir Alexander Carew of Antony House, a Parliamentarian commander at Plymouth, had been executed for treachery the previous month. Sir George Middleton, a Royalist Lancashire landowner had his house plundered by his tenants, and they broke down the enclosures of his park, turning his deer into venison and cutting down his timber. Powis Castle, captured by Parliamentary troops in 1644, was not returned to William, 3rd Lord Powis until after the Restoration of Charles II in 1660.

For individuals, the war brought acts of violence and destruction, hitherto unprecedented levels of taxation, levies of crucial goods – beds and bedding, food, carts, equipment and horses – the pressures of billeting, and plundering. The night before Naseby, William Jenaway had eight sheep stolen by Parliamentarians quartered nearby. Armies brought much devastation, but so also did local garrisons. The ordinary people suffered alongside the elite. The structure of government was turned to the ends of war. In 1643 Prince Rupert ordered nearby parish constables to provide labour for fortifying Towcester, adding: 'in no wise fail, as you will answer the contrary at your utmost peril; as the total plundering and burning of your houses, with what other mischiefs the hungry soldiers can inflict upon you'. There was also organised destruction. This ranged from the 'slighting' of captured Royalist fortifications, such as Corfe Castle,

Dunster Castle, Kenilworth Castle, and Dunseverick Castle in Ulster, to prevent them from being used in rebellions, to the destruction of the visible remains of 'superstition' in churches.

Military depredations encouraged the Clubmen movement in late 1644 and 1645 in which, in the Welsh Marches and the West Country, local people sought to keep troops out. These risings were a determined attempt to restore local control, and to limit the demands of garrisons such as Hereford and Langport. The last major Clubmen force, in Dorset, was dispersed by Parliamentarian troops in August 1644. The widespread impact of the war interacted with popular appeals for support by both sides to raise political and religious consciousness, thus helping both to give radicals voice and to make it harder to reimpose order.

The twelfth-century keep of Kenilworth Castle, Warwickshire. The former Royalist castle was slighted in 1643 to prevent it being used in rebellions. Throughout England, Royalist estates were sequestrated and only returned if their owners agreed to pay a fine and take the oath requiring reform of the church.

The regime of the Rump Parliament – so called because it comprised what was left after Pride's Purge of December 1648 – was bitterly divided and unable to agree on a religious settlement. It also became involved in an expensive war with the Dutch (1652–4) that brought victories, but no decisive success. In April 1653 Cromwell closed the Rump, which 'would never answer those ends which God, his people and the whole nation expected from them'. This made his intention to rule by military command blatantly clear, although there was significant civilian influence in his regime through a council and Parliament. At the end of the year, after the failure of the radical nominated Barebones Parliament (named after the London MP and religious Independent Praise-God Barebones), the disillusioned Cromwell became Lord Protector 'of England, Scotland, Ireland etcetera'. In 1657, he became hereditary Protector with a ceremony that included much of the ceremonial of English monarchy: a coronation oath and enthronement. Although he opposed the title of king, Cromwell lived in royal palaces with a pseudo-court including a household, guard and entourage, and as Lord Protector, he created two peerages: Lord Dacre in 1657 and Lord Burnell in 1658.

This man born into the Huntingdonshire gentry, who had had no tenants and who had worked for a living, was possibly the most dramatic example of upward social mobility in British history. Cromwell told MPs in 1657 that he had taken on his position 'out of a desire to prevent mischief and evil, which I did see was imminent upon the nation'. He ruled Britain until his death in 1658, even if he did not reign.

Cromwell's was a military regime, shot through with an intolerant sense of divine purpose. On 22 January 1655, he told Parliament:

> . . . I look at the people of these nations as the blessing of the Lord . . . And the people being the blessing of God they will not be so angry but they will prefer their safety to their passions, and their real security to forms, when necessity calls for supplies.

In 1655, largely in response to Royalist risings, authority in the localities was entrusted to major-generals, instructed to preserve security and create a godly and efficient kingdom – an unpopular step. The division of the country among the eleven

England's Arke Secured and the Enimyes to the Parliament and Kingdom Overwhelmed. *The Civil Wars led to an explosion of propaganda, with the publication of prints and news books. Both fed off the politicisation of the 1640s and helped polarise public opinion by demonising the other side and focusing on atrocities and sinister schemes.*

major-generals created a new geography. It was a geography of military control that totally ignored long-established patterns based on aristocratic estates and clientages. The major-generals might have a role akin to that of Tudor lords lieutenant, but their social background was different.

The Civil Wars had revealed the military redundancy of the traditional centres, although they were of considerable local importance. Garrisoned houses at Madresfield Court and Strensham helped the Royalists to hold southern Worcestershire. The Earl of Derby's house at Lathom was a Royalist stronghold in Lancashire. Nevertheless, garrisoned stately homes, such as Burghley House, Compton Wynyates, Coughton Court, and the Marquess of Winchester's seat at Basing House, fell to siege or storming. The major-generals were instructed to keep control over the JPs, and to take control of the militia. Compared to the former lords lieutenant, they lacked the local social weight necessary to lend traditional strengths to their instructions. They followed the pattern set by the Rump of alienating and trying to circumvent the established gentry elites; the county committees had played this role in the 1640s. Reliance on the major-generals made it harder to demilitarise the regime. It was unpopular not only with Royalists but also with many republicans. The Parliamentarian cause that had been so badly fractured by 1649 was increasingly divided. The unpopularity of the major-generals led Cromwell to change policy in 1657 and to seek to re-establish the role of JPs and traditional gentry families. Many of the latter, however, were unwilling to cooperate.

Meanwhile, hostility to an oppressive Puritanism that, for the sake of continued reformation and godliness, repressed popular rituals deemed superstitious or profane (such as Christmas and dancing round the maypole), fused with resentment of the illegal, radical and repressive regime. Staunton Harold Church in Leicestershire was one of the very few Anglican churches built in the period. Its builder, Sir Robert Shirley, was a Royalist plotter who was imprisoned in the Tower and died there in 1656.

The oppressive Puritanism was ineffective as well as unpopular. The Long Parliament had abolished episcopacy, so there was now no established church in England and Wales, and this weakened attempts at moral policing. The godly were divided. Religious radicals had no time for Presbyterians or moderate Independents. Presbyterians, such as John Robartes, were disillusioned with the regime, and he retired to Lanhydrock. Formerly persecuted groups, however, benefited from a degree of toleration. Baptists, for example, were able to build Loughwood Meeting House near Axminster in 1653. Yet such actions seemed menacing to the bulk of the population. The regimes of the 1650s found no system of legitimacy that brought them even a measure of popularity. The Puritan 'Cultural Revolution' was an arid failure – steps such as banning the 'Cotswold Olimpicks', games held at Dover's Hill since 1612, were not welcome. Several preachers compared England to Israel after Moses, ungrateful for the gifts of God.

An unpopular regime that was vulnerable to subversion and faced major financial problems, the Protectorate, nevertheless, was assertive abroad. The Rump had built up the navy. Between 1649 and 1660 some 216 vessels were added to the fleet, many of them prizes, but half the fruits of a shipbuilding programme. The earlier dependence on large merchantmen ended with the establishment of a substantial state navy, which in 1653 employed almost 20,000 men. The fleet was used to project English power – in the Mediterranean, the Baltic and further afield. Benefiting from the opportunities created by conflict between France and Spain, England embarked on a war with Spain in 1655–9, which led to the capture of Jamaica, but its expense caused a financial crisis.

Thanks to larger armed forces, government was becoming more expensive and taxation more onerous. A major change in the nature of government was beginning. It was not popular. The Puritan minister Vavasor Powell condemned the state in the winter of 1655–6 for its foreign policy, for high taxation, and for financial and spiritual corruption, adding, 'We withdraw, and desire all the God's people to withdraw, from these men as those that are guilty of the sins of the later days, and that have left following the Lord.'

Oliver Cromwell fell ill at the start of 1658 and died on 3 September, the anniversary of his victories at Dunbar and Worcester. Cromwell's successor as Protector, his son Richard, unable to command authority and, crucially, lacking the support of the army, was deposed in May 1659. The resulting political crisis that saw the bitterly divided army opposed to the reconvened Rump Parliament, which sought to end military rule, was only resolved with the Restoration: the army commander in Scotland, George Monck, marched south, occupied London, and restored order and a moderate parliament that on 8 May 1660 recalled Charles II. Oliver Cromwell's corpse was exhumed and hanged at Tyburn, but it would not be so easy to end the memory of the Interregnum.

EIGHT

The Restored Monarchy, 1660–88

Coronation Procession of Charles II to Westminster from the Tower of London, 23 April 1661, by Dirck Stoop. The coronation, on St George's Day, was disrupted by a thunderstorm.

Charles II (1660–85) possessed the skills his father so patently lacked. Approachable and charming, he was also flexible and pragmatic. Charles wished to get his way, but he lacked the intolerance and arrogance of his first cousin, Louis XIV, who assumed personal power in France in 1661.

The Restoration of the Stuart monarchy was popular. John Evelyn wrote in his diary:

On 29 May 1660, Charles II entered London with a triumph of above two hundred thousand horse and foot, brandishing their swords and shouting with inexpressible joy; the way strewed with flowers, the bells ringing, the streets hung with tapestry, fountains running with wine; the mayor, aldermen and all the companies in their liveries, chains of gold, banners; lords and nobles, everyone clad in cloth of silver, gold and velvet; the windows and balconies all set with ladies; trumpets, music and myriads of people flocking the streets and ways as far as Rochester . . . I stood in the Strand and beheld it and blessed God. And all this without one drop of blood.

Popular joy, however, did not solve political problems, and it did not last. Charles II neither set out to rule without Parliament, as his father had done, nor to restore the prerogative taxation and jurisdictional institutions of the 1630s, such as Ship Money and Star Chamber. The 'Cavalier Parliament' of 1661 decided that all legislation that had received the royal assent from Charles I should stay in place. This meant that the legislation of 1641 against the methods of the Personal Rule remained in force, although not the subsequent Acts of Parliament. There was to be no return to the policies of the 1630s. However, the *ad hoc* union with Scotland introduced under Cromwell was repealed.

Far from persecuting those who had supported the Parliamentarian cause in the 1640s and Oliver Cromwell in the 1650s, and using their estates as the basis for a substantial landed state under royal control, the Act of Indemnity of 1660 pardoned all who had not actually signed Charles I's death warrant. Nevertheless, lands confiscated from Royalists were generally returned. There was no thorough purge of

Timber-framed houses in Tewkesbury's High Street, the earliest dating from 1470. Thirteen of the town's twenty-four burgesses were purged in 1662 as punishment for its support of the Cromwellian regime.

officeholders. Many former Cromwellians and ex-Presbyterians continued as JPs, although individuals who were distrusted were removed.

Nevertheless, care was taken to lessen the chances of any new rebellion, although support for any such renewal of chaos was limited. Acts banned 'tumultous' petitioning of Parliament, and allowed the king to censor the press and (under the Act for the Well Governing and Regulating of Corporations of 1661) to purge boroughs of those regarded as disaffected. Those suspected of plotting rebellion, such as Sir John Hotham, were arrested, while most of the 'regicides', including John Carew of Antony House, were executed. So were others whose actions were seen as treasonable, such as Sir Henry Vane. Regicides who had already died were exhumed – a powerful example to the living. There were indeed conspiracies, such as the Northern Rising planned for 1663, but fewer than the alarms of the period would suggest. There were major alarms in the autumn of 1660, as well as in 1665 and 1667.

In 1662 an order was issued for the slighting of the walls and defences of major towns that had backed Parliament, such as Gloucester. This led to a very public imposition of control on such places, an imposition that was enforced by forces from surrounding rural areas: 'Upon the 10th day of July 1662 the Lord Lieutenant of the County of Northampton and the Deputy Lieutenant came to this town with some of the trained bands and . . . pulled down the town walls and gates . . . they also pulled down some part of the castle walls and they carried away all the arms and armour that was left in the town.'

Similarly the 1661 legislation for the purging of boroughs relied on local commissioners who were supposed to get borough officials to take the oaths of supremacy and allegiance and to remove the unwilling – or even those who were willing if they saw it as 'expedient for the public safety'. In Gloucester about three-quarters of the corporation's members were purged, although most were willing to take the oaths. Thirteen of the twenty-four burgesses of Tewkesbury were purged in 1662. Charles was unwilling to appoint former Cromwellians as lords lieutenant and deputy lieutenants and he adapted the lieutenancy to make it a more effective defence of the royal position. The elites had learned from the 1640s and 1650s that to turn against the crown was to invite widespread disorder and a general questioning of hierarchy. Furthermore, once dead, Charles I became a more acceptable symbol of monarchy. Charles as royal martyr helped to lead to a revival of the theory of the divine right of kings to rule.

Without much in the way of crown lands and granted the customs and excise on the basis of an inflated estimate of the levies' true income, Charles II had to rely on parliamentary taxation. As a consequence, he had to respond to parliamentary views. Due to anxieties about royal power, Charles II was only allowed a small army and the 'Cavalier Parliament' of 1661–79 pushed the malleable king into a more rigid religious settlement than he would have preferred. The Corporation Act of 1661 obliged town officials to accept an Anglicanism that clearly differentiated itself from nonconformity. The Act of Uniformity of 1662 led to the ejection of Presbyterian clergy from their parishes, and, under the Conventicle Act, worship with five or more people was forbidden unless it was in accordance with Anglican rites. The Five Mile Act of 1665 prohibited Dissenting ministers from living within 5 miles of any corporate town or place in which they had served prior to the act. They also had to take an oath of non-resistance to royal authority before they could teach. These acts were used against nonconformist preachers, such as Vavasor Powell, who spent most of the 1660s in prison and died there in 1670. The Test Acts of 1673 and 1678 excluded nonconformists from office and Catholics from office and Parliament.

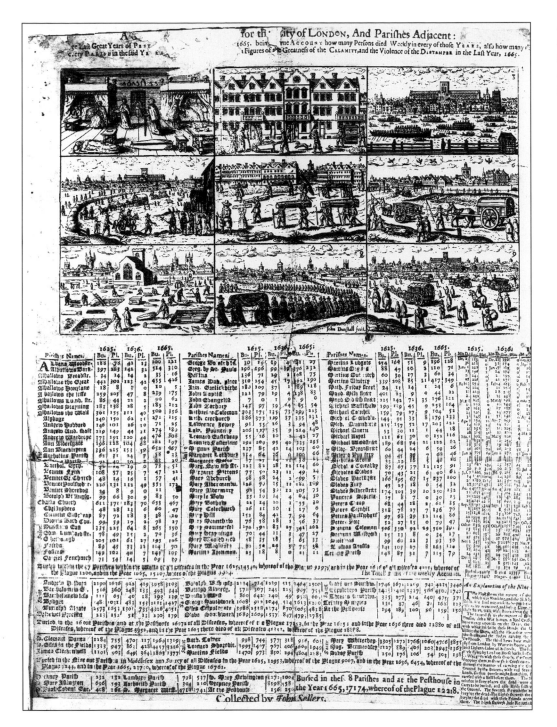

A contemporary broadsheet showing the numbers of deaths recorded in the Bills of Mortality *during 1665 and London scenes associated with the plague epidemic.*

This intolerance was a consequence of the drive for uniformity that a state church demanded in a climate of fear about the political, social and religious consequences of accepting diversity. Such fears had been underlined by the breakdown of order in all three spheres during the 1640s and 1650s. Puritanism was now regarded as a serious threat. Order was similarly reimposed in Scotland: Parliament, episcopacy and aristocratic power were all restored.

This reimposition of control was to unravel over the following three decades, but, in the meanwhile, the British were offered brutal reminders of the vulnerability of human society. Between 70,000 and 100,000 people died in England in 1665 during the Great Plague.

Politics and the Press, 1660–95

An active world of newspapers was an important aspect of seventeenth-century politics and society, and something that distinguished Britain from most other European countries. This world began in the Elizabethan period with the publication of news pamphlets, especially by the publisher John Wolfe. In 1620 the first English-language newspapers were imported from Amsterdam. They encouraged the publication of 'corantos' in London from 1621. The press was kept under control until the abolition of Star Chamber in July 1641 led to an explosion of publication. The press fed off the politicisation of the 1640s, but in 1655 most of the press was banned and a licensing system was restored. This censorship continued with the Restoration. The 1662 'Act for preventing the frequent Abuses in printing seditious, treasonable, and unlicensed Books and Pamphlets, and for regulating of Printing and Printing Presses' was based on the theory that the freedom to print was hazardous to the community and dangerous to its ruler, a threat to faith, loyalty and morality. The theme was control. Printing was strictly limited to the master printers of the Stationers' Company of London and the university presses. Only twenty of the former were permitted and appointments to vacancies were made by the Archbishop of Canterbury and the Bishop of London, who were troubled enough by the dissemination of heterodox opinions not to support a relaxation in the control of printing. Only four founders of type were permitted and vacancies were again filled by the two senior clerics. All master printers and founders were obliged to provide sureties of £300 not to engage in illegal printing. The number of apprentices, journeymen and presses per printer was regulated. The printing of material offensive

The Coffee House Mob *from* Vulgus Britannicus, 1710. *Newspapers lie on the table.*

to the Christian faith, the Church of England, any officer of the government or any private person was prohibited and a licensing system established to enable pre-publication censorship. The secretaries of state were given authority over publications dealing with 'affairs of state'. This authority was delegated in 1663 to Sir Roger L'Estrange, who undertook it in return for the profitable patent for the exclusive publication of all newspapers. Existing newsbooks were suppressed to make way for L'Estrange's monopoly with the publication of the Oxford Gazette *in November 1665. This became the* London Gazette *(or* Gazette *for short), the following year when the court returned to London after the plague. The Scottish Privy Council discouraged the printing of news relating to Scotland, and it was not until the parliamentary union of 1707 and the abolition of the Council in 1708 that the situation altered there.*

The Gazette *was not the sole means of spreading news. Although the trade and advertising newspapers set up after the Fire of London of 1666 contained no political news, this was not the case with manuscript newsletters. The lack of domestic news in the* Gazette *led readers who wanted political, and, in particular parliamentary, news to turn to newsletters. George Larkin's pro-government* Publick Occurrences Truly Stated *reported on 6 March 1688: 'I have set a friend of mine to consult the Letters, and haunt the confiding coffee houses, where the grave men puff out sedition'.*

It was not until the Popish Plot that the Gazette's *monopoly on printed news was breached. Public excitement, political commitment and the prospect of the expiration of the licensing provisions in 1679 led to a sudden proliferation of unlicensed newspapers, the first of which appeared on 3 December 1678. By the end of 1679 more papers were being published than at any time since 1649, an unwelcome development and comparison for the government. In response, a Tory press was founded. However, Charles II wished not to conduct a propaganda war but to terminate one. The judiciary supported the power of the royal prerogative to control the press, and prosecutions for seditious libel were launched. Chief Justice Scroggs directed that juries were only competent to determine whether the defendants had published the libel; judges alone could decide whether it was seditious, a ruling that greatly limited the role of juries. Certain of government support, officials of the Stationers' Company and the Secretaries of State enforced the law against illegal printers.*

Charles II stamped out the Whig newspapers, and in 1685 James II had Parliament revive the 1662 Printing Act. However, the disruption of the agencies that supervised printing in 1688–9 led to the appearance of new papers, all of them favourable to William III. Once in control, William moved to revive the machinery of press control, attacking unlicensed works.

In 1695, however, the Licensing (Printing) Act lapsed. It was felt that the existing system for the supervision of printing was inadequate, and plans were drawn up to prepare a new regulatory act. This failed because of parliamentary divisions and a lack of parliamentary time. Thereafter, despite attempts to revive a licensing system, the press remained free of pre-publication control. A spate of new titles followed. The first successful paper, the Daily Courant, *began publication in March 1702, and the first provincial paper, probably the* Norwich Post, *in 1701. A new world of print had been born.*

This brutal visitation of bubonic plague was to be the last major outbreak, and indeed Scotland had had its last in 1649, but the end to such epidemics could not be foreseen in 1665. Mutations in the rat and flea populations were probably more important in preventing a recurrence of plague than clumsy and erratic public health measures and alterations in human habitat thanks to construction with brick, stone and tile. Yet all this lay in the future, and in 1665 it was easy to see the Great Plague as a result of divine displeasure. Its impact was especially prominent, because London was hard hit.

Calamity was visited on the capital again the following year. The Great Fire of London raged for four days from 2 September 1666; it destroyed St Paul's Cathedral, the Guildhall, the Royal Exchange, 87 churches and about 13,200 houses, in total about two-thirds of the City of London. Charles II and his brother, James, Duke of York, took an active role in fighting the flames, filling buckets and encouraging the fire-fighters, but the blaze left the city devastated. John Evelyn, Christopher Wren and others produced plans for rebuilding London to a more regular plan, but resources and will were lacking, and the existing property rights of individuals were one of the chief stumbling blocks to an organised replanning. Wren had to be content with designing the new St Paul's and a large number of London churches. Fire also devastated other towns in this period, including Northampton in 1675, Kelso in 1684, Warwick in 1694, Blandford Forum, and Towcester in 1749, and was a reminder of the limited ability of humans to control their environment. In Honiton there were severe fires in 1672, 1699, 1747, 1765, 1790, 1797, 1817 and 1840. The royal palace in Whitehall burned down in 1698.

The political challenges of the reign were less calamitous, but were serious for the reputation and stability of the government. War against the Dutch in 1665–7 and 1672–4 brought only limited success, and in 1667 there was the humiliation of a Dutch raid on the English fleet in the Medway, in which seven English ships were lost. By the Secret Treaty of Dover of May 1670 with Louis XIV, Charles promised to declare war on the Dutch, to convert to Catholicism, and to restore the religion to England at some point later in his reign. Rumours about these secret clauses in the agreement soon leaked out, and suspicion about Charles's religious and political intentions bedevilled the rest of the reign. In 1672 the king issued a Declaration of Indulgence in which he claimed the prerogative right to vary the parliamentary settlement of religious affairs. He suspended the enforcement of the laws against worship by Dissenters and permitted Catholics to practise in their own homes. Such moves fanned fears about Charles as did the stop on payments out of the Exchequer in 1672, the joint attack with Louis XIV on the Dutch the same year, and Charles's favour for Catholics at court. Worries about the king increasingly overlapped with concern about the succession. A noted and fecund womaniser, Charles had no children by his wife and this left his Catholic brother James as his heir. Had Charles had a lawful heir, he/she would have been born to a Catholic mother. Charles himself seems to have fuelled some of the speculation regarding the possibility of his conversion. The discovery in 1998 of a 'flaming heart', an explicit Catholic symbol, in the Medici Panel (a gift from Charles to Duke Cosimo of Tuscany) suggests that the English king's Catholicism was an open secret in Europe.

Charles's reign is noted today for the laxity of its morals, a sexual permissiveness that was a

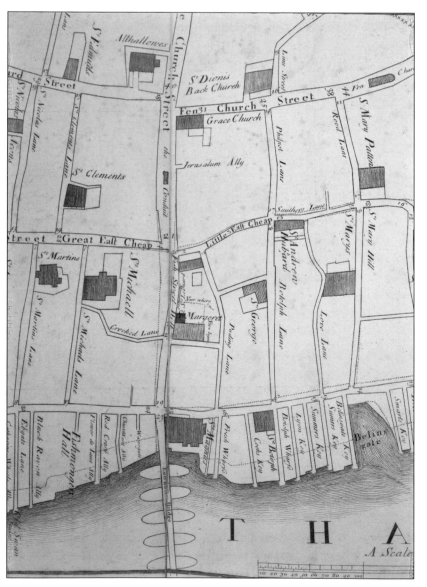

Map of Streets and Lanes in ruins after the Great Fire, 1666, detail of East Cheap and Thames Wharfe.

Sir Christopher Wren's St Paul's, built after its predecessor was destroyed by the Great Fire of London in 1666.

reaction to Puritan zeal. Contemporary commentators made similar comments. Engine, a maid in Edward Ravenscroft's play *The London Cuckolds* (1681), explained:

> This employment was formerly named bawding and pimping, but our Age is more civilis'd and our Language much refin'd. It is now called doing a friend a favour. Whore is now prettily call'd Mistress. Pimp; friend. Cuckold-maker; gallant. Thus the terms being civilis'd the thing itself becomes more acceptable. What Clowns they were in former Ages.

In practice, there was much disquiet about the morality of the court and suspicion that its laxity extended to tolerance of Catholicism. The prominence and role of Charles's mistresses, for example Barbara Villiers, who was created Duchess of Cleveland and Southampton in her own right, and the French born Louise de Kérouälle, who was made Duchess of Portsmouth, led to criticism. The instability of ministries, especially after the fall of Lord Chancellor Clarendon in 1667, exacerbated concern about the situation at court. George Savile, 1st Marquess of Halifax, who served Charles II as Lord Privy Seal, later wrote of the king: 'He lived

Charles II's mistress Barbara Villiers, Duchess of Cleveland, as St Catherine of Alexandria, 1665–70, by Sir Peter Lely.

with his ministers as he did with his mistresses; he used them, but he was not in love with them.'

The paranoid political culture of the period led in 1678 to the Popish Plot. An adventurer, Titus Oates, claimed that there was a Catholic plot to assassinate Charles and replace him with James. The murder of Sir Edmund Godfrey, the London magistrate who took Oates's evidence, and the discovery of suspicious letters in the possession of James's former private secretary, Edward Coleman, inflamed concerns. The revelation by political rivals that Charles's leading minister, Lord Treasurer Danby, had been negotiating with Louis XIV fanned the flames. Danby fell, court power collapsed, and the long-serving Cavalier Parliament was dissolved in January 1679. In a political atmosphere made frenetic by rumour and hard-fought elections (including two in 1679 which were, in part contested on party lines), the Popish Plot became the Exclusion Crisis (1678–81) – an attempt to use Parliament to exclude James from the succession and to weaken Charles's government. Its leading advocate, Anthony Ashley Cooper, 1st Earl of Shaftesbury, created what has been seen as the first English political party, the 'Whigs' – a term used initially to describe Scots Covenanters and then more generally for those who were against James, Duke of York. The Whigs' loyalist opponents were termed Tories, from *toraidhe*, Irish for cattle thief/bandit – an abusive nickname applied to those who backed James. The Tories denied that Parliament had the right to alter the succession and argued, also, that exclusion threatened the social order and might cause another civil war. The damage of the last was still being repaired, for example by the Myddeltons at Chirk Castle, and by the citizens of Worcester. Politicisation affected county communities, as in 1680–1 when Charles sought to remove Whig JPs.

Exclusion failed in the face of the political geography of the times, although there were other reasons for its lack of success. Unlike in 1638–42, the crown retained control of Scotland and Ireland. Covenanter opposition in Scotland was repressed. Within England there was a reluctance to risk civil war anew. Furthermore, Charles's right to summon and dissolve Parliament, which he used in his dissolutions of January and March 1681, and his strength in the House of Lords denied exclusion a constitutional passage.

The Whig failure to secure exclusion in 1681 was followed by a reaction that was made possible by Charles's ability to dispense with Parliament thanks to peace, a rise in customs revenues, and a subsidy from Louis XIV. Whig office-holders were purged, Sir John Hotham being excluded from the list of East Riding JPs, and the Whig leadership was compromised by the Rye House Plot – a 1683 conspiracy to assassinate Charles and James. The conspirators fled or were executed. In Scotland, Covenanters were similarly punished. Robert Baillie of Jervis was executed in 1684. Government control over town corporations, especially London, was strengthened and used to remove opponents. Charles relied on the support of the Tories, and his ability to do so brought a measure of stability. Charles II in these last years of his reign was more in control of his kingdom than any of his predecessors since Henry VII. Furthermore, unlike Cromwell, his position did not rest on force and he had the wholehearted support of the Church of England in upholding royal power. In return, Charles was willing to allow Tory churchmen to initiate prosecutions of Protestant Dissenters in the early 1680s on a more extensive scale than at any point in the reign. The addition to widespread support for the hereditary basis of monarchy of disquiet about his opponents ensured that there was a good popular basis for Charles's adroit management of the political situation.

JAMES II (1685–8)

Adroit is not a description that springs to mind when considering James II (VII of Scotland). He inherited his father's worst characteristics – inflexibility and dogmatism. His brother, however, left him a strong position, thanks to the reaction against exclusion, the crippling of the Whigs, and the support of the Tories. James was able to succeed his brother without difficulty.

His position was further strengthened by the attempts that were made to overthrow him in 1685. One of Charles's illegitimate sons, James, Duke of Monmouth (1649–85), sailed from his exile in the United Provinces and landed with eighty-two companions and a supply of arms at Lyme Regis on 11 June. The landing was unopposed, and, although a part of Monmouth's force failed to overwhelm the Dorset militia at Bridport, recruits joined the duke rapidly. Then a force of militia being assembled at Axminster to oppose the duke collapsed. Monmouth was proclaimed king at Taunton on 19 June and by the time he marched on Bristol on the 21st he had 8,000 men; this included little gentry support, however. Monmouth crossed the Avon at Keynsham, but was discouraged from pressing on by bad weather and the strength of Bristol's garrison. Instead of attacking the city or bypassing it to advance into the West Midlands, he headed for Bath, but it did not surrender and Monmouth lost the initiative. Falling back into Somerset, the duke attempted a night attack on the recently advanced royal army on Sedgemoor (6 July). But the advantage of surprise was lost and the poorly organised rebel army was defeated by its experienced opponents' superior firepower. Unlike Charles II in 1651, the fleeing Monmouth was captured in a ditch on 8 July. He was beheaded a week later after confessing to Archbishop Tenison the sin of revolt against a lawful authority. The bungling executioner required five blows with the axe.

Monmouth's rising was assisted in Scotland by Archibald Campbell, 9th Earl of Argyll, who also returned from the United Provinces for the invasion and rapidly recruited support. Argyll's operations, however, were hampered by divided counsel and the speed of the government's response, including the appearance of two frigates which took the earl's ships and handicapped his operations around the Clyde estuary. Argyll advanced with about 2,000 men to confront a royal army near Dumbarton. However, orders that his men fight were ignored and the troops retreated.

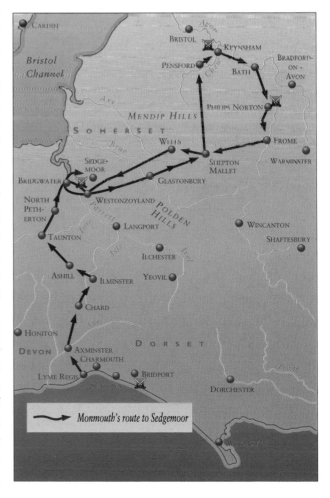

Monmouth's route to Sedgemoor

During the retreat, the cohesion of Argyll's force was lost, and its numbers fell as clansmen returned to their homes. Argyll was captured and executed.

Monmouth's rising is worth considering at length because it was the last major one in England and Sedgemoor the last significant battle on English soil. There might seem to be parallels in the events of the next century but in fact the Jacobite rising in northern England in 1715 was less important than that in Scotland, while in 1745 the Scottish Jacobite rising led to no independent action in England. James II was to be overthrown in 1688, but by a foreign invading force, under his nephew and son-in-law, William III of Orange, not by a domestic rising, although domestic discontents were directly related to William's decision to invade. In combination, the events of 1685 and 1688 reveal much about the political geography of Britain. As in France, where there was a contrast between the ability to sustain civil war against royal authority in the late sixteenth century and the failure of rebellions against Louis XIV in the seventeenth century, so also in Britain there had been a shift from the volatile situation of the late 1400s. This was disguised in part because the Stuarts were twice overthrown in the seventeenth century, but, as already mentioned, the overthrow in 1688 was by foreign invasion, and by another Stuart, not by domestic rebellion. Furthermore, the rebellions against Charles I in Scotland in 1638 and England in 1642 were not rebellions of the periphery against the centre – as the risings of the 1490s, 1530s and 1560s were – but, rather, rejections of royal authority by national bodies.

The events of 1685 and 1688 did not suggest that it would be possible successfully to defy governmental power – royal or otherwise – from the basis of a regional power nexus. Although it was a different kind of struggle, the Civil War in England can also be seen as the triumph of the national centre in this light, as the Royalist forces were worn down by Parliamentarians based in the wealthiest parts of the country, especially London. Scotland during the Civil War was somewhat different, because the Marquesses of Montrose and Huntly were still at large in 1646 when Charles I ordered them to lay down their arms. Indeed Huntly had just stormed Aberdeen.

Within a decade of this surrender in 1646, the potential of national forces to transform the political geography of Britain had been abruptly demonstrated. The republican regime that had executed Charles I had been faced with very different governments in Scotland and Ireland, and could not feel safe until these had been overthrown. In a remarkable display of military power, republican forces conquered both Scotland – a success that had eluded English monarchs throughout history – and Ireland, as well as the remaining English Royalist bases in the Channel Isles, the Isles of Scilly, the Isle of Man and English colonies. Thereafter, there was not to be a lasting difference in military-political control between England, Scotland and Ireland until the British state lost most of Ireland in 1922. Short-term variations in allegiance – between England and Ireland in 1689 or England and Scotland in late 1745 – were unstable, and seen as such on both sides. Thus, irrespective of their precise constitutional relationship, England, Ireland and Scotland had become an inter-connected unit in the geography of military power. This ensured that any attempt to overthrow James II would have to seek to supplant him in all three kingdoms.

James's victory over Monmouth in 1685 encouraged him to press on with unpopular policies. He increased his army. Parliament was opposed to this policy, and particularly anxious over the appointment of Catholic officers. Tension over the issue was increased by Louis XIV's abrogation of Protestant rights in France in 1685 with his revocation of the Edict of Nantes; this led to a flood of refugees into London. Unprepared to accept

Tresco Castle, Isles of Scilly, was built by Cromwell in 1651 as an artillery point to watch the channel below.

criticism and unable to understand views different to his aim, James prorogued Parliament in November 1685 and, with less constraint, moved towards the Catholicising of government, both central and local. The changes necessary to establish full religious and civil equality for Catholics entailed a series of unpopular steps: the destruction of the privileges of the Church of England, a policy of appointing Catholics to office, the insistent use of prerogative action (especially the extension of the claim to dispense with the law), the build-up of a large army with many Catholic officers, and preparations for a packed Parliament. Going much further than his brother had done in the wake of the Exclusion Crisis, in 1687 James established a commission to 'regulate' the parliamentary boroughs. Ninety-seven were purged in order to produce a pliant Commons. Dissenters and Catholics were installed as members of corporations. Catholics were made lords lieutenant. The dismissal of Lord Derby as Lord Lieutenant in both Cheshire and Lancashire was a breach with local patronage structures and assumptions of hierarchy. So also were the extensive purges of JPs in 1686-7. Yet there was no revolution, nothing comparable to the crisis of 1638-42, in part because there were no opportunities to reject James's plans, no crisis in Scotland or Ireland to force issues to the fore in England.

James VII of Scotland, II of England, in Garter robes, by Gennari. James (1633-1701) was king from 1685 until he was driven into exile in the winter of 1688-9. As lacking in ability as his father Charles I, James was more determined to introduce change. It is interesting to speculate how far history would have been driven had he been the eldest son.

Like those of the childless Mary Tudor, James's policies also appeared ultimately reversible. He had no surviving son by his second marriage to the Catholic Mary of Modena and the surviving children by his first marriage to the Protestant Anne Hyde were two daughters both married to Protestant, if not Anglican, princes: Mary to William III of Orange and Anne to Prince George of Denmark. The birth of a Prince of Wales on 10 June 1688 was therefore a major shock that transformed the situation. Despite reports that the baby was smuggled into the bedchamber in a warming pan, there is no doubt that the child was Mary's; although many wanted to believe otherwise.

Nineteen days later, the political temperature rose further when Archbishop Sancroft of Canterbury and six bishops were acquitted on charges of sedition for refusing to read James's order that the Declaration of Indulgence of 1687 granting all Christians full equality of religious practice (a challenge to the position of the established church) be proclaimed from all pulpits. They chose loyalty to the church above that to the king. James had received the petition of the seven in May 1688 with the exclamation 'This is a standard of rebellion', but it was only such because he chose to treat it thus.

The political culture of the period assumed deference in return for good kingship, expectations of political behaviour that involved a measure of contractualism. James spurned these boundaries. He had deliberately set out to find a new constituency of political support after his failure with the Tories in the Parliament of 1685. This steered him to his goal of a more secure position for Catholics as part of an attempt to create a wider-ranging religious toleration that would also benefit Dissenters. The attempt entailed an attack on the position of the church, and thus the views of the Tories. A minority of Whigs cooperated with James, but the majority remained suspicious of his intentions, opposed to his offers and readier to put their trust in his daughter Mary and her husband, William. They let it be known that they backed toleration for Dissenters without power for Catholics.

James's basis of support was therefore narrow, but, as under Oliver Cromwell, there was no clear and prudent political course for those who were disenchanted, no institutional expression of national discontent that could instigate a change in policy and recreate the consensus between crown and social elite that was the hallmark of early modern government.

THE 'GLORIOUS' REVOLUTION

The acquittal of the bishops was followed by an invitation to William from seven politicians to intervene in order to protect Protestantism and traditional liberties. The conspiracy, however, was of secondary importance to the invasion. William had already decided to try to take England in order, in an escalating international crisis, to keep it out of the French camp, and, instead, to ensure that English resources were directed against France. Nevertheless, the invitation was important to him, as he wished to arrive as a liberator, not conqueror, in order to increase his chances of success.

William's first invasion attempt in mid-October 1688 was defeated by storms at sea, with the loss of many supplies, including over a thousand horses, which were crucial to the mobility of any invasion force. Horses were especially liable to break their legs in storms because ships were not stabilized. William's second attempt was more successful, and England was invaded despite its possession of a large and undefeated navy and a substantial army. A strong north-easterly wind prevented the English fleet, then lying at the Gunfleet off Harwich, from leaving anchorage, and this allowed William to sail into the Channel. By the time the English commander, George Legge, 1st Lord Dartmouth, finally sailed on 3 November, the main Dutch fleet was already passing Dover.

William landed at Brixham in Devon on 5 November; the pursuing English fleet was no nearer than Beachy Head. A successful attack could still have weakened William, but, at a Council of War on 5 November, the English captains decided not to attack what they believed to be a larger Dutch force. Thereafter, first storms and then bad weather prevented the English fleet from acting until it surrendered to William's authority on 13 December. This was the most ignominious naval campaign in English naval history, a campaign that was flawed from the outset by a defensive, reactive mentality that owed something to England being formally at peace and much to division and discontent among the captains. Disenchanted with James, some of the English captains were less than fervent in their hostility to William.

On land William was outnumbered by James, who blocked the route to London with a force of 30,000 men on Salisbury Plain. William stayed at Exeter from 9 until 21 November, hoping to refresh his troops and win English support. He found Exeter unenthusiastic, although some, including Francis Luttrell from Dunster Castle, came

The image of victory, William III on a grey charger observed by Neptune, Ceres and Flora, by Sir Godfrey Kneller (1646–1723).

127

The north-west front of Sizergh Castle, Cumbria. Its owner Sir Thomas Strickland fled abroad with James II as William of Orange gained the support of London.

into the city to offer his support. However, indecision, ill-health, and desertion by a series of senior officers and his younger daughter, Anne, led James to abandon his army on 24 November, weakening his troops' morale. It had already been hit by dissension and conspiracy among the officers. James's position was also damaged by a number of provincial uprisings. By 5 December Derby, Nottingham, York, Hull and Durham had been seized for William, and the Anglican lords lieutenant had largely abandoned James, although the extent of loyalty towards James, and the role of local circumstances – particularly determined leaders – is suggested by the fact that Carlisle, Chester and Newcastle successfully resisted such attempts.

William refused to halt his march on London in order to allow negotiations to proceed, as the Tory leaders would have preferred, and James fled the capital. Captured and returned to London he was finally driven from it by Dutch pressure. James's captors had to encourage him to flee a second time by leaving him unguarded. This enabled William to claim that James had deserted. His supporters were purged, especially those who were Catholic. Stripped of his offices, Richard, Viscount Preston returned to Nunnington Hall. William Herbert, 1st Marquess of Powis, of Powis Castle, and Sir Thomas Strickland of Sizergh Castle fled abroad with James. Throughout Britain the 'Glorious Revolution' in part meant a shift in the local distribution of power, certainly as far as royal posts were concerned. Sir John Hotham, who had been forced into exile in 1684, landed with William of Orange and returned to Hull, now as Governor. In Warwickshire, a Protestant mob sacked Coughton Court, the house of the Catholic Throckmortons and the east side of the courtyard was destroyed. In Scotland, exiles such as Sir Patrick Hume and Robert Baillie, returned, regained their estates, and became influential. In turn, the Powis estates were granted by William III to two Dutch favourites, who he made Duke of Portland and Earl of Rochford. The Herberts were not reinstated until 1722.

THE REVOLUTION SETTLEMENT

A monarchical system abhorred a vacuum of power and, far from being willing to concede to his wife, William made clear that he wanted to be ruler. He declared on 3 February 1689 that he would be neither regent or prince consort (as Anne's husband was to be), and thus one of the many innovations of the Revolution Settlement was the creation of a joint monarchy, that of William (1689–1702) and Mary (1689–94). By the Bill of Rights of 12 February 1689, Parliament misleadingly declared that James had deserted the kingdom – a product of their preference for the view that James had abdicated, rather than the more radical notion that he had been deposed. Declaring, 'whereas it hath been found by experience that it is inconsistent with the safety and welfare of this Protestant kingdom to be governed by a popish prince, or by any king or queen marrying a papist', Parliament also debarred all Catholics from the succession. This ended the rights of James's son, the future 'James III'. Anne's rights as successor to the childless Mary were subordinated to those of William, a consequence of his intimidatory role in cajoling a settlement. The financial settlement, however, left William with an ordinary revenue that was too small for his peacetime needs, obliging him to turn to Parliament for support. This was a result of the distrust of the royal prerogative that had arisen as a result of Stuart rule. So also was the clause in the Bill of Rights prohibiting a standing army unless with the agreement of Parliament. In Scotland, the Scottish Convention of 1689 and the Claim of Right it issued in 1690 marked a firm rejection of royal authority: the offer of the crown to William and Mary was made conditional on their acceptance of the Claim, which stated that James VII had forfeited the crown by his policies and that no Catholic could become ruler of Scotland or hold public office.

As in 1485, England had been successfully invaded. But in 1688 the political situation was very different for a number of reasons, not least the validating role of Parliament in

England's Memorial to its Wonderful Deliverance from the French Tyranny and Popish Oppression. *Providence was seen at work in the struggle waged both within Britain and further afield. James II was presented as the agent of Louis XIV and the Pope.*

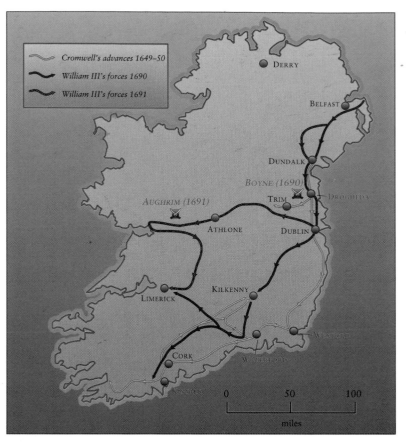

Legend:
- Cromwell's advances 1649–50
- William III's forces 1690
- William III's forces 1691

England, and the need to ensure that Scotland and Ireland were brought in line. Nevertheless, there was also a fundamental continuity. Political issues were settled by conflict. Furthermore, the dynastic position was crucial: political legitimacy could not be divorced from the sovereign and the succession. Both these factors ensure that the elements of modernity suggested by the constitutional products of the 1688 invasion – especially the Bill of Rights of 1689, and the moves towards regular parliaments and elections and a freer press – have to be qualified by reminders of more traditional features of the political structure. The foreign force invading England and the aristocrats rising against the king were reminiscent of the French-supported opposition to King John in 1216 and of Henry VII's French-backed seizure of power from Richard III in 1485. It is misleading to present the so-called Glorious Revolution of 1688 as an unqualified advance on the march to modernity.

An effective parliamentary monarchy, with parliamentary control over the finances of the state, had been the aim of many of the critics of Charles II. The Revolution Settlement created the constitutional basis for such a monarchy, but the instability of the ministries of the period 1689–1721 suggests that the political environment within which such a monarchy could be effective had not been created. Two major wars (1689–97, 1702–13) were financed by Parliament, albeit with considerable difficulty, in contrast to the débâcle of the last Stuart war, the Third Anglo-Dutch War of 1672–4 for which there had been no sound financial base. However, policy formulation and execution were handicapped and the confidence of allies sapped by frequent changes in government. At one level, these changes were not too serious: power remained the monopoly of the highest social groups and, despite Tory claims to the contrary, the Whigs were a party primarily of great landowners, not of bankers and Dissenters. At another level, the party politics and ministerial instability of 1689–1721 revealed the grave limitations of the Revolution Settlement. A parliamentary monarchy could not simply be legislated into existence. It required the development of conventions and patterns of political behaviour that would permit a constructive resolution of contrary opinions within a system where there was no single source of dominant power. The slowness of the development of these patterns was particularly serious as Britain was at war for much of the period and Jacobitism was a significant force.

While the 'Glorious' Revolution was an important advance for a particular view of England, it did not secure instant dominance for that view, or allow the nation to unite around it. In fact, the Revolution produced a number of competing theses of patriotism. Alongside praise for William as a Protestant and providential blessing on the nation were Jacobite, Tory and 'Country' views of the new king as a usurper and of an England suffering depredations under his tutelage, views that were perfectly viable and that attracted considerable support in the 1690s. These views remained marginalised – not because of any inherent absurdity, or necessary incompatibility with English national character, but because the circumstances of William's reign allowed him a political and polemical victory over his opponents. Most importantly, William proved able to win the military struggle over the British succession that followed 1688. He could, therefore, exclude his opponents from power, and condemn critics of his vision of nationality and political destiny as disloyal. In addition, William's military victory coincided with a dramatic expansion of public politics. In the 1690s, the advent of annual parliaments, the ending of pre-publication censorship, and the development of a considerably more active press, meant that polemical politics began to produce more and different kinds of material. As a result, the particular patriotic discourse associated with the victors of the revolution was widely disseminated, and gained the highest profile in the culture of print, as well as in government records.

Mary II (1662–94), wife of William III, by William Wissing or Wissmig. Elder daughter of James II by Anne Hyde, Mary married her cousin in 1677. She returned to England as queen in February 1689 and became joint monarch, acting as regent in William's absence, although he wielded the real power. She died, childless, of smallpox.

The consequence of the victory for Williamite patriotism has been to shape not only Georgian Britons' view of their world, but also later historical understanding of the period. The 'Glorious' Revolution was seen as the source of a 'matchless constitution'. Much of the scholarship dealing with the century after 1688 has been soaked in the sort of Whiggism promoted by that event, with the result that many of the ambiguities and complexities of the period have been lost. Until recently, historians of the 1690s and the eighteenth century were almost as effective as Williamite politicians in marginalising the Jacobite and other dissonant voices of the age. This was true both of academics and of more popular writers such as Macaulay and Churchill. Consequently, the Protestant and Whiggish vision associated with the victors has come to seem natural to the English, and the coherence and potential persuasiveness of alternative world views has been obscured.

Similarly, too little attention has been paid to the exclusivity and polemical nature of the eventually dominant patriotism. Its victory has hidden the fact that it was necessarily divisive because directed against critics of William, and that it derived much of its early drive from its partisan character. Civil war in Scotland and Ireland was the first consequence of the 'Glorious' Revolution.

NINE

The Facts of Life

It is as necessary to be wary of finding signs of modernity in the social and domestic life of the early modern period as in its politics. Visiting houses from the age it is all too easy to assume that life was in many respects similar to ours. Of course, the furnishings are different, but there are few signs for the superficial viewer of more profound contrasts, contrasts that assure us the very experience of life was totally different. This chapter will look at some aspects of difference, concentrating on the period from 1650.

It is best to start with the facts of life, or rather the fact of death. Individual and collective responses to the natural and built environments are affected by the age of the individual observer. The average experience of life for people in the past necessarily came at a younger age than for the average 21st-century person, and was shaped within a context of the ever-present threat of death, disease, injury and pain. There was still joy and pleasure, exultation and exhilaration, but the demographics were chilling. Alongside longlasting individuals, there were lives quickly cut short, in the case of women especially in childbirth. Sir Hugh Acland (1637–1713), the owner of Killerton, survived his son John and was succeeded by his grandson, another Hugh, who lived from only 1696 till 1728. Alexander, 20th Brodie of Brodie, died of consumption in 1759, aged eighteen. Edward Phelips IV (1678–1734) of Montacute married his cousin Ann (1687–1707), only for her to die after the birth of her second daughter. Ann's sisters, Elizabeth (1689–1750), who became Edward's second wife, and Edith (1694–1772), were longer lived, but Edith had no surviving children. Sir Barrington Bouchier of Beningbrough Hall had three wives, John Hobart, 2nd Earl of Buckinghamshire of Blickling Hall two, Sir Brownlow Cust of Belton also two. Of the Parkers of Saltram four of the five who headed the family between 1649 and 1840 had two wives. Several of these wives died young: after Frances, first wife of John Parker, 1st Lord Boringdon (1734–88), died in 1764, he married Theresa (1744–75), but she died soon after the birth of her second child, another Theresa. Other (sic), 3rd Earl of Plymouth, married Elizabeth Lewis in 1730, only for him to die aged twenty-five, his wife to follow a year later, and the estates to be inherited by the 4th Earl, at the age of eighteen months, under the guardianship of his grandfather. Wallington passed to the Trevelyans in 1777 because, with the death of his daughter Elizabeth (1735–52), Sir Walter Calverley Blackett (1707–77) had no surviving children. These were wealthy individuals with some change of quality living. The situation for the 'lower orders' was bleaker on average.

The Patient and the Doctor, *by Gabriel Metsu, 1660s. Medical care was of limited assistance in dealing with many problems as medical knowledge was often deficient. Medical treatments, such as blistering and mercury, were often painful, dangerous or enervating. Surgery was primitive and performed without anaesthetics.*

The aggregate results of such life expectancy were as blunt. After the growth of 1500–1650, Britain's population did not rise greatly for a century. In England it probably fell between 1660 and 1690 and in Ireland and Scotland in the 1690s. Declining fertility was certainly important in causing the fall between 1671 and 1691, but death rates were of greater importance thereafter: the death-rate crises of 1696–9, 1727–30 and 1741–2 wiped out the growth of intervening years. Figures are approximate – there was no official census until 1801 – but the population of England and Wales probably rose from 5.18 million in 1695 to only 5.51 in 1711, 5.59 in 1731 and 6.20 in 1751 – a rise of only 1 million in sixty years. Thereafter, as the demographic regime changed, it rushed ahead, to 8.61 million in 1801.

The relationship between population and household structure was very different from that in modern Britain. Barring occasional bigamies, wife sales and aristocratic

The south front, Blickling Hall, Norfolk. Rats were a problem in country houses like Blickling as well as in hovels.

Bills of Divorce, marriage was irreversible, and ended only with the death of one of the partners. Most childbearing was within marriage. Despite the absence of effective contraceptives, recorded illegitimacy rates were low, very low by modern standards, although it is impossible to say how much illegitimacy was concealed by infanticide. Marriages were also generally late. At the end of the seventeenth century, English men married at about twenty-eight and women at about twenty-seven. Childbearing was thus postponed until an average of more than ten years past puberty, which itself occurred later than in modern Britain. In addition, many men and women never married: about 23 per cent of people aged 40–4 were unmarried. By the start of the nineteenth century, there were major changes: the recorded illegitimacy rate had risen from 1.8 per cent to 5 per cent, and the average age at marriage fell to 25.5 and 23.7 for men and women respectively. Fewer than 9 per cent of people remained unmarried.

Disease remained a constant presence. Thirty-eight per cent of the children born in Penrith between 1650 and 1700 died before reaching the age of six. Very high child mortality figures continued to be recorded across Britain throughout the eighteenth century, although if childhood was survived, it was possible to live to a considerable age. Over 22 per cent of the congregation of Holy Trinity, Whitehaven, who died between 1751 and 1781 were over sixty. Defences against disease remained flimsy, not least because of the limited nature of medical knowledge. There was no comparison to modern suppositions that there should be a medical cure for everything, only folk remedies and prayer.

Yet there were advances. Smallpox was one of the most serious diseases. Among those it claimed was Queen Mary in 1694. Initially inoculation was of only limited value, not least because those treated, when not isolated, were a source of infection. Inoculation became safer after the Suttonian method of inserting only the smallest possible amount of infectious matter was widely adopted from about 1768. Vaccination – a safer method – was not performed until 1796. Typhus, typhoid, influenza, dysentery, chicken-pox, measles, scarlet fever, and syphilis were all serious problems. Other conditions that can now be cured or held at bay, were debilitating. Opium and alcohol were the only painkillers, and cheap laudanum was a universal panacea. There was much trust in quack medicines and, more effectively, herbal remedies. Their popularity reflected the sense that something could and should be done: there was no simple acceptance of the grim will of God. Troubled by failing eyesight, John Meller, owner of Erddig was recommended the herb eyebright by his sister: 'I had the distilled water of it and thought it no way unpleasant being sweetened with sugar. You may also make a tea of it or have it dried.'

Night, *by William Hogarth. Until gas lighting, and later electricity, transformed the situation, the change between day and night was far more abrupt than is the case today. Nighttime offered different sensations, experiences and dangers. For example, the role of moonlight was much more important than today.*

Jane Ebbrell, spider-brusher, aged 87, in 1793 by John Walters of Denbigh in the Servant's Hall at Erddig. The verse was added to the picture by Philip Yorke I some fifty years later. Servants were central to British society, not only to the life of the upper orders.

The virulence of diseases and the potency of crippling problems were more than a consequence of a lack of knowledge and treatments, especially antibiotics and anti-inflammatory drugs. Living conditions were also a major problem. Crowded housing conditions, especially the sharing of beds, helped spread diseases, particularly respiratory infections. Most dwellings were neither warm nor dry and sanitary practices were a problem. The privies developed by Alexander Cummings and Joseph Bramah, patented in 1775 and 1778, were used by few. There were few baths, washing in clean water was limited, and louse infestation was serious. Although outer clothes were worn for long periods, and were not washable, those who could afford it wore linen and cotton shifts next to their skin, and these shifts could be regularly laundered. However, most people wore the same clothes for as long as they could. Bed bugs were a real horror, because they were no respecter of persons. By modern standards, breath and skin must have been repellent.

Rats were also a problem – at country houses, such as Blickling Hall, as well as in hovels. The *Salisbury and Winchester Journal* of 27 September 1790 reported: 'A correspondent, about to lay flooring in a house newly built, asks how he may best prevent rats harbouring between the joists? We will thank the intelligent to inform him by a line to the printer.' The exposed state of man was further underlined by an item in the issue of 25 October 1790:

Last week died in a state of canine madness Miss Tomkins, near Exeter. What is very remarkable, this young lady had never been bit, but received her death, it is thought, by permitting a dog to run about the house after being bit by a mad dog. This should be a caution to many unthinking people, who suffer such dogs to run about the house, never considering that the poison remains on the coat of the animal, and by this means is communicated to their clothes etc.

A regulated society directed against the poor was the answer, suggested an item on 20 December 1790: 'A correspondent of Frome informs us, that in consequence of several persons of that town having lately been bitten by a mad dog, the parishioners, at a vestry, entered into a resolution of relieving no pauper who should keep a dog. A laudable example for other parishes to follow!' Rabies remained an issue. On 17 February 1792, the *Chelmsford Chronicle* offered its readers a cure for rabies 'handed to us by a neighbour'.

It is difficult to recreate an impression of the smell and dirt of the period. Ventilation was limited, drains blocked. Humans lived close to animals and dunghills, and this damaged health. Manure stored near buildings was hazardous and could contaminate the water supply. Effluent from undrained privies and animal pens flowed across streets and into houses through generally porous walls. Privies with open soil pits lay directly alongside dwellings and under bedrooms. Pump water was affected by sewage and river water in towns was often contaminated. In Leeds, public sewers passed effluent downstream to water-collection points. This unhealthiness was a cause and facilitator of disease, especially typhus.

Poor nutrition lowered resistance. Fruit and vegetables were expensive and played only a minor role in the diet of the urban poor, who were also generally ill clad. The poor ate less meat and, outside southern England, less wheat and more oats. Bad harvests led to higher death rates, as in Worcestershire in 1708–12, although there were no actual famines in England, unlike in Scotland and Ireland where there were severe crises, notably in Scotland in 1696–9 and Ireland in 1740–1.

Accidents were also a serious problem and it was frequently difficult to deal with their consequences. In 1786 Lady Margaret Duff, wife of James, 21st Brodie of Brodie, burnt to death, when peat from her bedroom fire set her nightgown alight. Accidents were common at birth. There were many crippled men and women who had been mangled in childbirth.

For those who survived, life could be very difficult, and this became more of a problem when the population rose from the 1740s. It led to increased pressure as more sought land, employment, food and poor relief, disrupting local economies and hitting living standards.

Agricultural labour was arduous, generally daylight to dusk in winter, and 6 a.m. to 6 p.m. in summer. Industrial employment was also hard – up to sixteen hours daily in the Yorkshire alum houses – and often dangerous. Millers worked in dusty and noisy circumstances, frequently suffered from lice and often developed asthma, hernias and chronic back problems. Disorders could result from the strain of unusual physical demands or postures, such as those required of tailors and weavers. Many places of work were damp, badly ventilated and/or poorly lit. Work frequently involved exposure to dangerous substances, such as arsenic, lead and mercury, or was dangerous in itself, particularly construction, fishing and mining. Many industrial processes were dangerous to others besides the workers: dressing and tanning leather polluted water supplies and were therefore kept outside cities, for example, on the banks of the River Wandle south of the Thames and away from London. The kilns of brick and tile works produced smoke and fumes.

Domestic service was less dangerous, but still arduous. At least 12,000 female domestic servants were probably employed in the four largest Scottish towns in the late seventeenth century, possibly 10 per cent of the 16–25 year old women in Scotland. When visiting the stately homes of the period, it is as well to remember the unpleasant tasks that faced these women such as the disposal of excreta. Water-carrying, generally a female task, could cause physical distortion. Cleaning and drying clothes involved much effort. As surviving laundries, such as that at Killerton and Shugborough suggest, the dirt had to be pummelled out of clothes with the use of lye, and some early mangles required much muscle-power.

The social world of the early eighteenth century was to dissolve as a result of the technological transformations, industrialisation and urbanisation that were to be associated with the Industrial Revolution, but this change took over a century, and much that was common in society in 1700 was still customary in 1860 despite railways, telegraphs and the expression of confidence in the future proclaimed with the Great Exhibition of 1851.

TEN

The Politics and Culture of an Aristocratic Society

For most of us politics means the world of political parties, but it is more appropriate when looking at its impact to begin by considering politics in its wider sense: the nature of power within society, and the practice of power. The fundamentals are apt to be overlooked, but they set the parameters within which politics, as it is narrowly and conventionally conceived, was conducted.

What then were the fundamentals? First, society continued to be male dominated. That did not preclude power on the part of individual women, most obviously for the eighteenth century 'royals', particularly Queen Anne (1702–14), and dowagers, especially Sarah, Duchess of Marlborough. Furthermore, personal relations were such that, at the individual level, the influence of women over their husbands or lovers could be considerable. Nevertheless, public practice and theory were male-centred. Women constituted one of the great silent majorities of the period.

A second excluded group was defined by age. Age wielded power and expected respect. This was integral to a propertied society in which inheritance was crucial to wealth. Most wealth was still tied up in land. The relationship between capital and income greatly favoured the former – as, in general, was true of British history until the economic growth of the nineteenth century – and the ability to create income without capital was limited. Imperial expansion and industrialisation were both to increase greatly the possibilities for self-advancement. In some cases this led to massive wealth – epitomised in the eighteenth century by Robert Clive, the conqueror of Bengal, who became an aristocratic landowner, and such manufacturers as Josiah Wedgwood and Samuel Crompton. Admiral Lord Anson (1697–1762) was a childless self-made man who left his fortune to his elder brother Thomas who used the money to extend the house and develop the park at Shugborough. These figures were still uncommon in the period, sufficiently so for there to be grave suspicion about the wealth produced by 'nabobs' who had made their money in India. Nevertheless, these men began to make their mark. Francis Sykes, who had done so, had a splendid Palladian mansion built for him by John Carr at Basildon Park in Berkshire in 1776–83, a property he had purchased in 1771. In 1746 Henry Talbot, an East India merchant, bought and remodelled Vintage House, near Dorking, one of the many stately homes now demolished. An equivalent of the nabobs, James Dawkins from

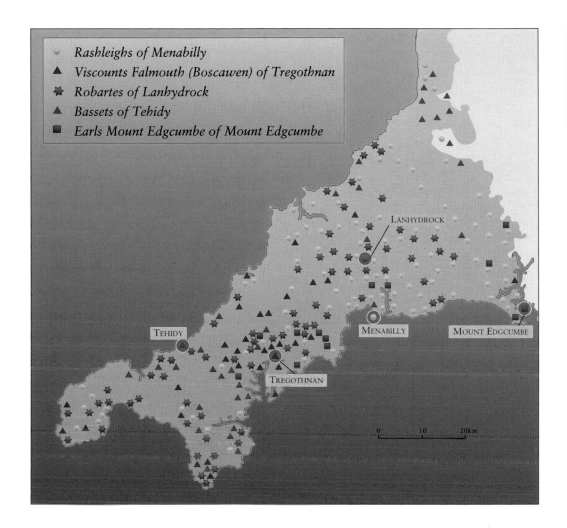

- Rashleighs of Menabilly
- Viscounts Falmouth (Boscawen) of Tregothnan
- Robartes of Lanhydrock
- Bassets of Tehidy
- Earls Mount Edgcumbe of Mount Edgcumbe

LANHYDROCK

TEHIDY

MENABILLY

MOUNT EDGCUMBE

TREGOTHNAN

0   10   20km

MAJOR ESTATES IN CORNWALL IN THE EIGHTEENTH CENTURY

The estates of the major families were often widely dispersed. This encouraged a sense of county rather than local identity. The majority of estates were let on three-life leases for ninety-nine years, encouraging the independence of tenant farmers. The crown, through the Duchy of Cornwall, was the greatest landowner. The major landowners shown on the map were resident families. Many enjoyed considerable power in Cornwall's large parliamentary representation.

Jamaica, purchased the Oxfordshire estate of Over Norton in 1726. He stood unsuccessfully as MP for Oxford in 1734, spending at least £1,000 on the election, but was elected unopposed for New Woodstock on the interest of the Duchess of Marlborough and sat for the constituency from 1734 until 1747.

There was an active land market and status could be readily acquired, but in most of Britain, especially in areas of established agriculture, the distribution of wealth did not change greatly in the eighteenth century, other than through marriage and inheritance. The pattern of estates also did not alter. Thus in Oxfordshire, the Churchill estate could be created only because there was a royal manor – Woodstock – to use. This affected the nearby parliamentary constituency of New Woodstock. The dukes of Marlborough became the hereditary high stewards, claimed the right to appoint the recorder of the borough (an influential figure at election time) and selected many of the MPs, including family members, such as the heir, the Marquess of Blandford, in 1727, John Spencer, grandson of the 1st Duke, in 1732, 1734, 1741 and 1744, and James Dawkins in 1734. Lord Charles Spencer, second son of the 3rd Duke, sat for the county from 1761 until 1801. His brother, Lord Robert, sat for New Woodstock (1768–71 and 1818–20) and Oxford (1771–90), as well as for two seats outside the county. Such individuals regarded membership of the Commons as a right. They were also the prime catches in the marriage market and thus best able to preserve and increase their wealth by marriage.

However, a remodelling of the local power hierarchy comparable to that produced by the creation of the Churchill estate was unusual. Indeed, the stability of the landed order was one of the striking features of the period. Such a remark might appear surprising given the aristocratic emphasis on longevity of lineage and continuity of control, but in the period 1400–1660 there had in fact been considerable disruption. The aristocratic feuds and the dynastic discontinuities of the fifteenth century had been responsible for major changes in landownership. Political and religious shifts in the sixteenth century had had the same effect, and after the execution of Thomas Howard, Duke of Norfolk, in 1572 there were no more dukes in England or Wales until George Villiers became Duke of Buckingham in 1623. The Dissolution of the monasteries and the sale of other church lands by Henry VIII and his successors had seriously disrupted established patterns of control. The same was true of the Civil Wars, although there had been a considerable restoration of Royalist landownership with the restoration of Charles II in 1660.

In contrast, there was much more continuity from 1660 and into the eighteenth century. There were no changes in England comparable to those suffered by Catholic landowners in Ireland in the late seventeenth century. Tories might complain in the reigns of George I (1714–27) and George II (1727–60) that Whig policies discriminated against the landed interest with which they liked to associate themselves, but Sir Robert Walpole, Whig Prime Minister 1721–42, brought land tax down from 3 shillings in the pound in 1717–21 to 2 shillings in the pound (10 per cent) in 1722–6, 1730–1 and 1734–9, and to 1 shilling in the pound (5 per cent) in 1732–3, and his protégé Henry Pelham, First Lord of the Treasury 1743–54, was similarly committed to peace and low taxation. Both were also members of the social elite, albeit not at the highest level, and were keen to establish themselves in landed society. Walpole came from the Norfolk gentry, built a lavish seat at Houghton and became Earl of Orford. Pelham, the younger brother of the Duke of Newcastle, whose seat was at Claremont, established himself at Esher Place. On the other side of the Commons, whatever the political proscription they suffered under George I and George II – which closed careers in government, the military, the law, and the higher reaches of the church to them – the Tories were not driven from the land.

Landed continuity had political, social and cultural consequences. It contributed greatly to the third of the fundamentals: exclusion by social status. This was a hierarchical society, and there were few challenges to the assumptions that reflected and sustained this situation. The distribution of governmental power and authority fundamentally accorded with the structure of the social system, not with democratic representation. There were shifts, not least an ecclesiastical pluralism that challenged religious authority following the Act of Toleration of 1689. Nevertheless, the ethos and practice of politics were more conservative than in the seventeenth century, and it was possible to encompass political and religious divisions, bar Jacobitism, within the system. Although much commentary naturally related to political tension and disagreements, the structure of politics and government, far from precluding debate and discussion, now expected them. Government relied on cooperation and lacked both a substantial bureaucracy and a well-developed bureaucratic ethos. Loyalties were still largely local and personal, rather than to the state as such. In politics, aside from the institutional framework of contention – elections and Parliament – the court and ministerial context of elite politics was not one of uniform opinions and an absence of debate. It would be wrong to suggest that the British *ancien régime* was stable if that label is intended to imply an absence of debate and of new ideas and initiatives.

After the defeat of Jacobitism (the cause of the excluded Stuarts), the state became more stable and this situation was sustained in England and Scotland until the challenge of the 1790s, although there was a collapse of authority in North America in 1775. In England and Scotland, this stability was not maintained at the cost of any permanent struggle with the world of extra-parliamentary politics. There was no such struggle, nor any rigid divide, nor, arguably, prior to the 1790s, a coherent challenge to the political structure. Indeed, the measure of the conservatism of the period was that stability was a case not of radicalism overcome or resisted, as in the early 1660s, but of a society with few radical options until the crisis created by the French Revolution and the accompanying development of British radicalism in the early 1790s.

This was clear in electoral terms. Oxfordshire, for example, might have had a large electorate of about 4,000 voters (the 40-shilling freeholders) but those elected as MPs were scarcely ordinary freeholders. From 1740 to 1790 the county was represented by Sir James Dashwood, George, Viscount Quarendon, Norreys Bertie, Thomas, Viscount Parker, Sir Edward Turner, Lord Charles Spencer, and Philip, 4th Viscount Wenman. The sole apparent non-aristocrat in this list – Norreys Bertie – was the grandson and great-grandson of MPs, and the grand-nephew of the 1st Earl of Abingdon.

The politics of the great houses remained important. This was true of the more numerous borough seats as well as of the county constituencies. Irrespective of whether they actually had any urban property, local aristocrats and gentry could be of considerable consequence in influencing borough representation – the Dukes of Bolton and Chandos in Winchester, the Robartes of Lanhydrock in Bodmin, the Luttrells of Dunster Castle at Minehead, the Dukes of Grafton and the Ickworth-based Earls of Bristol at Bury St Edmunds, and the Earls Gower at Newcastle under Lyme. This influence was not always uncontentious: in 1722 and 1748 Derby successfully resisted the usually dominant interests of the dukes of Devonshire and the earl of Chesterfield, and in 1747 the Ansons of Shugborough and Gowers of Trentham were only just able to overthrow the sitting Tory MPs in Lichfield, becoming very unpopular locally in the process. Yet, in general, particularly in smaller boroughs, the influence of the rural elite was strong. Many boroughs, such as Exeter, that in the seventeenth century had chosen townsmen as MPs, chose country

A View of the House of Commons, engraved by B. Cole (fl. 1748–75). In 1743, John Campbell MP noted 'some gentlewomen in our gallery, not being able to hold their water let it run on Mr Dodington and a Scots member who sat under. The first had a white duffel frock spoiled, the latter almost blinded.'

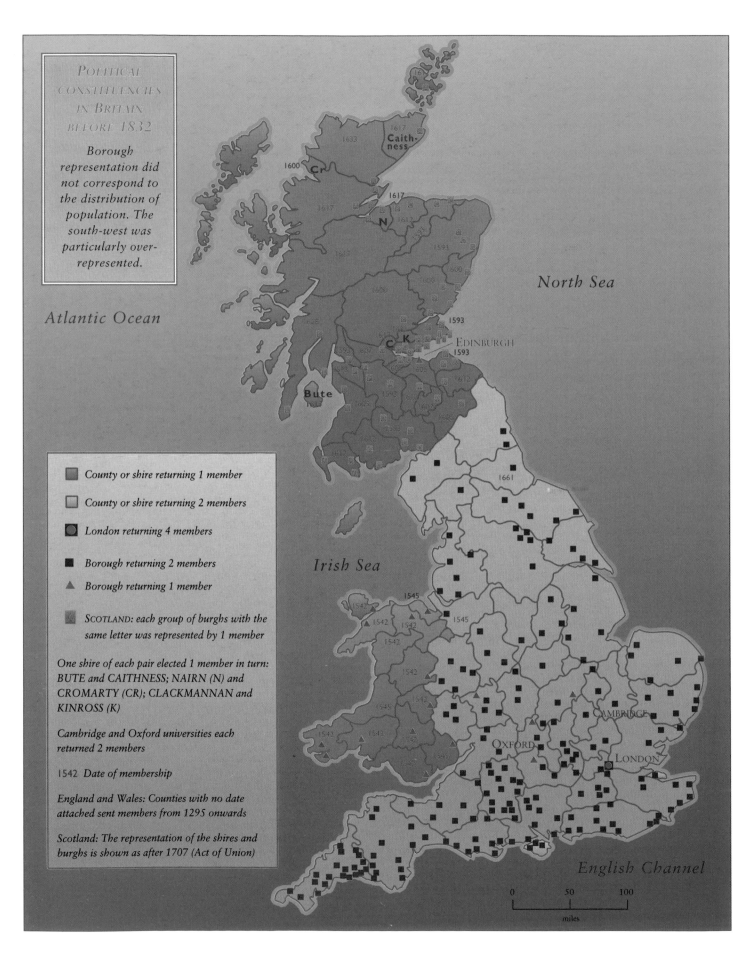

POLITICAL
CONSTITUENCIES
IN BRITAIN
BEFORE 1832

Borough
representation did
not correspond to
the distribution of
population. The
south-west was
particularly over-
represented.

Atlantic Ocean

North Sea

Irish Sea

Caith-
ness

Cr

N

C K

EDINBURGH

Bute

■ County or shire returning 1 member

□ County or shire returning 2 members

◉ London returning 4 members

◼ Borough returning 2 members

▲ Borough returning 1 member

SCOTLAND: each group of burghs with the
same letter was represented by 1 member

One shire of each pair elected 1 member in turn:
BUTE and CAITHNESS; NAIRN (N) and
CROMARTY (CR); CLACKMANNAN and
KINROSS (K)

Cambridge and Oxford universities each
returned 2 members

1542 Date of membership

England and Wales: Counties with no date
attached sent members from 1295 onwards

Scotland: The representation of the shires and
burghs is shown as after 1707 (Act of Union)

CAMBRIDGE

OXFORD

LONDON

English Channel

0   50   100

miles

gentlemen the following century. This was true whether or not the franchise was wide. In west Wales the occupant of the Cardigan Boroughs seat was chosen by the freemen of the four boroughs that shared the seat. Yet the county grandees dominated the 'election' of burgesses at their court leets, and there was something of a race to enrol large numbers of freemen in order to ensure the selection of favoured candidates. The electorate there was dramatically widened, but it was done so only to choose gentry candidates, the Pryses of Gogerddan and the Lloyds of Peterwell. Despite the preponderance of borough seats in Britain, the county elite dominated Parliament.

In Oxfordshire, elite influence can be seen at opposite ends of the spectrum – in both the two county parliamentary seats, and the single member constituency of Banbury, where only eighteen members of the corporation enjoyed the right to vote. Oxfordshire was uncontested between 1710 and 1754 and securely held by the Tories. Although an opposition group in Parliament, the Oxfordshire Tories scarcely came from the ranks of the socially excluded. Sir Robert Jenkinson, MP 1710–17, was a baronet and the son of an MP, and had houses in Walcot, Oxfordshire, and Hawkesbury, Gloucestershire. His brother, Robert Bankes Jenkinson, MP 1717–27, succeeded to the baronetcy, the country houses and the seat in Parliament. Both men were educated at Trinity, Oxford and Lincoln's Inn. The father of Henry Perrot, MP 1721–40, was nicknamed 'Golden Perrot' thanks to his wealth. Sir William Stapleton, MP 1727–40, was a baronet, was educated at Christ Church and married the granddaughter of an earl. Sir James Dashwood, MP 1740–54 and 1761–8, had estates that were so extensive that allegedly he could ride direct from Kirtlington to Banbury on his own lands. Educated at Eton, he built a house at Kirtlington second only in Oxfordshire to Blenheim in size. George Lee, Viscount Quarendon, MP 1740–3, was the heir to the 2nd Earl of Lichfield. Phillp, 3rd Viscount Wenman, MP for Oxford in 1749–54, who stood for the county in 1754, had large estates around his house at Thame Park.

In 1754, in possibly the most controversial county election of the century, the Oxfordshire Tory interest was challenged by the Whig or new interest. Sir Edward Turner and Lord Parker stood, supported by the Duke of Marlborough, Earl Harcourt and the Earl of Macclesfield. Parker was the heir to George, 2nd Earl of Macclesfield, Turner, a baronet with a seat at Ambrosden. Yet, as the defeated candidates were Dashwood and Wenman, it is a little difficult to present this as a case of social oppression. The Tories spent over £20,000 on the election, a double return was made, and the election was decided in favour of the Whigs by the partisan House of Commons.

Banbury was also influenced greatly by the landed elite. The major electoral interests at first were the Copes of Hanwell, two miles away, and the Norths of Croxton, a mile further. Sir Jonathan Cope was MP 1713–22, his relative Monoux Cope in 1722–7, but from 1740 the choice rested with the Norths. Frederick, Lord North, the Oxford-educated head of the government that lost America, was uncontested MP from 1754 until he succeeded his father as 2nd Earl of Guilford in 1790.

Of the other seats in Oxfordshire, Oxford was a freeman borough with 1,200 voters in 1722. Most elections were uncontested, and the corporation was the strongest interest. Between 1715 and 1784 there were contests for the parliamentary seat only in 1722, 1768 and 1780. The city was not a source of resistance to the Tory rural hinterland. Such a clash existed in parts of England, especially where towns dominated by nonconformist Whigs clashed with Church of England Tory hinterlands, but not across much of the country.

Sir Robert Walpole addressing his cabinet, by Joseph Goupy. In 1739, Walpole told the Commons, 'I have lived long enough in the world to know that the safety of a minister lies in his having the approbation of this House. Former ministers neglected this and therefore they fell! I always make it my first study to obtain it, and therefore I hope to stand.'

In the case of Oxford, a common Toryism lessened tensions, as did the economic role of the borough as county capital and market centre, rather than, for example, an 'enclave' port and industrial town, such as Whitehaven. Oxford MPs did not all have country houses. Thomas Rowney, MP 1695–1722, lived in St Giles's in the city. Matthew Skinner, another lawyer, MP 1734–8, and Recorder of Oxford, lived at St John the Baptist's, Oxford. However, other Oxford MPs were country gentlemen, while the landed order itself had much influence in the city. This was especially true of the Tory Earls of Abingdon. Montagu Bertie, 2nd Earl, was High Steward of Oxford until 1743, and a supporter of Matthew Skinner. His steward's son, George Nares, was Town Clerk 1746–56, Recorder 1766–71 and MP 1768–71, although by 1768 he was elected as MP on the Marlborough interest. Despite the corporation's criticism of the Earl of Abingdon in 1768, it is difficult to see the election of that year as a rejection of aristocratic influence. The other MP returned for Oxford in 1768 was the Honourable William Harcourt, son of the 2nd Viscount, a local aristocrat, and himself a lieutenant-colonel in the Dragoons.

If the elections for the borough seats suggest social cohesion, rather than social chasms, Oxford University and its parliamentary representation were redolent of ideological division. The university was a Jacobite stronghold, and proud of its strong Toryism. After its Jacobite Chancellor, James Butler, 2nd Duke of Ormonde was attainted in 1715, he was succeeded by another Jacobite, his brother, Lord Arran, who held the post until his death in 1758. George Lee, 3rd Earl of Lichfield, formerly MP for Oxfordshire and another Jacobite, was High Steward of the University in 1760–2 and Chancellor from 1762 until 1772. The MPs representing the institution were all Tory and the absence of a royal right to create honorary doctors prevented the government from increasing Whig influence as it did at Cambridge. Oxford acted as a centre of Tory intellectual activity, and this had serious implications, given the role of the two English universities in training the clergy of the Church of England. The government did not press plans for extending regulation of Oxford that were considered in 1719 and 1749. Such a step would have been contentious and a reminder of James II's unpopular attack on the rights of the fellows of Magdalen College after they failed to accept his candidate as president. In addition, it did not accord with Whig caution about infringing the rights of the propertied. Shorn of its early radicalism, the Whig government was now very much located within the context of maintaining established rights.

Ideological division over the succession helped split the elite from the 'Glorious' Revolution of 1688 until George III (1760–1820) ended the proscription of the Tories after his accession in 1760. This division provided much of the dynamic for local politics, providing real bite to personal and family rivalries. In 1698 Sir Henry Hobart of Blickling Hall, a firm Whig, was killed in a duel with his Tory neighbour, Oliver Le Neve, that arose from election-time allegations. Hobart had alleged that Le Neve had accused him of discreditable conduct at the battle of the Boyne in 1690 and that this had affected the 1698 election. Le Neve fled the country. After they came to power in 1714, the Whigs carried out a purge of many of the Tory JPs. This purge had achieved its aim by 1719, ensuring that the Tories had only minority status in the commissions of the peace, and Walpole made no effort to complete it. It sufficed that the Tories were not strong enough to dominate the commissions; there was no attempt to remove them completely from positions of authority. Yet, the purge of other local offices (lord lieutenancy, deputy lieutenancies, custos rotulorum (a senior JP who held the records of the quarter sessions), duchy offices in Cornwall and Lancaster) was more complete than that of the JPs. Furthermore, many of the new Whig JPs were not of gentry origins, and this was greeted with outrage in what was still a hierarchical society that assumed office should equate with social status. The Tories pressed for higher landed qualifications for JPs, as they had done successfully for MPs.

Walpole's policy was to avoid provoking the Tories, but this did not mean that they were satisfied. Their opposition was contained, not conciliated, and, in some respects, their exclusion echoed that of Catholics. Yet hostility was not generally pushed as far as actual conflict. Anglican neighbours were willing to hold Catholic property in trust for Catholic friends after 1715 in northern England. Most of England, including all of the south, was not directly affected by the Jacobite risings in 1715 or 1745. Thus there was no immediate issue to provoke clear signs of allegiance.

The Column and Statue of Liberty, Gibside, Tyne and Wear, was one of many monuments and buildings constructed to 'enhance' the landscape with inspiration from the classical world.

As a consequence, it is possible to emphasise the general success of the eighteenth-century English political system in preventing civil conflict, rather than to stress the divisions within it. This emphasis on consensus appears most appropriate in the cultural context. There were differences between Whig and Tory cultural preferences, seen very clearly by visitors to the grounds of Viscount Cobham's seat at Stowe, with its sculptural lessons about the value of Whiggery, and the need for true Whiggery. Yet, shared values were of greater importance. This was true of elite lifestyle and culture. Both are now mostly recalled through the built landscape of stately homes and the less obviously reformulated landscape of their parks. Landscape gardening, for which England became famous on the continent during the century, represented an Anglicisation of classical notions of rural harmony, retreat and beauty, and both Tories and Whigs embraced these trends. Some landscapes were 'enhanced' by buildings that referred directly to the classical world, such as Henry Flitcroft's Pantheon at Stourhead and the Column and Statue of Liberty at Gibside, the second a Roman Doric column topped by a statue of Liberty dressed in classical drapery and carrying the Phrygian cap, the cap of Liberty. The imitation of the Temple of Theseus (or Pephaestus) at Athens designed for the grounds of Hagley Hall by James 'Athenian' Stuart in 1758 was the

The Grand Tour

The tension between cosmopolitanism and xenophobia was important to the sense of foreignness that helped to define the mental space between Britain and the continent. This was greatly expanded in the fifteenth and sixteenth centuries. The loss of possessions in France was an important political discontinuity with wide-ranging cultural, economic and social consequences. The Protestant Reformation widened the divide. This was obviously true of Catholic Europe, especially as a result of the political and religious vigour from the 1560s of the Catholic Counter-Reformation and its consequences for the defensiveness of English and Scottish society. The Protestant Reformation was also significant, because England ended up with a distinctive church settlement that was challenged by alternative non-episcopal Protestant models, especially the Presbyterianism of Calvin's Geneva, and Knox's Scotland, and the more liberal situation, but still one dominated by Presbyterianism, in the United Provinces (modern Netherlands).

A sense of difference from the continent persisted in the seventeenth century, in particular as a result of the widely-held belief that the age of religious wars had not stopped. Concern over Catholicism and Catholicising tendencies within Britain was directed as much against James II as it had been against his father, Charles I. Louis XIV's Revocation of the Edict of Nantes in 1685 and the flight of the Huguenots (French Protestants) that followed helped keep religious tension alive. This all had a geographical component. Rome was the centre of the evil empire; Ireland, Lancashire or Whitehall were its outliers. Jacobitism lent fresh force to this concern: the exiled James II was supported by Louis XIV and his relics were kept in Paris after his death in 1701; his son, James III, held court in France and Italy.

In such a context, travel could be regarded as dangerous or suspicious, but in the eighteenth century a substantial number of British men and women journeyed for pleasure. The process had really begun in the seventeenth century, but it greatly increased in scale in the eighteenth. The cultural impact of this tourism was considerable and can be seen in the stately homes of the period. Many British artists travelled in Europe and were influenced by what they saw. Tourists were painted, frequently in elevating poses in classical surroundings. Pompeo Batoni painted at least 154 British tourists, including in 1766 Colonel William Gordon who was shown being awarded an orb of command and a victor's wreath by a statue of Roma (Fyvie Castle). There is also a fine collection of Batonis and Grand Tour furnishings at Uppark. Not all depictions were so exalted as Colonel Gordon: the English painter Thomas Patch produced caricatures of many young Englishmen passing through Florence, some of which can be seen at Dunham Massey.

Tourists frequently commissioned paintings of places they had seen. Many purchased views of Venice. Canaletto painted several hundred, virtually all of which were sold to British buyers. There were four in the dining-room at Farnborough Hall, which William Holbech remodelled in the late 1740s to display what he had collected abroad. Felbrigg Hall was similarly reorganised from 1749 to accommodate souvenirs of the Grand Tour. Some tourists commissioned reproductions of paintings that they liked:

The Red Drawing Room at Uppark. The room was redecorated for Sir Matthew after his return from the continent in 1751.

Henry Hoare had Batoni and Jeremiah Davison paint copies of four Renis and one each of Veronese, Guercino, Bourdon and Van Dyck for Stourhead. Reni's Aurora was copied for at least nine houses, including Shugborough and West Wycombe. Philip Yorke, later 3rd Earl of Hardwicke, commissioned a set of busts for his library at Wimpole and ordered paintings. Other tourists bought old masters.

Architecture attracted great attention, for a lively interest in it was regarded as an attribute of gentility, and British architecture was heavily

A caricature group in Florence, c. 1760, by Thomas Patch (1720–82).

influenced by continental models. Frederick Augustus Hervey, the Earl of Bristol and Bishop of Derry, planned the building of Ickworth while in Italy. The Mussenden Temple, a domed rotunda built for Derry at his Irish estate at Downhill in 1783–5, was based on the Temple of Vesta at Tivoli.

Tastes varied, but there was a marked preference for the classical over the Gothic that led most early tourists to ignore or dislike the architecture of Germany and most of provincial France. In turn, tourists paid great attention to Palladian buildings. Many of the buildings that were admired were relatively modern and classical or baroque in style – St Paul's in London, Les Invalides in Paris, palaces such as Versailles, and the Upper and Lower Belvederes in Vienna were praised. The response to older buildings was generally unfavourable unless they dated from classical times, although in the second half of the century an appreciation of Gothic did begin to emerge. The strong influence of a classical education and of a public ideology that drew heavily on classical images and themes helped counteract the pernicious consequences of Italy being the centre of Catholicism. Roman works were purchased and displayed. The discovery of Pompeii and Gavin Hamilton's excavations around Rome stimulated great interest in sculpture. William Weddell MP, who went to Italy in 1765, sent back nineteen cases of classical statuary to create a collection that is still complete at Newby Hall. A fine collection of classical statuary built up by Charles Wyndham, 2nd Earl of Egremont, survives at Petworth.

Tourism served to enrich the British elite culturally, but this did not commend it to critics who depicted a failure to defend the integrity of British life and society in the face of all things foreign. Criticism of patrons of Italian opera, particularly in the 1720s, and of French theatre, especially in the 1730s and 1740s, focused on their supposed role in spreading alien values. Cultural nationalism was also encouraged in a positive direction, with the development of vernacular, ballad opera, most famously John Gay's Beggar's Opera (1728), and oratorio, pre-eminently the achievement of Handel, the rediscovery of Shakespeare and the foundation of the Royal Academy.

Despite criticisms, there was relatively little unthinking assumption of foreign customs, manners and mores. The elite was open to continental influences, but displayed both self-confidence and national pride, and was unwilling for the most part to compare Britain and British manners unfavourably with continental Europe. Only a tiny proportion of travellers enjoyed their tour so much that they opted to live abroad, like George, 3rd Earl Cowper (1738–91) who, along with the long-serving British envoy, Sir Horace Mann, became a pillar of late eighteenth-century Florentine society.

The Circus at Bath by John Wood the Elder, 1758. The development of Bath as a city of orderly leisure owed much to Richard 'Beau' Nash, who in 1705 was appointed first Master of Ceremonies. His Rules for the behaviour of visitors were first published in 1742. William Pitt the Elder paid £1,200 for number 7.

first copy of a Greek Doric temple. The new design derived from artistic models, especially the presentation of the landscapes of Roman Italy in the paintings of Claude Lorraine which influenced the banker Henry Hoare when he laid out the gardens at Stourhead after he inherited the estate in 1741. Far from reflecting a lack of confidence in British products, such landscapes were part of the appropriation of the classical past to contemporary purposes. A sense of Britain as the new Rome developed as imperial responsibilities accumulated and taste became more refined. Similarly, classical ideas and designs came to inform British architecture, aspects of a redefinition of taste and style that reordered fashion and acceptability. This led to significant expenditure, as country houses were built or rebuilt and townscapes created.

Aside from prominent new works – such as Stowe and Blenheim, Bath and the New Town of Edinburgh (the last unique in the scale of support it received from the Convention of Scottish Burghs), there were also less well known but still important construction projects, such as Penrice Castle in Glamorganshire, where work on a new house designed by Anthony Keck, begun in 1773 and finished in 1783, cost nearly £7,000. Between 1660 and 1760, 389 new country houses and villas were built in England; more were constructed towards the end of that period than earlier, although some impressive houses were built in the late seventeenth century, including Ashdown House for William, 1st Lord Craven in about 1663, the first Cliveden for the 2nd Duke of Buckingham, Belton House, Felbrigg Hall, Kingston Lacey, Sudbury Hall, and Uppark. Older houses, such as Canons Ashby, were altered. Ham House was enlarged by the Duke of Lauderdale and exhibits all the richness of the Restoration period.

In the eighteenth century, fashion, interest in architecture and gardening, and concern with social status combined in an upsurge of activity. Some stately homes, such as Blenheim, Castle Howard, Stowe, and Wentworth Woodhouse, were monuments to ostentation that dominated the countryside. Architecture and portraiture promoted stability by emphasising the power and immutability of the elite leadership of society. Ralph, 1st Duke of Montague had his coat of arms and family tree carved on his staircase at Boughton House to promote the idea of an unchanging family succession.

Blenheim, Castle Howard and Seaton Delaval were the work of Sir John Vanbrugh (1664–1726), a leading exponent of the English baroque. Other major baroque monuments are Sir Christopher Wren's St Paul's Cathedral, and a number of buildings in Oxford, including the Radcliffe Camera and the interiors of Queen's and Trinity chapels. Vanbrugh displayed a degree of spatial enterprise similar to that of the architects of princely palaces on the continent, but his heavy style invited a critical response. A less grandiose baroque can be seen at Beningbrough Hall, built under the supervision of William Thornton. Thornton worked under Vanbrugh at Castle Howard and Beningbrough has a two-storey hall of architectural quality and fine plasterwork, both aspects associated with the baroque. There were also important foreign influences at Wimpole Hall, Clandon Park, and Dyrham Park. Other important stately homes of the period include Calke Abbey, built in 1701–4.

In contrast to Vanbrugh, the Scottish architect Colen Campbell (d. 1729) was influenced by the style of the sixteenth-century Italian architect Andrea Palladio and by Inigo Jones, as was his principal patron, Lord Burlington, who was responsible for Chiswick House. Both sought to encourage what they saw as a distinctly British style in contrast to the continental baroque of Wren, Vanbrugh and Nicholas Hawksmoor. Campbell's works included Wanstead House, Mereworth and Stourhead. Palladianism also influenced the extension of the fashionable spa town of Bath with John Wood the Elder's Queen's Square (1728–34) and Circus (1754–64), his son's Royal Crescent (1767–74), and Assembly Rooms (1769–71), and the Palladian Bridge created in the nearby gardens of Prior Park. William Pitt the Elder had a house in the Circus and was MP for the city.

There was also a continuing interest in the Gothic style, but it was employed largely in rebuilding – Alnwick Castle from 1750, Welbeck Abbey from 1752 – rather than for new seats. Horace Walpole's Gothic suburban villa at Strawberry Hill was unusual in being a new house, as was Thomas Johnes' Hafod in the 1780s. Castle Ward in County Down was a curious example of classical and Gothic. Built between 1762 and 1770, it has a classical east side and a Gothic west, due to the contrasting tastes of Bernard Ward, later 1st Viscount Bangor, and his wife, Lady Anne. Gothic was not generally regarded as a style equal to classicism until the work of architects such as James Wyatt at the close of the century.

The stately homes of the eighteenth century were a testimony to wealth, confidence, the income generated by rising demand for crops after the sustained population growth that began in the 1740s, the profits of agricultural improvement, the greater social stability that followed the restoration of Charles II, and increased political stability. Costs were high and the expense could be ruinous. William Stanton was paid around £5,000 in 1685–8 to build Belton House; Erddig bankrupted Joshua Edisbury for whom it was built. Over £8,000 was spent on it.

Major figures proclaimed their prominence with new or greatly rebuilt mansions, such as William Cavendish, 1st Duke of Devonshire's Chatsworth, Sir Robert Walpole's Houghton, the Duke of Chandos's Canons, the Earl of Hardwicke's Wimpole, Sir George Lyttelton at

The entrance hall at Osterley Park, part of the remodelling of the house carried out by Robert Adam.

Hagley Hall, the Ansons at Shugborough, Thomas, 2nd Lord Onslow's Clandon Park, and William Duff, 1st Earl of Fife's, Duff House. Competition was important. Ralph, 2nd Lord Verney, rebuilt much of Claydon House in order to rival Earl Temple's work at nearby Stowe. Duff House was designed by the Scot William Adam, whose influential brother Robert (1728–92) rebuilt or redesigned many stately homes, including Culzean, Croome Court, Harewood House, Hatchlands Park, Kedleston, Luton Hoo, Osterley Park, Mellerstain, Shardeloes, Syon House for the Duke of Northumberland, Kenwood for the Earl of Mansfield, Bowood and Lansdowne House for the Marquess of Lansdowne, Ugbrooke for Lord Clifford, and Saltram for Lord

SUFFOLK, THE GREATER
HOUSES IN 1674 AND
PARKS IN 1783

*Large houses and estates
were widely distributed,
but in general the
aristocracy and gentry
found it difficult to build
up estates on the heavier
soils of High (central)
Suffolk. There was much
continuity between 1674
and 1783, but nearly
thirty major parks were
added by the latter date.*

Boringdon. There was no regional pattern; this was a national style. There was also more modest building and remodelling, for example at Dinefwr Park.

Houses were enhanced by gardens and parks (grounds of houses). British gardens in the early decades of the period were created in the formal, geometric patterns that characterised continental designs. There was a clear segregation between gardens and the surrounding estate. Gardens were an opportunity for ostentation and display. Those of Hampton Court have recently been returned to their original geometric form. Formal gardens of the period include the Dutch-style water area at Westbury Court, and the French-style creation at Dunham Massey; there was also a baroque water garden at Powis Castle though it does not survive.

The separation of garden and park ended under the influence of William Kent (1684–1748). Kent developed and decorated parks at, for example, Stowe, Chiswick, Claremont, and Rousham, in order to provide an appropriate setting for buildings. He used the 'ha-ha', a ditch, sunk from view, to create a boundary between garden and

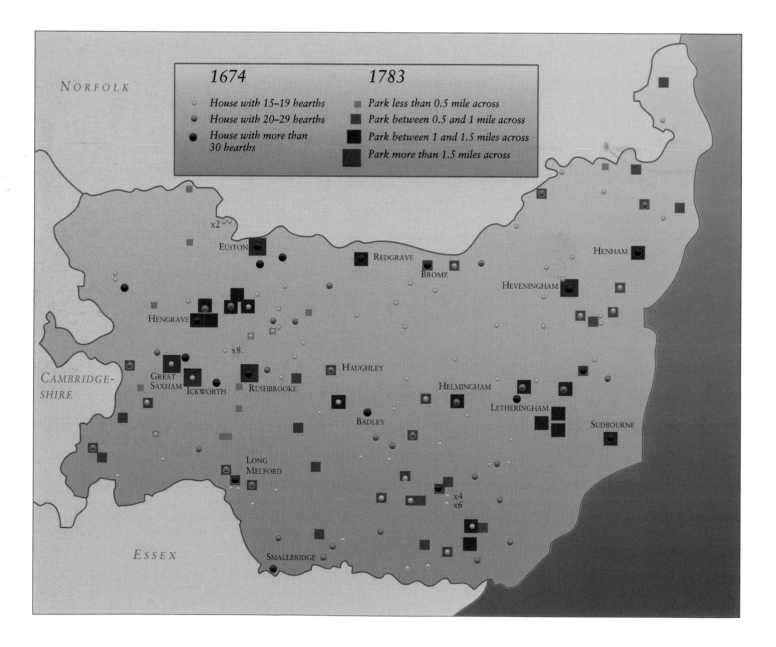

park that did not interrupt the prospect but did prevent animals from entering the garden: sheep were decorous and utilitarian, but at a distance. Sunken fences were employed to conceal the limits of the property.

Trained under Kent, Lancelot 'Capability' Brown (1716–83) rejected the rigid formality of geometric models and contrived settings that appeared natural but were, nevertheless, carefully designed for effect. His landscapes of serpentine lakes, gentle hills, copses on the brow of hitherto bare hills, and scattered groups of newly planted trees swiftly established a fashion. Having made his reputation at Croome, Brown laid out or remodelled the grounds of 180 houses, including Audley End, Berrington Hall, Blenheim, Chatsworth, Claremont, Eywood, Heveningham Hall, Ickworth, Ingestre, Kew, Kirtlington, Nuneham Courteney, Petworth, Sheffield Park, Trentham, Wimpole, Ashridge for Francis Egerton, 3rd Duke of Bridgwater, the 'Canal Duke', and Burton Pynsent for Pitt the Elder. At Charlecote Park, Brown redesigned the grounds, removing the water gardens and changing

The grounds at Blenheim were among 180 properties laid out or remodelled by Lancelot 'Capability' Brown. Work on the great house designed for John Churchill, Duke of Marlborough, by architect Sir John Vanbrugh, began in 1705. Vanbrugh's work was finished off by Nicholas Hawksmoor between 1722 and 1725.

the course of the River Hele so that it tumbled into the Avon within sight of the house. He also advised on the landscaping of Dinefwr Park. His work brought him substantial wealth, and, having begun work as a kitchen gardener, he ultimately became High Sheriff of Huntingdonshire.

Brown and Kent's system was criticised for the formalism it retained by Sir Uvedale Price, who argued in favour of a wilder and apparently untamed, more natural and 'picturesque' beauty that would accord with 'all the principles of landscape-painting'. This influenced Humphry Repton (1752–1818) who transformed about 220 gardens, including Attingham Park, Hatchlands Park and Wimpole, and developed Brown's ideas in accordance with the concept of the 'picturesque'. This stressed the individual character of each landscape and the need to retain it, while making improvements to remove what were judged blemishes and obstructions, and to open up vistas, as at Attingham Park. At

Antony House, Repton swept away the formal parterres. He called Sheringham Park his 'most favourite work'. Claremont and Stowe evolved from the major early eighteenth-century gardener Charles Bridgeman through Kent to Brown and Repton.

More famous landscape gardeners were emulated by a host of others. At Saltram, where the deer park had been created in the early 1740s, John Parker MP, later 1st Lord Boringdon, employed a Mr Richmond from 1769 to develop the park in the Capability Brown style. An orangery was built between 1773 and 1775, and a chapel, a garden bower, and a battlemented octagon were also constructed in the park, which was visited by George III in 1789. Between 1767 and 1789, William Emes advised Philip Yorke at Erddig where he created hanging gardens and 'natural' clumps of trees, and was also responsible for the landscaping at Chirk Castle and Powis Castle, and for work at Wimpole. Stephen Wright landscaped Clumber Park for Henry, 4th Duke of Newcastle. At Dyrham Park, Charles Harcourt-Master replaced the formal Dutch water garden of the 1690s with a classic park with picturesque clumps of trees. At Raby Castle, Thomas White altered the park for Gilbert, 2nd Lord Barnard; the moat was drained later in the century.

Many landowners took a close personal interest in landscaping. This was true of Lord Cobham at Stowe, George Bowes at Gibside, Thomas Johnes at Haford, which was landscaped in the 'picturesque' style by 'Warwick' Smith, John and William Aislabie at Studley Royal, and Pitt the Elder. British landscape gardening was increasingly admired and copied abroad. In Russia, British experts created and looked after Catherine the Great's imperial gardens and parks.

The stately homes that were built had to be decorated and furnished, leading to an explosion in the patronage of all kinds of work from frescoes to furniture. Thomas Chippendale (d. 1779) from Worcestershire, who became one of the leading London furniture-makers, dedicated his book of design to Hugh Smithson, Earl of Northumberland. Given his acquisition of the title, he sought to legitimate his earldom by ostentation. Patronage was a means to establish the 'taste' of the earl, although support for great cultural development occasionally had no impact on the patron. The 11th Duke of Norfolk, a prolific patron and President of the Society of Arts who died in 1815, was notoriously filthy, leading to the epitaph:

> The first in rank for filth and birth,
> Here rots a vile old sinner's earth.
> His history lies in this short placard.
> He lived a beast and died a blackguard.

The new and embellished houses also required large numbers of books for the libraries, which became an established feature, and of portraits for the large spaces created in their public rooms, such as the grand entrance halls at Beningbrough and Blenheim.

Many members of the elite were keen collectors of paintings. An important theme was aristocratic recreations, especially horses and hunting, as in the works of George Stubbs. John Wootton's painting of *Dancing Dogs* (1759) hangs in the Staircase Hall at Wallington, the home of Sir Walter Blackett, Newcastle MP and coal trader who bred Bedlington terriers. The classical interests of patrons and artists combined in the depiction of antique landscapes and stories, the heroes of the ancient world being suitable companions for the portraits of modern aristocrats. At Petworth, the Duke of Somerset invited artists and craftsmen to produce pieces for particular places and

spaces. Joshua Reynolds, a regular visitor at Saltram, went hunting and shooting with his host whom he painted in a portrait that is still at the house. Saltram also has several other of Reynolds' paintings, including a loving painting of Parker's children, that reflects the contemporary emphasis on domestic affection, and a portrait of Paul Ourry, who was eventually an admiral, an MP, and Commissioner of Plymouth Dockyard. There is also a portrait of Reynolds himself by the Swiss-born Angelica Kauffmann that was commissioned by John Parker. The elite in Ireland, Scotland and Wales responded to and shaped the same cultural impulses as their English counterparts, and their patronage of distinctive cultural traditions, such as bardic poetry, declined, although Scottish cultural traditions, such as Highland dancing, were being renewed by 1780.

The role of wealthy landowners as patrons and leaders of fashion ensured that they played a crucial role in the artistic world. Display was a major part of the nature of patronage, and the conspicuous consumption of culture emphasised social status. Major stately homes, such as Castle Howard, Houghton and Stourhead, were open to respectable-looking passing visitors, and acted as display models for architectural, artistic and landscape styles. Kedleston was always open to the public and was perhaps the most admired. Guidebooks for the most notable houses were published from mid-century.

It is necessary to remember the social politics on which landed patronage rested. The rural population was dominated by an economy of proprietary wealth, a system built around rent and also poor remuneration for labour in the context of a markedly unequal distribution of land. Alongside the stately homes mentioned above, there were less grand farmhouses, such as Townend in Cumbria and Braithwaite Hall in North Yorkshire, both of which date from the seventeenth century. Most of the rural population were less kindly housed. Whitegates Cottage on the Gunby Hall Estate in Lincolnshire, is a small thatched

Hambletonian by George Stubbs, 1800. Stubbs (1724–1806) produced very popular paintings of racehorses. Born in Liverpool, Stubbs was an expert in anatomy who published The Anatomy of the Horse *(1766). His paintings reflected his applied knowledge. In 1790–3 he painted sixteen of the leading racehorses and in 1800* Hambletonian beating Diamond *at Newmarket, his largest painting. Stubbs also produced many pictures of a scene he saw at Ceuta, a lion attacking a white Barbary horse.*

153

Travel in Britain

British domestic travel and tourism boomed in the eighteenth century. As roads were improved, not least by the turnpike trusts that were responsible for many major routes by mid-century, journey times shortened dramatically and became more predictable. More frequent coach services appeared on major routes and facilities, such as coaching inns, increased. Maps and other information for domestic travel appeared in greater quantities, charting the widespread improvement.

The great stress on health and sociality ensured the triumph of the spa. Numerous watering places were founded or expanded, mostly inland, although, towards the end of the century, coastal resorts developed under royal patronage – Weymouth benefited from the visits of George III, as Brighton was to do from the residence of the Prince Regent, later George IV (1820–30). Other coastal resorts became popular without royal support. The Salisbury Journal of 22 July 1754 listed eighteen 'persons of distinction' who had arrived at Lymington 'to drink the sea water and take the diversion of the place', while the issue of 2 September 1754 named a further thirteen. More generally, the development of the leisure facilities of many towns made them attractive to visit.

George III bathing at Weymouth, 1789, by John Nixon (1760–1818).

Domestic tourism, however, was neither unlimited nor without its problems. Scotland, Ireland and Wales received relatively few tourists, British or foreign, and played a smaller role in travel than Bath or Tunbridge Wells. Those who did visit them were struck by the lack of facilities. The attitude of royalty was indicative of a wider lack of interest within the élite. In the eighteenth century no monarch visited Ireland, Scotland or Wales – or, indeed, the north of England or most of the Midlands. Georges I (1714–27) and II (1727–60) knew nothing of Britain beyond south-east England, although they frequently went to Hanover. George III (1760–1820), in contrast, never went to Hanover, and, instead, got as far as the south-west, including Cotehele and Saltram, which he visited in 1789. He also travelled to Worcester in 1788 for the Three Choirs Festival, a major celebration of sacred music launched in the eighteenth century. After 1763, more Britons travelled abroad, but there was also an expansion of domestic tourism. Visits to literary shrines, country houses, picturesque ruins and the natural landscape all became fashionable. This became even more the case when the French Revolution and the subsequent war brought the Grand Tour to a close; while a greater interest in landscape in the second half of the century, that reached its peak in romanticism, led far more visitors to the Lake District, North Wales, the Wye Valley, and the Scottish Highlands. Travel to these areas was aided by the development of roads from mid-century.

home built in about 1770 to provide accommodation for estate workers. Its mud and stud walling was very different to the red-brick panelled Gunby Hall, and would also have been colder, darker and wetter. Such contrasts can be all too rarely glimpsed.

The poor were badly affected by the decline of some rural industries, by enclosure and by any factor, short- or long-term, that pressed on real wages. Heavy rent rises led to the emigration of about 20,000 Scots to North America between 1769 and 1774, the Reverend William Thom reflecting in his *Candid Inquiry into the Causes of the Late and Intended Migrations from Scotland* (Glasgow, 1771) that 'in whatever country the whole property is engrossed by a few, there the people must be wretched'. Yet, sympathies should be distributed widely. The burden of poor relief could be considerable and often it was shared among a small number of ratepayers, and the heaviest proportionate burden of poor relief was paid by those just above the level of income eligible to receive it.

Enclosure, which entailed either the reorganisation of fragmented holdings in open fields or the subdivision of common pastures, affected the landscape of much of England, particularly the Midlands. Original enclosures were unofficial, but parliamentary means were extensively employed in the second half of the century. Although there were enclosures by small landholders, for example in Upper Wharfedale, the dominance of both centre and localities by the landed elite was expressed by enclosure Acts. In order to facilitate a reorganisation of the rural landscape that enhanced the control and profits of landlords, 1,532 enclosure Acts were passed between 1760 and 1797. Formerly common land, Alderley Edge was planted by Lord Stanley from 1745 and enclosed in 1779. The 420 acres of the Great Field of Cley on Cley Hill in Wiltshire were enclosed in 1783.

Enclosure made it easier to control the land, through leases and hence higher rents, and was often accompanied by a redistribution of agricultural income from the tenant farmer to his landlord as rents rose more than output. There was an increasing gulf between the landowner and the tenant in terms of disposable income, although tenant farmers, as distinct from owner-occupiers, did not pay the costs of enclosure.

Enclosing landowners alarmed much of the rural population and created wide disruption of traditional rights and expectations, common lands and routes. This disruption interacted with the more general impact created by rising population on the rural economy. Demand for foodstuffs rose, but English agricultural wages remained below fifteenth- and early sixteenth-century levels in real terms throughout the eighteenth century. This eased the position of those employing labour, but hit the labourers themselves.

Enclosure was helped by the extent to which, unlike on much of the continent, peasant ownership of the land was limited. Those who had previously relied on access to common land, and thus enjoyed a degree of insulation from general movements of prices and wages, were hit hard. In some areas, such as Hampshire and Sussex, enclosure was by private agreement and caused less tension, but in others enclosure led to a bitter response. In Northamptonshire an alliance of small occupiers and landless commoners resisted parliamentary enclosure with petitions, threats, attacks on gates, posts, fences, and other crimes. The enclosure of the former Malvern Chase led to riots in 1777–80. This was not a rural society simply of deference and order, but one in which aristocratic hegemony was seen as selfish and disruptive by many. The vicious mantraps on the ballroom staircase at Powis Castle are a reminder of the nature of control in society. Enclosure dislocated the senses of place and identity for many who worked the land.

Survey map of Kedleston, Derbyshire, 1769, by George Ingham. The village was swept aside to make way for an extended park around the house.

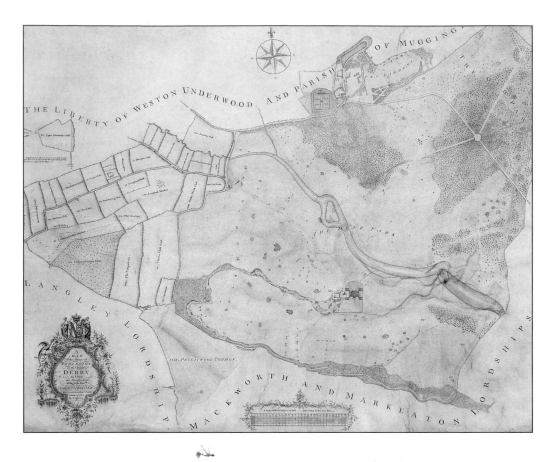

This was taken furthest where settlements were moved, as when the medieval Oxfordshire village of Nuneham Courtenay and its church were destroyed to make way for Earl Harcourt's new park in 1759, although Harcourt did provide the displaced villagers with well-built, spacious houses. The village at Shugborough was bought up and demolished by Thomas Anson between 1731 and 1773 in order to create open parkland in front of the house. To improve the park at Attingham, Tern Mill was demolished in 1787–9, the village of Berwick Maviston was pulled down in 1802 and part of the town of Atcham in 1806, while in 1779–80 the London–Holyhead road was moved away from the house and in the 1790s a branch of the Shrewsbury canal was abandoned when half dug. Villages were also swept aside for Kedleston, Stowe, and Wimpole. The route of the London–Portsmouth road was altered to allow improvement of the gardens at Claremont, while in the 1770s the public road that ran under the northern battlements of Powis Castle was diverted. Oliver Goldsmith complained in the *Deserted Village* (1770) about the tyrant that had destroyed 'sweet Auburn' village:

> . . . The man of wealth and pride
> Takes up a space that many poor supplied;
> Space for his lake, his park's extended bounds,
> Space for his horses, equipage and hounds.

This social politics had many other manifestations, ranging from the seating arrangements in churches and the treatment of the dying and their corpses, to the response to crime. The Game Act of 1671 made hunting the exclusive preserve of the landed gentry in England and Wales, and was matched by legislation in Scotland and Ireland. Viewed as an unfair challenge to livelihoods, it was enforced in a sustained conflict with poachers. From the late 1770s game preserves were protected by spring guns and mantraps. The nature of hunting was affected by the reorganisation of rural space and control encapsulated in the enclosure movement. Fox-hunting became immensely popular in the second half of the century, and many great landlords had their own private packs, while others were maintained by subscription. Hunting led to the construction of stables and kennels on a more elaborate scale than previously and tree planting in the open country was often undertaken to provide cover for the fox. These copses were sometimes given names resonant of contemporary events like 'Botany Bay' in the Quorn country of high Leicestershire.

Although the hanging of Earl Ferrers for murder in 1760 and of the cleric Dr William Dodd for forgery in 1777 were cited as evidence of the universality of the law, it was rare for members of the elite to suffer execution or imprisonment unless involved in treason, while aristocratic debtors escaped imprisonment for debt. The lower orders were handled less gently, but there is also evidence that the law served all social groups, albeit without equal access or favour. For example, the use of legal redress in civil disputes was widespread. In Surrey an appreciable percentage of prosecutions were initiated by labourers or servants. In general, it was the unemployed, the unconnected and immigrants who were treated worst by the judicial system.

Some of the humbly born made it to the bench of bishops, and John Potter, Archbishop of Canterbury 1737–47, was the son of a Wakefield linen-draper and from a Dissenting background, but connections and patronage ensured that a large share of good livings went to clerics from an elite background. Potter himself disinherited his eldest son for marrying a domestic servant. The money, instead, went to his second son, Thomas, who received the fortune of nearly £100,000 and was a rake who compromised the daughter of a Sussex rector but yielded to paternal pressure to marry her. He subsequently became an MP. The family could have provided characters and plot for a book by Henry Fielding or Samuel Richardson, who popularised the English novel in the 1740s; but for the absence of the humour enjoyed by the first and the redemption sought by the second. Richardson reputably wrote much of one of his morality novels, *Sir Charles Grandison* (1753), at Canons Ashby.

In comparison with the following 200 years, the rate of social change in the eighteenth century was relatively low. That does not imply that there was little movement by individuals. Social mobility was helped by primogeniture and the consequent need for younger sons to define and support their own position, and also by the relative openness of marital conventions that in particular allowed the sons of land to marry the daughters of commerce, although the opposite was far less common. Partly as a result of this, the social elite in England was far less exclusive and far more widely rooted in the national community than was the case in most continental countries. Yet this mobility strengthened, rather than weakened, the social hierarchy. There were relatively few signs of the kind of tensions that developed between Lloyd George and the aristocracy at the beginning of the twentieth century.

One obvious point of contrast is between the situation in Britain and that in the rebellious colonies of North America in 1775. In the latter, a political breakdown helped lead not only to a new state, the USA, but also to a more fluid society. British American society had always been more fluid anyway, not least because of the opportunities to expand the frontier of settlement, but differences became more pronounced and important after independence. The newly independent state had its landed estates and stately homes, for example along the Hudson and James rivers (such as Montgomery Place), but its upper

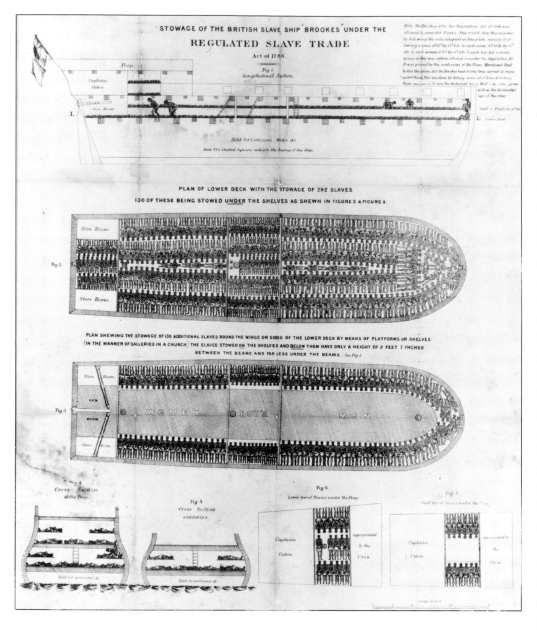

'Stowage of the British Slave Ship Brookes under the Regulated Slave Trade Act of 1788'. Abolitionism became stronger with the foundation of the British Society for Effecting the Abolition of the Slave Trade This used public meetings, subscriptions and the press to urge an end to the slave trade.

house, the Senate, was not based on a hereditary aristocracy. Furthermore, the president was a leader chosen for his merit, not a monarch who was the apex and political rationale of a hereditary system. It is worth considering American developments, for they indicate how a society in the British world could be very different, and, possibly, how Britain could have been very different. There was no preordained pattern of development. Yet the American example also serves as a testimony to the conservatism of the British world. There was a marked reluctance to opt for independence, even after fighting broke out in 1775. The newly independent state also retained differences based on gender. Established churches continued to be important. Despite the universalist principles of the Declaration of Independence (1776), slavery persisted.

Elsewhere in the British world, there was a considerable flexibility in social organisation. Slavery was crucial to the economy of the British West Indies, but the judgement in the Somerset Case of 1772 was generally regarded as ending slavery in England. In Ireland, the Catholic majority lacked the vote and suffered serious legal prohibitions on their activity, although minor concessions were made in the early 1790s. In Bengal and the Carnatic (South East India) a small number of officials of the East India Company made substantial sums as a part of the governing class. In each case, the British position rested on force, the force that had established British control, and, in the case of the slaves, had led to their seizure in West Africa.

There was a measure of resistance, for example from the Maroons, escaped slaves, in Jamaica, and from rural opposition movements in Ireland, such as the Whiteboys and the Oakboys. Yet, it is also necessary to note the cooperation upon which British control rested, and to consider the comparisons with the situation within Britain. Slavery would have been impossible without the collusion of powerful African rulers, such as the kings of Dahomey, who seized and sold slaves. The British traders on the coast, both the Royal Africa Company and the independents, were in no position to intimidate these rulers. In India, the British position was in part dependent on cooperation with native rulers. This was true for example of Clive in the Carnatic in the 1750s and of the campaigns against Tipu Sultan of Mysore in the 1790s in which Maratha and Hyderabad cavalry played an important role. It was also true of cooperation with local mercantile and landholding elites within the areas the British came to control. In Ireland, the bulk of the Catholic population accepted British control; resistance was limited, crucially so during the Jacobite uprisings in 1715 and 1745, and even during the 1798 rising in Ireland most of the population did not rebel. Moreover, important sectors of Catholic society did find it possible to cooperate with British rule.

Thus, within the empire, the same social dynamics that can be discerned in England were repeated. This owed much to a similar context. In India and West Africa, Ireland and northern Scotland there were no traditions of democracy or egalitarianism. Indeed, the most subversive legacy was, paradoxically, within England itself: the Civil War, and the consequent abolition of monarchy, established church and House of Lords. Yet, this was not a living legacy in the eighteenth century, and this fact was both cause and consequence of the essential stability of the period. Republicanism had very few adherents. The ideal of moderation was the backbone of a society sensibly wary of enthusiasm and excess; indeed, moderation was advocated for aesthetic, ethical and political reasons. Until the 1790s, there was no need for a coalition of the property-owning classes to defend property and order, and the crisis of the 1790s was to be only temporary.

By modern and contemporary standards there was only limited policing, and the army deployed in Britain, especially in England, was small. Nor was there any programme within England of fortification against domestic opponents. New fortifications were limited and the major plans that were rejected in 1786 were for works at Plymouth and Portsmouth to be directed against the French. Elsewhere, city walls and fortified positions fell into disrepair or were demolished, rather than being improved. Most castles decayed because they were uncomfortable to live in. In 1672, 272 wagon loads of lead and timber were taken from Warkworth Castle when the widow of Jocelyn Percy, 11th Earl of North-umberland gave the materials to one of the estate auditors. Tattershall Castle passed in 1693 into the ownership of the Fortescue family who held it until 1910 without living there. The moats were filled in and the tower used as a cattle shed. In 1739 the castle at Tonbridge began to be used as a quarry. The city walls of Carlisle were partly demolished, while the keep at Dunster Castle was levelled. Compared to the three previous centuries, England and Wales were peaceful. Troops had to be deployed to restore order when the

Plan of the East India Company's fortification works at Calcutta, c. 1750. In June 1756, the Nawab of Bengal, Siraj-ud-daula, stormed poorly defended and fortified Fort William after a brief siege, confining his captives in the 'Black Hole'. Sent from Madras, Robert Clive regained Fort William, largely thanks to supporting naval fire.

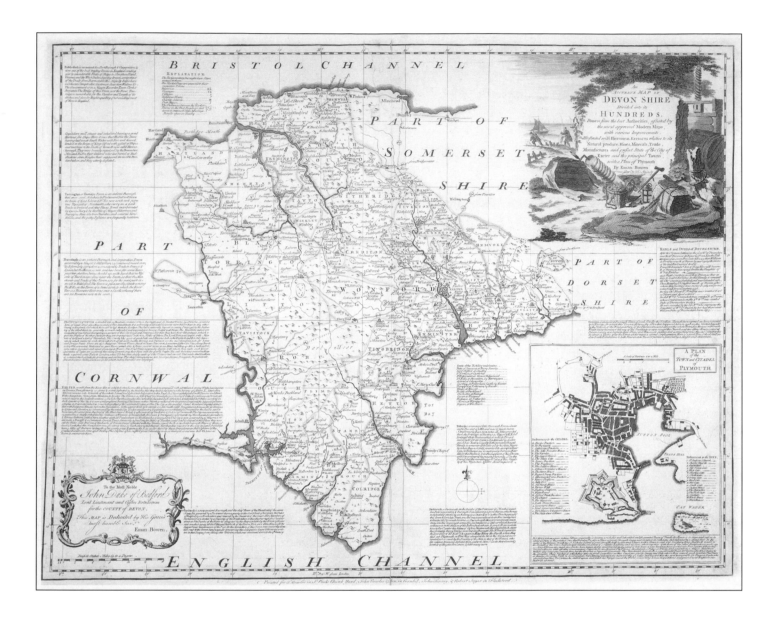

Copper plate hand-coloured map of Devonshire by Emanuel Bowen, c. 1754. Bowen cooperated with Thomas Kitchen in engraving maps for the Large English Atlas. *The forty-five maps were sold as a complete volume from 1760, the seventh edition appearing in 1787.*

Cornish tinners rose in 1757 and 1773 to seize grain, but there was no comparison with earlier risings in the south-west. The Jacobite rising in Northumberland in 1715 was the last in northern England, and again no comparison with earlier risings. By 1700 there were no 'no-go' areas, beyond the reach of government, law and order, except for the Scottish Highlands where the clan chiefs still held sway. This had not been the case a century earlier. There seemed little reason to believe that British society would collapse from within.

MAPS AND MAPPING, 1700–1800

The habit of referring to maps increased in the eighteenth century. Land surveyors were numerous and cadastral maps (showing the extent, value and ownership for taxation purposes) were produced in large numbers. Landowners could thus give a sense of place to reports from distant estates: in 1739–42 Wadham College, Oxford, had five maps made of its Essex estates. Aside from estate maps, there were new initiatives in the production of printed county maps in the mid-eighteenth century. Hitherto the

Elizabethan maps had been reprinted with scant alteration, due to the absence of new field work. Now new surveys of entire counties were undertaken and maps produced on detailed scales: one or more inches to the mile. The work from 1759 was in part encouraged by prizes awarded by the Royal Society of Arts, one of the major 'improving' bodies of the period. The first of the county maps – that of Cornwall by Joel Gascoyne, appeared in 1699. By 1750 only eight counties had been mapped at one-inch to a mile or larger, but by 1775 nearly half of the English counties had been thus surveyed. Essex, for example, was surveyed by John Chapman in 1772–4 and the resulting maps published in 1777.

Maps came to play a greater role in politics. In 1718 a map formed part of the Anglo-Dutch treaty delineating the frontier between the Dutch and the Austrian Netherlands, and the same year all MPs received a copy of Reeve Williams' pamphlet defence of British foreign policy, *A Letter from a Merchant to a Member of Parliament* which included a map. There was a growing market for maps, part of the expanding culture of print. In 1700 Edward Wells, an Oxford academic who was very interested in geography, published his *New Set of Maps Both of Antient and Present Geography*. His *Treatise of Antient and Present Geography, Together with a Sett of Maps in Folio*, first published in Oxford in 1701, appeared in a fifth edition in 1738. Enclosure maps reflected cartography as an aid to control, and there could be a hostile response to surveying: hostility to the enclosure of the former Malvern Chase in 1776 led local people to prevent John Andrews, the surveyor, from marking out the enclosure boundaries. He had produced a topographical map of Kent in 1769.

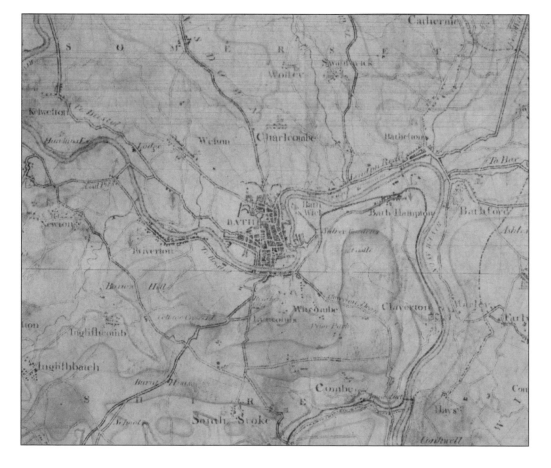

Detail from a geological map of the neighbourhood of Bath, engraved of John Cary and then hand-coloured by the artist, c. 1799. The versatile Cary was a map seller who also produced terrestrial and celestial globes, astronomical books, road books and maps, and canal plans. In 1798 he printed a new edition of Ogilby's Britannia *and in 1815 William Smith's* Delineation of the Strata of England and Wales with part of Scotland.

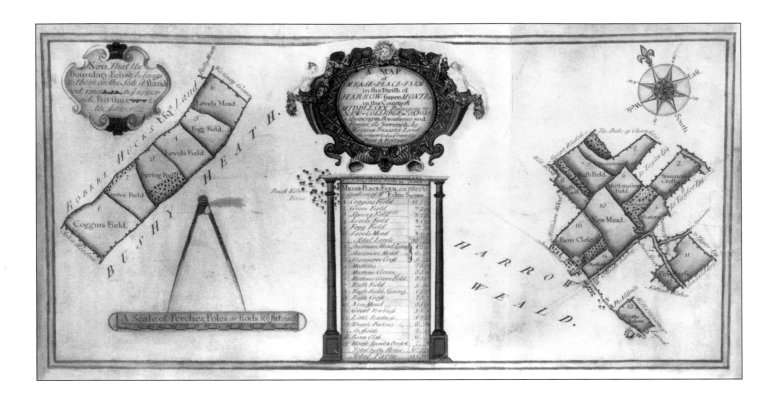

Map of Mease Place Farm in the parish of Harrow, belonging to New College, Oxford, 1736, by William Brasier. Land management encouraged a great increase in estate mapping in the eighteenth century.

The government survey of Scotland between 1747 and 1755 in order to produce a map that would, it was hoped, enable the army to respond better to any repetition of the Jacobite rising of 1745, was another aspect of mapping as an aid to control. Six surveying parties were employed in a move that was to parallel the road and fortress-building of the same years. Fortresses anchored the government position and maps provided guidance in the planning and use of force, offering the prospect of a strategic, Scotland-wide response to any future uprising.

Britain's maritime role and ambitions also led to a greater interest in charting the wider world. Aside from explorers, most famously Captain James Cook, who probed the Pacific, there was also a major effort to discover a method of determining longitude at sea: Parliament offered a reward in 1714 if a means could be successfully devised. With George III's support, John Harrison devised a marine chronometer that erred by only eighteen miles in measurement of the distance of a return journey to Jamaica in 1761–2. Between 1698 and 1700 Edmund Halley and HMS *Paramour* had discovered the extent of magnetic variation and the precise longitude and latitude of the American Colonies.

More generally, cartography was a crucial aspect of the ability to synthesise, disseminate, utilise and reproduce information that was crucial to British hegemony. The movement of ships could be planned and predicted, facilitating not only trade but also amphibious operations. Maps served to record and replicate information about areas in which Britain had an interest and to organise, indeed centre, this world on themes of European concern and power. The sprinkling of much of the world with British placenames reflected not only British explorers and power, but also its registration through surveying, charting and cartography.

ELEVEN

Towns and Trade

If we remember the eighteenth century through its stately homes, we also think of the townscapes of the period, especially the squares of the West End of London, Bath, Dublin and the New Town of Edinburgh. Many other cities also have important eighteenth-century areas, including Liverpool. A major expansion of urban life lay behind these Georgian buildings, constructed in a new, regular, 'classical' style, often in terraces that lined new boulevards, crescents, squares and circles. Urban life became more influential in Britain, especially England. The percentage of the population living in towns – defined as settlements with more than about 2,000 people – rose from about 17 in 1700 to about 27.5 in 1800, and at a time when the population was rising. Aside from London, which in 1700 had more than half a million people and in 1800 more than a million, there were only five English towns with more than 10,000 inhabitants in 1700: Norwich, Bristol, Newcastle, Exeter and York. By 1800 there were more than twenty-seven, including important industrial and commercial centres in the north and the Midlands, such as Manchester, Leeds, Sheffield, Sunderland, Bolton, Birmingham, Stoke and Wolverhampton.

Smaller towns also expanded. Stockton, an important port for North Sea trade, acquired a new parish church (1712), customs house (1730), town hall (1735), a theatre (1766) and a grammar school (1786). There was also major urban growth in Scotland, especially in Glasgow and Edinburgh, but also, by 1800, in industrial centres such as Paisley and Greenock, just as the iron-making centre of Merthyr Tydfil became the largest town in Wales. The largest in Ireland – Dublin, Cork, Belfast, Drogheda, Limerick and Waterford – were ports, their prosperity dependent on the growing commercialisation of the Irish economy.

By 1800 London had the largest population of any European city and was over ten times bigger than the second city in England. It established notions of urban life. Aside from the enormous growth of the city's trade, London also benefited from the increasing importance of its dominance of the world of print, the shaper of news, opinion and fashion. London newspapers circulated throughout England and were also crucial sources for the provincial press. The annual sale of London papers elsewhere in England rose from 1.09 million in 1764 to 4.65 million in 1790.

The turnpike and postal systems centred on London, reflecting and sustaining London's economic importance. London-based insurance companies, such as the Sun Fire Office, and the banks were able to organise business throughout the country. They

Georgian houses on Tombland, Norwich. One of only five English towns with more than 10,000 inhabitants in 1700, Norwich grew substantially in the eighteenth century.

163

were helped greatly by the expansion of the transport system. Stagecoaches regularly left London inns such as the George at Southwark. On 19 June 1773 *Jackson's Oxford Journal* reported:

> The difference in the number of stage coaches, etc. travelling on the Western road, within these few years, is not a little remarkable. About ten years ago there only passed through Salisbury in the course of a week, to and from London and Exeter, six stage coaches, which carried six passengers each, making in the whole (if full) 36 passengers. At present there constantly pass, between the above places, in the same space of time, 24 stage coaches, carrying six passengers each and 28 stage chaises, carrying three each making in the whole, if full, 228 passengers.

As a result of major expansion from the 1750s, by 1770 there were 15,000 miles (24,000 kilometres) of turnpike road in England, and most of the country was within 12.5 miles (20 kilometres) of one. The first Cheshire turnpike act had been in 1705, the next one not till 1724, but from the 1750s the situation in the county improved: cross routes were turnpiked, including Macclesfield to Buxton in 1758 and Chester to Northwich in 1769. Turnpike roads were constructed by turnpike trusts authorised by Parliament to raise capital for such purposes and to charge travellers. Although turnpike trusts reflected local initiatives, a national turnpike system was created. Parliament oversaw the system through renewal and amendment acts that reflected the strength of local interests. Maps, such as that of Staffordshire by William Yates in 1775, recorded the introduction of turnpikes and canals, and this information reflected the concern with travel routes. Travel was made faster by the cross-breeding of fast Arab horses, while further improvement came from the replacement of leather straps by steel coach springs and the introduction of elliptical springs. The time of a journey from Manchester to London fell from three days in 1760 to twenty-eight hours in 1788.

New Horse Guards from St James's Park, by Canaletto (1697–1768). Canaletto employed talents developed to depict Venice in order to show the glories of modern London. A neo-imperial, modern pride in London was expressed in his views of new buildings such as the Greenwich Observatory, Somerset House and Westminster Bridge.

The development of the turnpikes was central to the creation of regular long-distance horse-drawn wagon services, and the latter also benefited from the construction of bridges. Thus, whereas Kendal in Cumbria had been served by regular packhorse trains moving goods as far as Bristol, London and Southampton from the fifteenth century, in the eighteenth century horsedrawn wagon services with their greater capacity for moving goods took over long-distance and regional routes to and from Cumbria. Similarly, wagon access to Liverpool began in the 1730s and a direct coach service thence to London in 1760.

The *Atlas Historique* of 1705, dedicated to John Churchill, 1st Duke of Marlborough, and generally attributed to Henri Abraham Châtelain, described Britain as 'like a well-steered big boat'. This nautical comparison was appropriate. London was the focus of a growing global trade system. Britain became the leading trans-oceanic trader, dominating commerce with North America, India and China. Average annual exports rose from £4.1 million in the 1660s to £12.7 million in 1750 and £18.9 million in 1790, and that in a period of low inflation. Government sought to help trade. In 1722 the export duties on most British manufactured products were abolished. Import duties on foreign raw materials required for

Dyrham Park, South Gloucestershire. The china and other decorations in the house reflect the growing trade with other nations during the eighteenth century.

these products were reduced or abolished. Potential competitors within the British empire, in Ireland and North America, were hindered. British trade diversified, in both markets and products, and shipping tonnage rose greatly. Trade brought money into the country and encouraged industry. It also brought in goods that can still be seen in houses of the period: china, as at Attingham Park, Beningbrough Hall, Dyrham, Ham, and Saltram, and the lacquer furniture and embroidered silk bed hangings in the state bedroom at Erddig. The diet was changed by the import of sugar from the West Indies, while tea, coffee and chocolate also all had an impact, and led to the production, purchase and use of new goods, such as teapots.

Urban economies were also helped by the growing commercialisation of life. The infrastructure of, and for, money transformed the nature of the domestic market and of townscapes. New covered markets and shops were opened, as were banks and insurance offices. Advertising grew and trade directories were produced. In a world of 'things', where increasing numbers could afford to purchase objects to bring them pleasure, there was much buying of books, paintings and musical instruments. Rising prosperity helped towns grow, although much of this prosperity reflected their role as social centres and providers of service activities, as much as commercial and industrial functions.

In London, Thomas Wriothesley, 4th Earl of Southampton, laid out Southampton (now Bloomsbury) Square in the 1660s, while the West End estates of landlords such as Sir Richard Grosvenor and Lord Burlington were developed as fashionable residential properties. Celia Fiennes recorded 'There was formerly in the City several houses of the

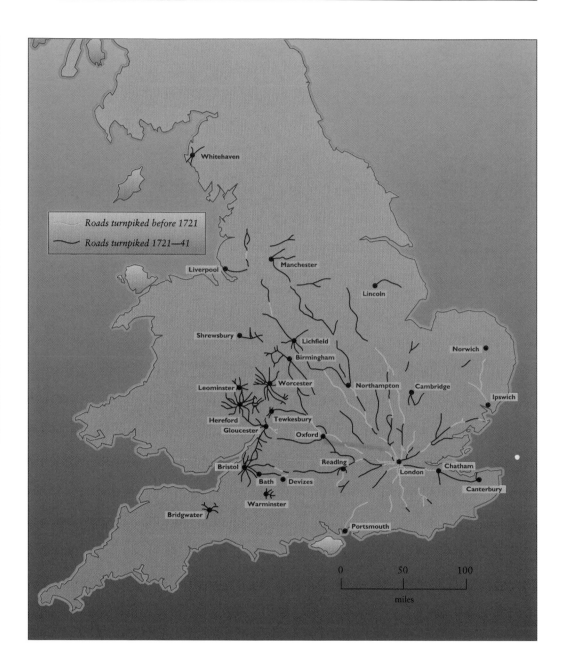

THE TURNPIKE ROAD NETWORK IN 1741

Turnpike roads were constructed by turnpike trusts authorised by Parliament to raise capital for such purposes and to charge travellers. Thus the road system came in part to reflect the degree of dynamism of individual trusts and the ability of particular routes to produce revenue, a consequence essentially of the strength of the regional economy and the role of the route in intra-regional communications. Parliament oversaw the system through renewal and amendment acts.

noblemens with large gardens and out houses, but of late are pulled down and built into streetes and squares and called by the names of the noblemen, and this is the practise by almost all'. Mayfair and St James's became select areas and roads, such as Oxford Street, were given the name of politicians. London was the major centre of consumption and leisure. There was constant activity, and a world very different to the rhythms and sensations of rural and small town life. 'All the world's a desert beyond Hyde Park', complained Sir Fopling Flutter in Sir George Etherege's comedy *The Man of Mode* (1676). In his successful play of 1696, *The Relapse*, John Vanbrugh referred to London as 'that uneasy theatre of noise'. The amount of fixed specialised investment in leisure rose greatly with theatres, pleasure gardens, James Wyatt's Pantheon in Oxford Street, a grand assembly room completed in 1772, and other facilities, ranging from auction houses to brothels. Although large, London was compact, not yet suffering from the congestion and sprawl of the following centuries.

Great wealth could be made in London. Sir Francis Child, a goldsmith banker who came from a clothier family in Devizes, became Lord Mayor in 1698 and an MP and was able to purchase the Osterley estate in 1713. His grandson, Francis, was able to spend £17,700 buying Upton as a country seat for hunting in 1757, as well as £1,200 on his election as an MP in 1761. His brother Robert was estimated to earn at least £30,000 per annum from the bank. Frances Bankes, daughter of a London merchant, brought £100,000 when she married Sir Brownlow Cust of Belton in 1775. Growth in London was continuous, the world of business digesting what had come before. Clarendon House, Piccadilly, a spectacular palace built in 1664–7 for the Lord Chancellor, the 1st Earl of Clarendon, father-in-law of James, Duke of York, was sold after the Earl's death in 1683 to 'certaine rich bankers and merchants', who demolished the house and developed the site.

Other towns expanded greatly. This was true of regional capitals, such as Norwich and Nottingham, county centres, such as Warwick, and developing entertainment centres, particularly spa towns, such as Bath, where the first Pump Room was built in 1706. Industrial growth led to more trade, and provided opportunities for investment. Thus, Bristol financiers developed copper works near Swansea from 1717, as well as iron and coal workings in south Wales.

The number of provincial newspapers, all of which were published in towns, grew – from twenty-four in 1723 to thirty-five in 1760 and fifty in 1782 – and their distribution networks became denser. In place of the seven agents of the *Chelmsford Chronicle* who were outside Chelmsford (including one in London) in 1764, the paper listed six London agents and another twenty outside Chelmsford in 1792. In January 1779 the *Hampshire Chronicle*, recently launched in Southampton, offered a list of agents, including seven London coffee-houses, and others in eighteen towns, including, Bath, Bristol, Chichester, Poole and Reading. A national press also developed in Scotland. The *Herald* was founded in 1783, the *Scotsman* in 1817. Newspapers were an aspect of an expanding world of print that was fostered by entrepreneurial publishing and bookselling.

The title page of the first edition of Dr Johnson's English dictionary, 1755, a major work in the eighteenth-century classification of knowledge.

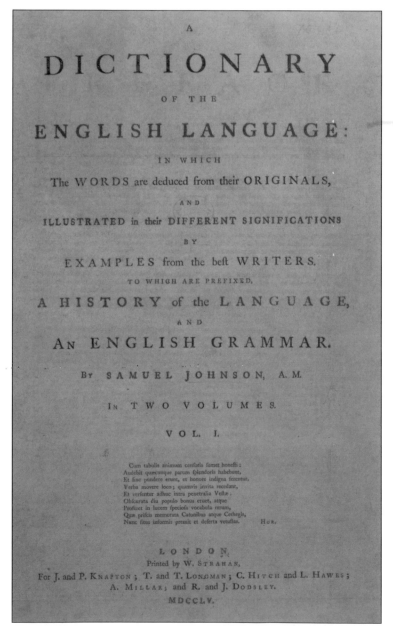

A

DICTIONARY

OF THE

ENGLISH LANGUAGE:

IN WHICH

The WORDS are deduced from their ORIGINALS,

AND

ILLUSTRATED in their DIFFERENT SIGNIFICATIONS

BY

EXAMPLES from the best WRITERS.

TO WHICH ARE PREFIXED,

A HISTORY of the LANGUAGE,

AND

AN ENGLISH GRAMMAR.

BY SAMUEL JOHNSON, A.M.

IN TWO VOLUMES.

VOL. I.

Cum tabulis animum censoris sumet honesti;
Audebit quæcumque parum splendoris habebunt,
Et sine pondere erunt, et honore indigna ferentur,
Verba movere loco; quamvis invita recedant,
Et versentur adhuc intra penetralia Vestæ,
Obscurata diu populo bonus eruet, atque
Proferet in lucem speciosa vocabula rerum,
Quæ priscis memorata Catonibus atque Cethegis,
Nunc situs informis premit et deserta vetustas. HOR.

LONDON,
Printed by W. STRAHAN,
For J. and P. KNAPTON; T. and T. LONGMAN; C. HITCH and L. HAWES;
A. MILLAR; and R. and J. DODSLEY.
MDCCLV.

The process of public description through print played an increasingly insistent role. Its manifestations were varied. John Slezer arrived from the continent in 1671 to take up the post of Chief Engineer with the Scottish Army. During the course of his duties over the following two decades, he travelled widely and made drawings of many of the major sights of Scotland. In 1693 he was granted a royal licence by Queen Mary to publish a book of the views that he had recorded. Called *Theatrum Scotiae*, this was the first pictorial record of Scotland. The accompanying descriptions were drafted in Latin by the Geographer Royal, Sir Robert Sibbald, but translated for publication. The Giant's Causeway on the coast of Ireland became famous when Susanna Drury's pictures were published as engravings.

Publishers sought a mass market. The first folio edition of Dr Johnson's *Dictionary*, published in 1755, cost £4 10 shillings (£4.50); 2,000 copies were printed. It was soon followed, however, by a second edition, published in 165 weekly sections at sixpence (2½ new pence) each.

Government increasingly involved standardised paperwork. There was a growth of bureaucracy with larger numbers of questionnaires to be sent back to Whitehall by JPs and other officials, and with a growing reliance on printed forms. London stationers provided poor law documents: such forms were part of a regular process by which information was gathered and disseminated, and instructions transmitted. The association of the printed word and authority continued to be strong.

The growth of the press was an important aspect of urban expansion and influence. So also was the world of fashion, for which towns served as display cases as well as retail sources. Provincial architects, such as Joseph Pickford in Derby and Richard Gillow and Thomas Harrison in Lancaster, were responsible for fine buildings in a large number of centres. Thus, the social world that fostered the demand for buildings, such as theatres and assembly rooms, was matched by entrepreneurial activity, artistic skill and the wealth of a growing economy. Houses were decorated according to a whole new range of styles and filled with new products. Wallpaper became fashionable, carpets more common and furniture more plentiful. Alongside light, roomy and attractive private houses for the middling orders – such as Fenton House in Hampstead, Maister House in Hull, Lawrence House in Launceston, and Wordsworth House in Cockermouth, and the Georgian terraces of Bath, the Clifton section of Bristol and other cities – numerous public buildings were constructed.

Old gates and walls were demolished, and theatres, assembly rooms and subscription libraries opened, as were parks and walks. Philanthropic foundations were responsible for new hospitals and schools. In Newcastle, a fortress against Jacobitism in 1715 and 1745, most of the gates and walls were demolished between 1763 and 1812; in their place major public buildings were constructed, including the Assembly Rooms in 1776 and the Theatre Royal in 1788. Stamford in Lincolnshire received a smart new Palladian assembly room just as the medieval gates obstructing traffic on the Great North Road were taken down.

The new theatre in Newcastle was indicative of the major expansion of provincial culture during the century. This was focused on the 'middling orders', or, to use a later and somewhat misleading terminology, the 'middle class'. This section of society both grew and acquired more disposable wealth, a consequence in part of economic expansion and of the growth and development of pro-fessionalism in a range of activities including the law and medicine. Unable to provide sustained large-scale patronage, the middling orders both participated in such patronage through public performances of works and public markets for the arts, and provided a crucial source of patronage at a less exalted scale. The patronage of the anonymous public was also crucial to the performers chosen: singers at the concerts in the leading London pleasure gardens at Vauxhall in the second half of the century knew that their future engagements depended on the number of encores the audience demanded.

Court and other institutional patronage in England had long been concentrated in or close to the metropolis. The public sphere of

The Guildhall, High Street, Worcester. Designed by Thomas White and constructed between 1721 and 1727 this was one of the many municipal buildings created during the period of Georgian urban expansion.

169

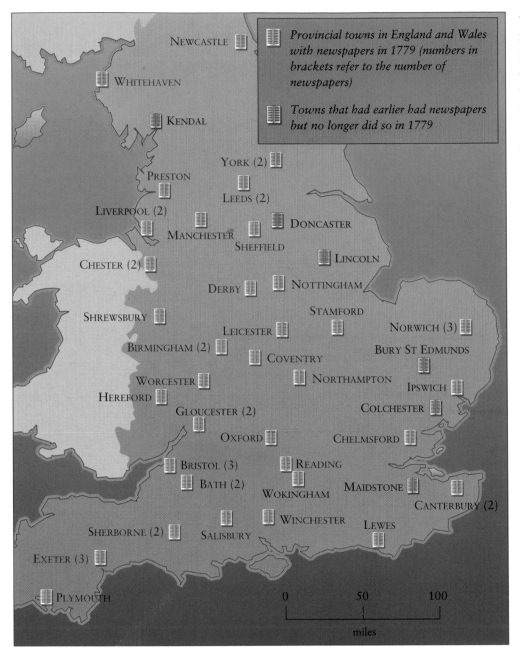

NEWCASTLE

WHITEHAVEN

KENDAL

Provincial towns in England and Wales with newspapers in 1779 (numbers in brackets refer to the number of newspapers)

Towns that had earlier had newspapers but no longer did so in 1779

YORK (2)

PRESTON

LEEDS (2)

LIVERPOOL (2)

MANCHESTER   DONCASTER

SHEFFIELD

CHESTER (2)

LINCOLN

DERBY   NOTTINGHAM

SHREWSBURY

STAMFORD

LEICESTER   NORWICH (3)

BIRMINGHAM (2)

COVENTRY   BURY ST EDMUNDS

WORCESTER   NORTHAMPTON

HEREFORD   IPSWICH

GLOUCESTER (2)   COLCHESTER

OXFORD   CHELMSFORD

BRISTOL (3)   READING

BATH (2)   MAIDSTONE

WOKINGHAM   CANTERBURY (2)

WINCHESTER

SHERBORNE (2)   LEWES

SALISBURY

EXETER (3)

PLYMOUTH

0   50   100

miles

the new cultural patronage was more extensive. It brought renewed energy to the cultural life of many towns. In Hertford there were subscription concerts in a specially built concert-room from 1753 to 1767 and in the 1770s concerts took place in the new Shire Hall, completed in 1771, which had assembly rooms built for such functions. Similarly, many provincial towns became centres of cultural 'production' and 'consumption', not that, as with amateur music-making, the two processes were necessarily readily separable. Regional circuits developed out of the routes of strolling players and they increasingly acted in purpose-built playhouses. When in 1786 the leading theatrical company in East Anglia, the Norwich Comedians or the Duke of Grafton's Servants, ceased to tour smaller towns, it was still able to concentrate its attentions on Norwich, King's Lynn, Yarmouth, Barnwell (Cambridge), Bury St Edmunds, Colchester and Ipswich. The Theatre Royal in Bristol was built in 1766 with a capacity of about 1,600. It was modelled on the leading London theatre at Drury Lane. A more intimate theatre, built in 1819, survives as the Theatre Royal at Bury St Edmunds. There was a similar expansion in Scotland and Ireland.

Similarly, more provincial centres could now boast professional painters. This was not only true of major centres, such as Bath and Norwich. Painters in country towns were patronised by the local gentry, as well as by townspeople. Mary Beale and Sarah Curtis were examples of women excelling as painters, and both in the fiercely commercial world of portraiture. Towards the close of the century, a taste for picturesque landscape was widely diffused and it served to help direct popular tastes towards romantic values.

Yet in this climate of expansion and increasing prosperity there were also serious problems. Some towns did badly, especially if they suffered from poor communications, such as Hereford, or were affected by competition, as Gloucester was from Bristol. Yarm declined once the bridge over the Tees at Stockton opened in 1769 and created a lower

PROVINCIAL CULTURE AT THE END OF THE EIGHTEENTH CENTURY

The press proved a crucial medium in developing the provincial culture of the period. Provincial papers were not local papers in the modern sense. Most towns of publication did not offer a large enough market. Thus the provincial press had to be regional, not local.

crossing point. There were also serious problems of regulation and control facing urban communities. Poverty and crime were concentrated in towns, as were problems of sanitation and health. Many lived in precarious circumstances, often in disrupted family situations and outside established patterns of hierarchy. Urban crowds could prove volatile. There were serious challenges to government authority, especially in Edinburgh in 1736, and London in 1733, 1736, 1768 and 1780. Riots in Glasgow in 1725 against the imposition of a new malt tax led to the deployment of troops and the killing of nineteen rioters. Food riots were also a major cause of disturbance and the use of troops did not always overawe the rioters. At Dysart in Scotland in 1720 the mob attacked soldiers and seized their weapons. Elizabeth Montagu, a 'bluestocking' (intellectual) wife of an MP, was shocked by the extent of critical sentiment in London in 1762:

> the Daemon of discontent is murmuring and whispering in well bred society, and bowling and scolding among the mob. Every species of abuse comes forth in print or pamphlet, and all the garretteer scribblers are treating the characters of great persons with a scurrility nothing but shameless vice could utter. I do not wonder the wretches sunk in infamy and poverty should be guilty of these outrages, but I'm surprized their works should be brought up in the manner they are . . . all mankind are philosophers and pride themselves in having a contempt for rank and order and imagine they show themselves wise in ridiculing whatever gives distinction and dignity to kings and other magistrates, not considering that the chains of opinion are less galling than those of law, and that the great beast the multitude must be bound by something. Alexander the Great was treated with contempt by a certain philosopher in a tub, but in this enlightened age, the man who made the tub would use him with the same scorn.

This was not only an issue in London. Elizabeth Montagu was depressed on a visit to Newcastle that autumn: 'There is an universal dejection amongst honest people. The public papers, absurd as they are, have made deep impressions.' Five years later, Elizabeth Grenville, wife of a major politician and former Prime Minister, George

Norwich Market Place, 1799, by Robert Dighton (1752–1814). Norwich city gates were taken down between 1791 and 1801 and the city gained a lunatic asylum (1714), a new shire hall (1749), assembly rooms (1754), a theatre (1756), a hospital (1771–2), a public subscription library (1784) and a new county gaol (1792–3). In 1806, Dighton admitted stealing etchings from the British Museum.

Grenville, was concerned about her husband's safety amidst 'the tumults and disorders' in London: 'It is indeed come to a most shocking pitch. God grant you safety in the midst of a wild tumultous and daring mob.'

Urban life had distinctive characteristics. It offered freedom and opportunity, although not equality of opportunity. The social system was more fluid in towns: mobility was greater and control laxer. Town life provided new ideas and offered new experiences. It was easier to bridge social divisions, whether in disseminating new fashions, such as the wearing of calicoes and the drinking of tea, or in expressing new political views. Migrants, however, could find that rural penury became urban poverty and without the community support that was stronger in the countryside. New townscapes, their associated cultural 'infrastructure', and their celebration in paintings were also expressions of social differentiation. The New Town in Edinburgh was not only the product of new architectural taste and of burgeoning prosperity for some sections of urban society, but also set the seal on emerging social divisions. Similarly, in London, Newcastle and many other towns, there was a growing social and spatial segregation in residential areas based on wealth and status.

The world of the poor, of expedients, did not extend to the purchase of luxuries, such as musical instruments, Wedgwood pottery, or indeed, for most people, newspapers. Similarly, illiteracy acts as a fundamental qualification of any description of the period in terms of the culture of print. Although the number of charity schools, such as the Blewcoat School founded in London in 1709, increased, the formal education of the bulk of the population remained limited. Yet the poor were a far from undifferentiated section of the population. Forms of status and security were attainable, although they were precarious. Far less work has been devoted to the cultural life of this section of the population than to the middling orders and it is all too easy to resort to a simple picture of exclusion and/or limited culture. The notion of a gulf between elite and popular culture was a schematisation imposed by later historians. Instead, it is far more likely that the situation was diverse and varied greatly by region and locality. A section of the poor was certainly receptive to printed political debate. In 1792 a fellow of Magdalen College, Oxford who sought government support to write a pamphlet costing 2d explained:

I have heard it frequently lamented that among the different pamphlets which have appeared, not one has been published, in favour of the constitution of this country, upon a very cheap plan, and in language suited to the comprehension of the common people: but on the contrary the pamphlet entitled 'the rights of man', has been published for three pence each, and in many places distributed gratis, which has been attended with very pernicious consequences.

Hannah More (1745–1833) soon filled the gap with her homely and accessible writings in support of morality and order

A growing urban sector coexisted with landed society and this helped to ensure a two-way flow in social and cultural attitudes. Urban development altered the institutional and cultural landscape of well-populated regions, and was crucial to a growing self-image of Britain as an improving society. Towns were also the forcing houses of the commercial economy and culture of print through which Britain became not only a world power but also a political society that saw domination as its national destiny.

TWELVE

The Politics of a World Power

In 1688 Britain had been successfully invaded. By 1763 it was to be the strongest power in the world. This is the global theme that has to be remembered when considering British politics in the period. It is all too easy to concentrate on the details of parliamentary groups and to forget the larger picture. The two were related: the domestic political situation proved propitious for imperial expansion, but this relationship was not the entire story. The course of military campaigns, the nature of international relations, and the strength and policies of Britain's opponents, especially France, were also important. By 1688 Britain had seized no major territories from France or Spain; by 1763 the situation was very different.

William of Orange landing at Torbay on 5 November 1688, by Sir James Northcote (1746–1831), engraved by James Parker, 1801. Such works were part of the beatification of the 'Glorious' Revolution.

War with France is a central theme, for it links Britain's transoceanic successes, both against the Bourbons (France and Spain) and their allies among native peoples of North America and India, with British policy in Europe, the conflict with Jacobite supporters in the British Isles, and the course of domestic politics. Britain and France were at war between 1689 and 1697, 1702 and 1713, 1743 and 1748, 1756 and 1763, 1778 and 1783 and from 1793 into the next century. The 'Glorious' Revolution led William III's views to shape policy and thereafter discussion of the national interest focused on hostility to France. Ideas of national interest, however, are inseparable from the

The victory of William III over James II at the battle of the Boyne in Ireland, 1 July 1690, engraved by Dirk Maes. William outmanoeuvred the outnumbered James. Under heavy pressure and concerned about the dangers of being surrounded, the Jacobites retreated. Having abandoned Dublin, they regrouped at Limerick.

ideologies that define a country's role and destiny, so enmity with France was only 'natural' to people who had already decided that Catholicism, Bourbon absolutism and continental predominance were the antithesis of Englishness or Britishness.

In the first bout of hostilities, that of the Nine Years' War or the War of the League of Augsburg (1689–97), William III stemmed the French advance in the Low Countries and defeated James II's supporters in Scotland and Ireland, especially with his victory at the Boyne in 1690. This secured the Protestant Ascendancy in Ireland and England's control over its politics and economy. The cost of the war also forced William to accept the discipline of parliamentary monarchy. There had been no such monarchy between 1682 and 1688 for, despite calling Parliament in 1685, James II rapidly dispensed with it. But both Charles II in his later years and James had had the benefit of peace. William had no such freedom. James II's policy of attempting to 'regulate' Parliament was abandoned. The Bill of Rights proclaimed that elections 'ought to be free'.

They certainly became more frequent. The Triennial Act of 1694 ensured regular meetings of the Westminster Parliament, and, by limiting their life-span to a maximum of three years, required frequent elections. There were ten elections between 1695 and 1715, and this helped to encourage a sense of volatility. The war also led to the regularisation of public finances that introduced principles of openness and parliamentary responsibility. The funded national debt, guaranteed by Parliament and financed by the Bank of England, which was founded in 1694, enabled the government to borrow large sums of money at a low rate of interest. After the Nine Years' War was over William was forced to accept an unwelcome degree of parliamentary influence over the pace of demobilisation and strong criticism of his advisors and policies.

In the War of the Spanish Succession (in which Britain was involved from 1702 to 1713) an army under John Churchill, 1st Duke of Marlborough, drove the French from Germany and the Low Countries, but other British forces were less successful in Spain. Marlborough's major victories were Blenheim (1704), Ramillies (1706) and

Oudenaarde (1708). He was less successful at Malplaquet (1709). The war ended with the Peace of Utrecht (1713) which brought France's recognition of its failure to dominate Western Europe. Wartime British gains, such as Gibraltar (1704), Minorca (1708) and Nova Scotia, were formally ceded to Britain. By the Act of Settlement of 1701, the house of Hanover, descendants of James VI and I through his daughter, were promised the succession in England.

The war was also important for the parliamentary Union of England and Scotland in 1707. A lack of certainty over the fate of an independent Scotland when Queen Anne (1702–14), who had no children to survive into adulthood, died and the danger that France might exploit the situation encouraged English politicians to press for Union. Many Scots were angered by the neglect displayed by William III and there was little support for Union in Scotland, but there was little choice. The Scottish economy was in a poor state and the civil war of 1689–91 that had followed the 'Glorious' Revolution had underlined the divisions in Scottish society and indicated the difficulty of independence from England. There was no good Protestant alternative – the refusal of the exiled Stuarts to convert to Protestantism lessened Scottish options.

The passage of the Act of Union through the Scottish Parliament in 1706 depended both on a determination not to be shut out of English and colonial markets and on corruption. The Scots lost their Parliament in Edinburgh but gained representation in Westminster. The distinctiveness of the Scottish legal system and established church – Presbyterian since 1690 – were, however, maintained.

The Act of Union was the culmination of a process that was already apparent in 1650–2, 1660 and 1689–91: England and Scotland were no longer to go different ways. In the risings of 1715–16 and 1745–6, the Jacobites sought to restore the situation as it had been before 1707 and thus break the Union. Their defeat was crucial to the political geography of modern Britain and to the success of the British state. For much of the period Britain was at war with, or under the threat of war with, France, and an independent, autonomous or rebellious Scotland would have provided the French with many opportunities for intervention or, at the very least, for distracting British resources. This prospect af alliance with a continental

John Churchill, Duke of Marlborough, by Adriaan van der Werff. The masterly British general in the War of the Spanish Succession was also skilful in holding the anti-French coalition together. Under Marlborough, the British army reached a peak of success that it was not to repeat in Europe for another century. He made his cavalry act like a shock force, and handled the artillery well. Marlborough was particularly successful in coordinating the deployment and use of infantry, cavalry and cannon on the battlefield, and in integrating operations across an extended front.

Articles of Union of England and Scotland. Union ensured that Scottish parliamentary politics would be waged in a parliament (Westminster) where Scotland's representation was limited: 45 MPs and 16 representative peers out of 558 MPs and about 200 peers. Equally, it became necessary for English ministers seeking to secure Parliament to control the votes of Scottish representatives.

enemy had been a threat from across the border for centuries and the removal of this threat should be seen as crucial to the geopolitics of the British state. Furthermore, Scotland now contributed powerfully to the resources of the British state. Without Scottish troops, the British army would have been less successful in the eighteenth century. Thus, the Union had a compound effect on the growth of British power.

Had the Union been opposed successfully by the Edinburgh Parliament then there would have been a variety of sources of resistance to incorporation in Britain. Instead, resistance was largely limited to, and defined by, Jacobitism – the cause of the exiled Stuarts. There were a number of challenges after the Union, including a planned French invasion in 1708, and an unsuccessful Spanish invasion in 1719, also on behalf of the Stuarts. The most serious were the '15 and the '45. Both were risings that began in the Highlands, the first at Braemar, the second with the landing of Bonnie Prince Charlie – Charles Edward Stuart, the eldest son of 'James III and VIII' – in the Western Isles. In each case, efforts were made to seize centres of power. The '15 was directed against George I (1714–27), the first of the Hanoverian dynasty. He replaced Queen Anne's Tory ministers with a Whig ascendancy that left the Tories no options in government service. This reflected George's distrust of the Tories, whom he saw as sympathetic to Jacobitism, and also the difficulty of operating a mixed Whig-Tory ministry.

In the '15 a number of important towns, such as Perth, were captured, but when the Jacobite forces, under John Erskine, 11th Earl of Mar, advanced on Stirling, they were blocked at Sheriffmuir by government forces under John Campbell, 2nd Duke of Argyll. Mar had a larger army, but he was a poor general and failed to grasp and retain the initiative. (Marlborough would have had little trouble in winning with the forces at Mar's disposal.) Thereafter, the '15 was on the decline, even though James III reached Scotland on 22 December 1715. A rising in Northumbria and the Borders led to an advance on Preston where the Jacobites were defeated, as the invading Scots had been by Cromwell in 1648. In early 1716 Argyll advanced against the outnumbered Jacobite forces in north-east Scotland and they melted away, James fleeing back to the continent. The rising led to a revival of concern about the defensiveness of country houses. In 1716 the Earl of Sutherland wrote to the pro-Hanoverian James, 18th Brodie of Brodie, 'Allow me to call your seat Castle Brodie, instead of House, since it has been garrisoned in so good a cause'.

For nearly three decades Jacobitism remained a threat, but not one that was central to political life. Indeed, between 1717 and 1720 divisions among the Whigs over foreign policy and ministerial office took precedence. The opposition Whigs, then led by Robert Walpole, cooperated with the Tories in order to thwart contentious government legislation. This focused on plans to reverse Tory Acts of Parliament against the Dissenters, and an attempt to secure a permanent pro-government majority in the House of Lords. Walpole returned to court in 1720. Benefiting from the fall-out of the South Sea Bubble, a major financial scandal, and from the unexpected deaths of his two leading Whig opponents, he swiftly rose to dominate politics. Walpole was invaluable to the Georges, as government manager and principal spokesman in the Commons, and as a skilled finance minister. He also played a major role in the elections of 1722, 1727 and 1734, which were all victories for the pro-government Whigs. Aside from his policies, Walpole was skilful in parliamentary management and in his control of government patronage.

He was far less successful in the election of 1741, in part because of the active hostility of the leading patron of the opposition Whigs, Frederick, Prince of Wales, who never became king because he died before his father, George II (1727–60). Under growing pressure in the Commons, Walpole resigned in February 1742. His protégé Henry Pelham, however, was able to become First Lord of the Treasury in 1743, and from 1746 was in a position to pursue Walpolean policies: fiscal restraint, unenterprising legislation, maintaining a Whig monopoly of power and the status quo in the church, and seeking peace.

The '45 was a more serious affair than the '15, in large part because, unlike in 1715, Britain was already at war – with France and Spain – while Bonnie Prince Charlie proved, at least initially, a better and more

Stirling Castle. The Jacobite forces under John Erskine, 11th Earl of Mar, advanced on the town in 1715 but were blocked at Sheriffmuir by government forces under John Campbell, 2nd Duke of Argyll.

THE JACOBITE
INVASION OF 1745

William III's success in
1688 had shown that
England could be
successfully invaded. The
closest to success later
was the Jacobite invasion
of 1745, but there was no
effective coordination
with the French, and the
Jacobites received little
support in England. On
the other hand, they
encountered no effective
opposition. Wade was
out-marched and
Cumberland
outmanoeuvred.

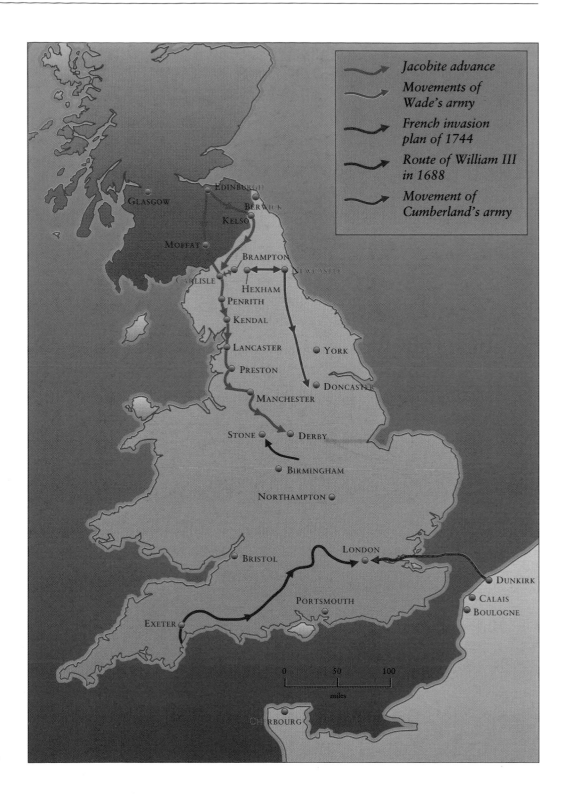

successful general than Mar had done. He outmanoeuvred the government forces in
Scotland under Sir John Cope and entered Edinburgh. Cope advanced to challenge the
Jacobites, but his army was wrecked at Prestonpans by a surprise attack: the Highland
Charge proved effective against unprepared forces.

Prestonpans did not bring all of Scotland to the Jacobites, but it gave them their
strongest position there. Yet, that was not enough. For Bonnie Prince Charlie to secure
his objectives, it was necessary to conquer England. Irrespective of the prince's wishes,

Culloden:
The Last Major Battle in Britain

On Drumossie Moor the terrain suited Cumberland's defensive position. Cumberland's forces also outnumbered his opponent's, 9,000 to 5,000, and the Jacobites were outgunned. The circumstances were not suitable for a Highland charge, not least because Cumberland's numbers permitted defence in depth. Any gaps in the front line could be filled. His artillery, firing canister shot, and infantry so thinned the numbers of the advancing clansmen that those who reached the royal troops were driven back by bayonet. The artillery was far more effective than at Prestonpans. Controversy surrounds the effectiveness of Cumberland's bayonet tactics, specifically the instruction to thrust forward and to the side, and thus rely on the next soldier for cover. However, the reliability of this method was not called into real question because of the role of firepower. The general rate of fire was increased by the level ground and the absence of any serious disruptive fire from the Jacobites, while the flanking position of the royal units forward from the left of the front line made Culloden even more of a killing field. Many factors led to

Culloden Moor.

confusion among the Jacobites: the slant of their line, the nature of the terrain, which was partly waterlogged, tiredness, lack of supplies, the difficulty of seeing what was happening in the smoke produced by the guns, and the independent nature of each unit's advance. John Maclean, a Jacobite officer, recorded,

> When all that pleased or was able to follow ther Collours marched out and was Drawn in order of Battel about 2 muskets shot from the Enemy they was waiting us in very good order with their Artilary befor them and the wind and snow in ther Backs. After a short stay and all the Disadvantages an Army could meete with as to ther numbers they Doubled or tripled ours and all advantages of Ground and wind and weather our Canon began to play upon them and they upon us. After we stayed about 10 minutes we wer ordered to march hastily to the Enemy which we did Boldly. They began a smart fire of their Small Guns and Grape Shots from there Cannons till we wer Beat Back with Great Losses our Right wing was flanked and surrounded by the horse which did Great Execution.

In celebration, Viscount Tyrconnel commissioned a bust of Cumberland, now in the Marble Hall at Belton. In contrast, the Jacobite Alexander, 17th Laird of Drum, escaped the battlefield, hid in a secret room at Drum, and fled to France.

a Hanoverian England would not allow a Jacobite Scotland. The government assembled an army at Newcastle under Field Marshal Wade, using the sea route up the east coast as a logistical axis, but the Jacobites avoided it by invading via Carlisle, which fell on 15 November after a short siege. Wade's slow advance via Hexham to relieve Carlisle was hampered by winter weather, and the faster moving Jacobites advanced unopposed towards London through Lancaster, Preston and Manchester. Another government army under George II's second son, the Duke of Cumberland, moved into the West Midlands to block the Jacobite advance. It was outmanoeuvred, misled by deliberately circulated reports that the Jacobites intended to move via Chester and North Wales, and exhausted by its marches in the West Midlands. Despite this failure of effective opposition, the Highland chiefs were discouraged by a lack of English support for the cause and by the absence of a promised French landing in southern England. They forced Bonnie Prince Charlie to turn back at Derby on 6 December 1745, a defining moment in eighteenth-century British history.

Government troops sought and failed to block the retreat. Once back in Scotland, a Highland charge was again decisive in giving the Jacobites victory at Falkirk (17 January 1746), although a defensive volley was also important in breaking the advance of the government troops. Government troops were also affected by growing darkness, the heavy rain wetting their powder, ineffective artillery, and a lack of fighting spirit: 'our foot gave a faint fire and then faced to the right about, as regularly as if they had the word of command, and could not be rallied until they got a considerable distance'.

Falkirk, however, was the last Jacobite victory. Charles Edward was short of money and the dynamic of Jacobite success had been lost. The inexorable nature of the deployment of resources by the British state, when its cohesion was not challenged by losing the initiative, was readily apparent in the preparations made by Cumberland. A large army was built up at Aberdeen, and Cumberland then advanced on Charles Edward's base at Inverness. Charles Edward failed to use the terrain to his advantage. Cumberland's crossing of the Spey was not contested and Charles Edward took no steps until, with an underfed and underpaid army, he attempted a night attack on Cumberland's camp, an advance that was mishandled and then abandoned before any assault could be mounted.

At the battle of Culloden on 16 April royal forces under the Duke of Cumberland finally shattered the rebel army. Charles Edward fled into exile. The results of Culloden, not least the heavy Jacobite casualties, marked the military end of Jacobitism as a serious force. Charles Edward's idiosyncratic and undisciplined behaviour in the following years greatly reduced foreign support, so that the Jacobite movement ceased to be of major importance in diplomacy or international relations. Charles Edward's conversion to the Church of England on a secret visit to London in 1750 did not lead to any rallying to the Jacobite cause, and the Elibank Plot of 1751–3, a scheme for a *coup d'etat* in London involving the kidnapping of George II, was betrayed.

Jacobitism represented an attempt to challenge developed and strengthening patterns of control: of Ireland by England, of Scotland by England, of northern Scotland by the Presbyterians of the Central Lowlands, of northern England by the south, and indeed of the whole of Britain by its most populous, wealthy and 'advanced' region: south-east England. Jacobitism thus represented an attempt to reverse the spatial process of state formation that had characterised recent (as well as earlier) British history. Proximity to centres of power, such as London, the Ile de France, and the Scottish Central Lowlands, brought a greater awareness of the political reality of 'England', 'France' and 'Scotland' than life in many other regions that were far from being economically and politically marginal. Such proximity was crucial to processes of state formation and resource mobilisation.

At one level, Jacobitism sought to resist this process in Britain. It was the expression of the northern Scottish and Irish desire for autonomy. However, Jacobite opposition in Scotland was not restricted to the Highlands and Islands. Indeed, most ideological Jacobites were lowlanders. Aberdeenshire and Angus produced more recruits than all Scotland west of the Great Glen and the majority of Jacobite commanders were not Highlanders. Culloden ensured that the new British state created by the parliamentary union of 1707 would continue to be specifically Protestant and with a political tone and agenda set in London and southern England. This was the basis of British consciousness, a development that did not so much alter the views of the English political elite, for whom Britain was essentially an extension of England, but, rather, that reflected the determination of the Scottish and Irish Protestant elites to link their fate with that of the British state.

William III's defeat of Jacobitism in Ireland in 1690–1 ensured that the Catholic challenge to this process was crushed there. In strategic and geopolitical terms this was of tremendous importance: an autonomous or independent Ireland would probably have looked to the major maritime Catholic powers, France and Spain, and this challenge to English power within the British Isles would have made it difficult to devote sufficient resources to the maritime and colonial struggle with the Bourbons. Jacobitism was also, particularly in England and at the court of the exiled Stuarts, an attempt not to dismember Britain or to alter the spatial relations within the British Isles, but rather to restore the male line of the Stuarts.

Bonnie Prince Charlie, by John Pettie. Charles Edward Stuart, 1720–88, was the eldest son of 'James III'. He had his moment of fame in 1745 when he came close to overthrowing the Hanoverian regime. After defeat at Culloden in 1746, he spent the remainder of his life as an increasingly drunken failure.

NATIONAL CULTURE

The defeat of Jacobitism helped to overcome or lessen the impact of long-lasting divides in British society, for example between Gaeldom and the world of English in Ireland and Highland Scotland, between English and Scots in Lowland Scotland, between

The Painted Hall at the Royal Naval College, Greenwich, by Sir James Thornhill (1675–1734), who became Serjeant-Painter to the king and King's History Painter in 1720.

Catholic, Anglican and Presbyterian in Ireland, and between Highland and Lowland and Presbyterian and Episcopalian in Scotland. Instead, there was a process of identification around English norms, as in John Walker's *Pronouncing Dictionary of English* (London, 1774), which provided 'rules to be observed by the natives of Scotland, Ireland and London, for avoiding their respective peculiarities'.

This was an aspect of the codification of the period that was, in part, a product of the culture of print and, in turn, whatever the caveat about London accents, reflected the primacy of the capital and of metropolitan norms. Many of the books published in Edinburgh and Dublin were reprints of London books. The authority of print, and the processes and pressures of commercialisation, served to lessen differences within Britain.

The fifth edition of the *Grammar of the English Tongue* by Sir Richard Steele and others appeared in 1728, and Robert Lowth's *Short Introduction to English Grammar* in 1762. Other aspects of culture were also codified in terms of rules and correctness, a public standardisation validated and enforced by print. Batty Langley, a gardener who became the prime exponent of the neo-Gothic, published *New Principles of Gardening* (London, 1728) and his rules for the neo-Gothic, *Ancient Architecture Restored* (London, 1741–2), the second edition of which was entitled *Gothic Architecture*,

The Distribution of the Premiums in the Society of Arts, *by James Barry, painted c. 1778–1801. It depicts members of the society including Samuel Johnson and Arthur Young. The Prince of Wales, a potential patron of the Scoiety, is shown in his Garter robes.*

Inside the Rotunda at Ranelagh, Chelsea, London. The pleasure gardens at Ranelagh became fashionable in the 1740s and 1750s, as a place to see and be seen, set and spot fashion, find spouses and whores. Horace Walpole noted, 'The company is universal: from His Grace of Grafton down to children of the Foundling Hospital.' Marylebone and Vauxhall were other fashionable gardens.

improved by Rules and Proportions (London, 1747). William Hogarth wrote a treatise on aesthetics, *The Analysis of Beauty* (London, 1753), in order 'to fix the fluctuating ideas of Taste' and define the principles of beauty and grace. This process was institutionalised with the Royal Academy, established in 1768 and designed to elevate 'fine art'.

Johnson's *Dictionary* was the first authoritative treatment of the language, and one that brought final stability to spelling. As the *Dictionary* plan of 1747 declared, 'The chief intent . . . is to preserve the purity and ascertain the meaning of our English idiom'. Johnson's citations reflected his sense of the role of a national canon of literature: half of all the quotations in the *Dictionary* came from only seven sources: Shakespeare, Dryden, Milton, Addison, Bacon, Pope, and the Authorised Version of the Bible, all works produced over the previous 170 years, and many of them over the previous 80, and thus an affirmation of the value of recent literature. Johnson also published a ten-volume *Lives of the Most Eminent English Poets*, creating a national heritage of literature. The 'discovery' of Shakespeare was related to a greater interest in the country's cultural past, part of the process by which a more self-confident nation focused on native values and models. Shakespeare was praised as the National Poet, and a monument in his honour erected in Westminster Abbey. There were no fewer than six major editions of his complete works in the century: by Rowe (1709), Pope (1725), Theobald (1753), Warburton (1747), Johnson (1765), and Malone (1790). Garrick was responsible for his plays being staged more frequently and he actively promoted the Shakespeare Jubilee in 1769. Even a Shakespeare forgery industry developed.

There was also a stronger interest in English music, particularly the works of Purcell and Handel. This focused on cathedral festivals of music, the foundation of the Academy of Ancient Music, and the mighty Handel commemoration celebrations in 1784. The last were so successful that they were repeated in 1785–7, 1790, and then in 1791 with over 1,000 performers and in the presence of George III.

In literature, there was a movement away from classical and towards British values and models. This entailed the searching and utilisation of a polyglot cultural inheritance in order to serve the needs of a distinctive British culture. A quest for what could be presented as Britishness and a celebration of the modern entailed an Anglicisation of classical and Hebraic forms, techniques and preoccupations. John Dryden Anglicised the epic, and Abraham Cowley the ode, while the novel presented a new and accessible (to the literate) form. In the theatre, Garrick developed a nationalistic school of acting believed to be superior to continental acting methods.

The new literature was also distinctly vernacular. Whereas cosmopolitan languages – French, German and Italian – were the languages of the European elites, or, at least, of much of their culture, in Britain the elite and imperialising language was English. Whereas in the United Provinces the major newspapers were published in French, in

Britain French-language periodicals were few and short-lived. The use of the vernacular allowed a degree of democratisation and inclusion in religion, culture, society and government. Thus, the hymns of the period, the work of such masters as Charles Wesley, Christopher Smart, Isaac Watts, William Cowper and John Byrom, could be sung by people of very different backgrounds. Novels created and responded to a large readership. They were not dependent on a distinguished list of subscribers or on political patronage. The variety of novels reflected the size and diversity of the reading public. Samuel Richardson's *Pamela* (1740), a very successful work on the prudence of virtue and the virtue of prudence, was countered by Henry Fielding's satirical *Shamela* (1741) and his popular *Joseph Andrews* (1742). John Cleland employed the epistolary style of *Pamela* in his pornographic novel *Fanny Hill; or, Memoirs of a Woman of Pleasure* (1744–9).

There was also greater self-confidence in British painting. In 1720 James Thornhill, a painter much favoured by the Whigs, became the first English artist to be knighted. Prior to that, the great names in British painting had been foreign, Anthony Van Dyck, Peter Lely and John de Medina becoming knights and Godfrey Kneller a baronet. Charles II had turned to Antonio Verrio to work at Windsor Castle between 1675 and 1682, and he also worked at Chatsworth, Burghley and Hampton Court. Thornhill's masterpiece was his painting of the Painted Hall in Wren's Royal Hospital at Greenwich (1708–12), an explicitly British grand state painting and a depiction of naval power. Thornhill also worked in Chatsworth, Hampton Court and St Paul's Cathedral, and decorated the staircase at Hanbury Hall. Later prominent portraitists, English and Scottish, included Henry Raeburn, Archibald Skirving, Ramsay and Joshua Reynolds.

Another product of the metropolitan forcing-house of artistic activity and cultural values, Hogarth, Thornhill's son-in-law, advocated a specifically English style. It appeared that the country of Isaac Newton had little to learn from the continent, and, if it did, a

Hampton Court Palace, where British painter James Thornhill completed the ceiling of the Queen's Bedroom in 1715. George I stayed in the palace the summers he was in England.

process of Anglicisation occurred, as with the Palladian style of architecture which was presented through works such as Colen Campbell's *Vitruvius Britannicus* (1725).

There had been an important shift in attitude towards Britain's cultural relations with the rest of Europe. By the end of the 1750s – thanks to a growing economy, an expanding population, an apparently successful political system that had crushed the Jacobite threat, and a great and powerful world empire – there was less of a sense of inferiority than there had been in the seventeenth century, and, instead, a marked feeling of superiority. Whig confidence broadened in mid-century into the cultural moulding of the notion and reality of a united and powerful country.

The Whig myth was successful and lasting in creating and sustaining values and standards by which Britain appeared superior to foreign countries. It was no coincidence that 'Rule Britannia' (first performed at Cliveden) emerged in mid-century; while 'God Save The King' became a popular song and an indication of loyalty – it had originated as a song in honour of Louis XIV and had been sung by Jacobites. Greater domestic stability and international strength both enhanced national self-confidence and led to greater praise from foreign commentators. Greater national wealth also had direct benefits for cultural activity. Between 1777 and 1783 James Barry produced a set of paintings to decorate the Great Hall of the Society for the Encouragement of Arts, Commerce and Manufactures, a body that produced decorative medals and premiums which rewarded innovations in various fields including the arts. The array of philosophers, scientists and others portrayed reached back to the ancient world and forward to modern British talent, for example poets from Homer to Goldsmith. To Barry and his patrons, the British were the new Olympians, equal to the greatness of the past.

PITT THE ELDER

William Pitt the Elder, 1st Earl of Chatham (1708–78), was a statesman whose personality and views greatly affected British politics from the mid-1740s until his death. His career is worth examining in some detail as it throws much light on the nature of the political system as Britain reached for empire. Pitt was particularly important as the great war leader in 1756–61. Then, he was one of the two Secretaries of State, not obviously the leading minister in the government, but someone who dominated it by ability, determination and force of personality. Personality is, indeed, the key to Pitt's rise. Despite appearances to the contrary, he was in part a political outsider, although this was more a matter of temperament than birth. His paternal background offered an instructive example of the flexibility of the English *ancien régime*, its ability to absorb new wealth and rising men, although this should not be exaggerated. Pitt's father was an MP, and one of his uncles by marriage, James, Earl Stanhope, a leading minister. Pitt himself was a protégé of Richard, 1st Viscount Cobham and spent much time at the latter's seat, Stowe.

Yet, in many significant respects, he was an outsider. In a number of ways, both subtle and obvious, his position in the 'establishment', however defined, was weak. Every ruling order, though presenting the appearance of a monolith to the unperceptive observer, has in reality many fine distinctions. Pitt's note was not one that would readily be heard naturally, his orbit not the most spectacular. Crucially, he was a second son, and one with little money. He was dependent on the patronage of others in order to get into Parliament in 1735, 1741, 1747 and 1754. In the first two cases he was elected by Old Sarum, a family pocket borough with five voters. In 1757 he was elected for Seaford, a constituency substantially influenced by Thomas Pelham-Holles, Duke of Newcastle, and in 1754 for another Newcastle seat, Aldborough. In 1756, Pitt was elected for the Grenville pocket borough of Buckingham and his own family's seat at Okehampton. He never sat for a county seat, the common aspiration for those with social standing, nor faced a popular contest.

Politically, Pitt had no secure base within a coherent group. He suffered from his lack of a large parliamentary connection. His career was based on standing in the House of Commons, especially on his oratorical vigour, not on connections. He came into high office without major obligations to any patron, and this independence ensured that he was very much his own master when it came to the crucial decisions. His ability to take a major role in the Commons depended on his ability to pose as the politician of conviction and argument, not the dispenser of loaves and fishes to backbenchers. As a tactic, it could work well. Pitt had a pre-eminence that in some respects was greater than that of Sir Robert Walpole, because Walpole could not take advantage of 'Patriot' rhetoric and pose as a man totally and selflessly dedicated to the good of his country.

William Pitt the Elder by William Hoare of Bath. Horace Walpole described his speech on the Address in 1755: 'How his eloquence, like a torrent long obstructed burst forth with more commanding impetuosity! . . . haughty, defiant, and conscious of injury and supreme abilities.'

Pitt's rigorous criticism of government, whether from outside, when in opposition, or of ministerial colleagues, when in office, was not simply a tactic designed to gain attention and to encourage others, not least the ministry, to use his support. He was happier criticising than defending and this aggressive position was best presented by attacking government, even from within. Pitt pushed his views without moderation. He had a sense of his own ability that he felt was most challenged by governmental complacency protecting ministerial mediocrity. He did not feel at home in the world of court society.

Many contemporaries saw him as a megalomaniac determined to bend national politics to his will. In 1761 John Carteret, 1st Earl Granville, remarked that Pitt 'was taking more upon himself than any man had a right to, approaching to infallibility'. Earlier that year, Bussy, the unsympathetic French envoy, reported:

This minister is the idol of the people, who regard him as the sole author of their success, and they do not have the same confidence in the other members of the council. The court and its partisans are obliged to have the greatest regards for the fantasies of a fiery people, whom it is dangerous to contradict. Pitt joins to a reputation of superior spirit and talent, that of most exact honesty . . . With simple manners and dignity, he seeks neither display nor ostentation . . . He is courageous to the point of rashness, he supports his ideas in an impassioned fashion and with an invincible determination, seeking to subjugate all the world by the tyranny of his

Thomas Pelham-Holles, 1st Duke of Newcastle (1693–1768), left, with his brother-in-law Henry Clinton, 7th Earl of Lincoln (1684–1728), by Sir Godfrey Kneller (1646–1723). A major electoral manager and firm Whig, Newcastle was a longstanding Secretary of State (1724–54) then served as Lord Treasurer before and during the Seven Years' War (1754–6, 1757–62).

opinions. Pitt seems to have no other ambition than to elevate Britain to the highest point of glory and to abase France to the lowest degree of humiliation.

Although the desire to bend politics to their will is common to many politicians and political circumstances, few politicians possessed this aspiration to the same degree as Pitt. The hostile Charles Townshend remarked that 'that animation of language and sentiment, which is allowed to the orator in political conflicts . . . has no place in a sober discussion'. Henry Harris wrote of Pitt's parliamentary performance in 1755 that he would 'keep any administration in fine breath – he was born for opposition – more excelling in his manner, in his language, and in high invective, than all the public speakers I ever heard of'.

Pitt was helped by the weakness of several ministries. He was totally different to Newcastle (1693–1768), the most prominent of the Old Corps Whigs, those Whigs who stayed in office throughout the reigns of George I and George II. Owner of Claremont, Newcastle played a crucial role in maintaining Old Corps cohesion in the difficult years after the fall of Walpole in 1742. He was a Secretary of State from 1724 to 1754 and First Lord of the Treasury from 1754 to 1756 and 1757 to 1762. Newcastle was a master of patronage, but was hit by the impact of difficult political circumstances in a political system that lacked both clear conventions for ministerial responsibility and an understanding of the position of prime minister as entailing clear-cut powers to direct government business and deploy ministerial patronage.

Newcastle had neither the personality nor the position to sustain the political structure that his paranoia dictated: a concentration of decision-making and power on his own person. He could not be a second Walpole. He was not strong enough to take and, more crucially, bear responsibility for decisions, and his anxiety led to indecisiveness. Newcastle wanted strong colleagues, able to take such responsibility, and for that reason operated best with his brother Henry Pelham and with Pitt successively. Yet he wanted these colleagues clearly subordinate and could not psychologically accept his own dependence on them; he was weak, but did not wish to acknowledge this weakness.

Aside from lacking the character necessary for the successful retention of high office, Newcastle also did not hold an office that would free him from, or at least lessen, his anxieties. For all his frenetic activity, and the time and personal wealth he devoted to patronage, Newcastle was only the most important member of the ministry. The king was the head of the government, and played a crucial role in political manoeuvres. Although willing to accept Newcastle, George II was not close to him, and this was a major source of the duke's anxiety.

Similarly, Newcastle was unsure of Parliament, unable, as a peer, to lead the Commons, but reluctant to allow anyone else to do the job, fearing (rightly) that he would be overshadowed. The absence of a reliable party unity on which government could rest left Newcastle, like other politicians, feeling vulnerable to attack. More generally, Newcastle's problems reflected, in part, the narrowing of the established Whig tradition during a period of growing change in political culture. Whiggery had originally been an opposition movement, but the Old Corps were establishment politicians who had little knowledge or understanding of populist, let alone radical, dimensions to Whiggery.

Pitt, in contrast, sought to be a populist. He did not come to office until 1746 when he became Paymaster General, not a major post, although a potentially lucrative one. He was a Secretary of State from December 1756 until September 1761, and Lord Privy Seal in 1766–8. For the rest of his life, he was without office. His last political cause was the conciliation of the American Colonials, not a popular one in governmental circles. Thus, for most of his political career, he did not hold major office, a situation very different from that of Walpole, Newcastle, and those other second sons, Henry Pelham and Pitt the Younger. Being without office, Pitt could more easily lend himself to the nexus of dissatisfaction, populism and radicalism generally known as 'Patriotism'. Thus, in the 1730s he attacked Walpolean corruption, in the 1740s Hanoverian subsidies, in the 1760s peace with France, and in the 1770s policy towards America. In each case, Pitt appealed to the notion that the government was betraying national interests. Politically potent and charged, this was part of a process by which he identified himself with such interests. This process was eased by the junior status of the paymastership, by the less controversial nature of

politics and government in 1746–53, certainly compared to the period 1738–45, and by the degree to which Pitt in office was associated with war. He was thus less publicly tarnished with the exigencies and compromises of office than other leading politicians, while he also avoided, for much of his career, the difficulties of opposing government during a period of success in war. Pitt's prominence indicated the growing role of public politics.

Other politicians, however, could not have expected anything like the public support that Pitt received in April 1757 when he was dismissed as a result of George II's hostility. The circumstances of his departure led to the so-called 'rain' of golden boxes, the presentation to him of the freedom and compliments of thirteen cities. The Common Council of London thanked Pitt for his attempt to 'stem the general torrent of corruption' and for his 'loyal and disinterested conduct'. Such motions were the consequence not simply of a spontaneous outburst of public zeal, but also of manoeuvres by Pitt's supporters, but Pitt benefited greatly from being able to present himself as the spokesman of opinion 'out of doors'. This was a particular skill and most politicians were not taking part in politics to such a public extent: the political milieu of the Dukes of Newcastle and Devonshire was very different from that of Pitt and, partly as a result, his potential importance was highly rated, possibly overrated. In many respects he benefited from being able to act as an apparent link between the world of the royal court and high politics, and that 'out of doors', an ability that owed much to his being in many respects temperamentally a political outsider. Pitt's apparent indispensability in the House of Commons led to his return to office in June 1757.

It is with war that Pitt is most associated, with British success in the Seven Years' War (1756–63). In and after the Second World War, comparisons were made with Winston Churchill. Since then, there has, however, been a process of revision, which has questioned Pitt's high standing. Nevertheless, there is no doubt that he was a crucial figure. Pitt wanted to send troops to conquer the French colonies and to Germany to prevent the French from overrunning Prussia. To secure these ends he actively pressed for the raising of fresh troops in Britain and refused to be distracted by the prospect of French invasion in 1759. He was against withdrawing any troops from America to Europe.

Pitt reaped his reward in 1759, the 'year of victories'. British forces took Québec, defeated the French at Minden in Germany and their fleet at Lagos (coast of Portugal) and Quiberon Bay (Brittany). He became even more popular with contemporaries and was, thereafter, closely associated with national triumph. However, Pitt's ability to capitalise on these advantages was limited as far as contemporaries were concerned. A new king, George III, who came to the throne in 1760, was determined to break with the personnel and policies of his grandfather's government. In particular, he wished to include Tories in the ministry and to negotiate peace. War-weariness, and concern about the cost of the conflict, was also rising within the government, especially on the part of Newcastle.

In this context, of a general British desire for peace, Pitt was politically foolish to hinder attempts to avoid war with Spain in 1761. Charles III of Spain was, in fact, moving closer to France and war might have been difficult to avoid, but Pitt was regarded as unnecessarily provocative to Spain and France in abortive peace talks in 1761. He outraged his colleagues by demanding that he get his own way over war with the Spanish. On 2 October 1761, when Pitt attended the Council and argued that Britain must attack Spain in the face of opposition from his colleagues, he delivered a valedictory assessment of his years as Secretary of State. Newcastle recorded:

> Mr Pitt in his speech recapitulated his own situation, called (as he was without having ever asked any one single employment in his life) by his Sovereign, and he might say in some degree by the voice of the people, to assist the State, when others had *abdicated* the service of it . . . that he was loaded with the imputation of this war being *solely his*;

that it was called his war; that it had been a successful one, and more than hinted that the success was singly owing to him . . . That in his station and situation he was responsible, and would not continue without having the direction; that this being the case, nobody could be surprised that he could go on no longer; and he would repeat it again, that he would be responsible for nothing but what he directed.

Resigning, Pitt became a symbol of opposition, both to George III's favourite, John Stuart, 3rd Earl of Bute, and to the return of some colonial conquests to France and Spain in the Peace of Paris of 1763. Thereafter, his career was less glorious. He held peacetime office as first minister without conspicuous success in 1766–8, and his government then diminished his status as a 'patriot' in the eyes of his former supporters. In his last years, Pitt opposed war with the American colonists.

Unlike many, Pitt's fame was not expressed by a mere list of the posts he held and the committees he sat on. Instead, Pitt had a clear vision of national greatness. His determination to confront France in the maritime and colonial sphere and his conviction that Britain must make substantial territorial gains was of material importance in global history for it was in his period of power that Britain became the most important power in the world. He was a man with whom the national interest could be associated, not simply because he made the claim, but also because he seemed apart from the world of court and connection. His funerary monument in Westminster Abbey included the passage:

> WILLIAM PITT EARL OF CHATHAM
> During whose Administration
> In the Reigns of George II and George III
> Divine Providence
> Exalted Great Britain
> To an Height of Prosperity and Glory
> Unknown to any Former Age.

THE IMPERIAL POWER

The defeat of Jacobitism was the crucial prerequisite not only for the stability of the Revolution Settlement and the Hanoverian succession – the domestic political consequences of 1688 – but also for Britain's success in emerging as the leading world power. This it did in the Seven Years War (1756–63), which is known in the USA as the French and Indian War, and dated 1754–63, because fighting in North America began in 1754, although war was not declared until 1756. The war ended with the Thirteen Colonies on the eastern seaboard of North America, and the British possessions in India, secure, with Canada, Florida, and French bases in West Africa and the West Indies captured, and with the Royal Navy unchallengeable at sea.

These victories were the achievement of a number of able military leaders, including Edward Boscawen and Edward Hawke at sea, Robert Clive in India, and James Wolfe in Canada. They left an architecture of victory, although none matched Blenheim, the nation's gift to John Churchill, 1st Duke of Marlborough, for his victory at Blenheim on the Danube in 1704. Boscawen had Hatchlands Park built, Clive built a new house at Claremont and altered the garden, and his family, having inherited Powis Castle in

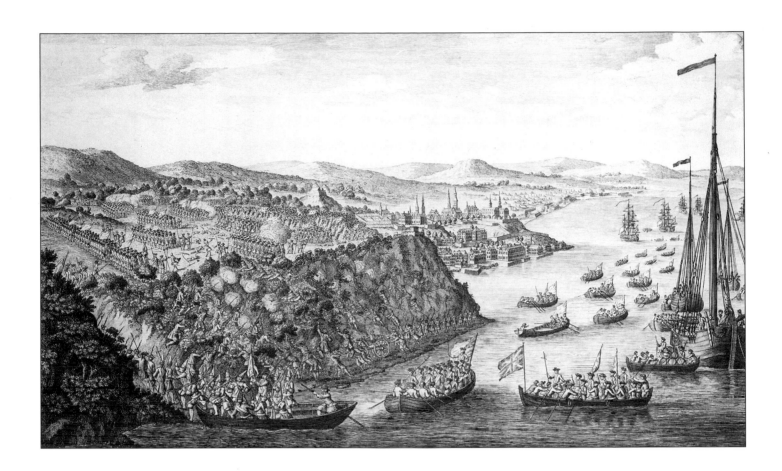

1801, repaired and richly embellished it. Wolfe, who spent his early years in what came to be called Quebec House, was commemorated with the Quebec Monument at Studley Royal and a hundred-foot column at Stowe.

Clive's victory at Plassey over Siraj-ud-daula, the Nawab of Bengal, in 1757, laid the basis for British control of Bengal, one of the wealthiest parts of India. Clive deployed his men, about 850 British troops and 2,100 sepoys, in front of a mango grove with an acute angle of the river behind him, the sepoys on the flanks and his ten field-guns and howitzers in front; fifty sailors acted as artillerymen. An artillery duel began and Clive withdrew his men into the grove, where they sheltered behind the mudbanks and among the trees. The Indians, about 50,000 strong, made no real effort to attack the British position, with the exception of a cavalry advance that was driven back by grapeshot. Clive had reached an agreement with Mir Jaffir, one of the Nawab's generals, and Mir Jaffir's men were totally inactive. A torrential midday downpour put most of the Nawab's guns out of action, but the British kept their powder dry. As the Indian artillery (operated by Frenchmen) retreated, Clive advanced to man the embankment surrounding the large village pond to the front of his position. An Indian infantry attack was repelled by Clive's artillery and infantry fire and, as the Indians retreated, Clive's men advanced rapidly, storming the Indian encampment. The Nawab had already fled. Clive's force suffered about 60 casualties, his opponent's only about 500 dead; but the political consequences were important. The battle was followed by the defection of Mir Jaffir whose son had the Nawab killed. Mir Jaffir was installed as the Nawab's successor and Clive received over £250,000 from him. French forces in India were subjugated in 1760–1, and Britain emerged as the most powerful European influence there.

A view of the taking of Québec by General Wolfe, 13 September 1759.

193

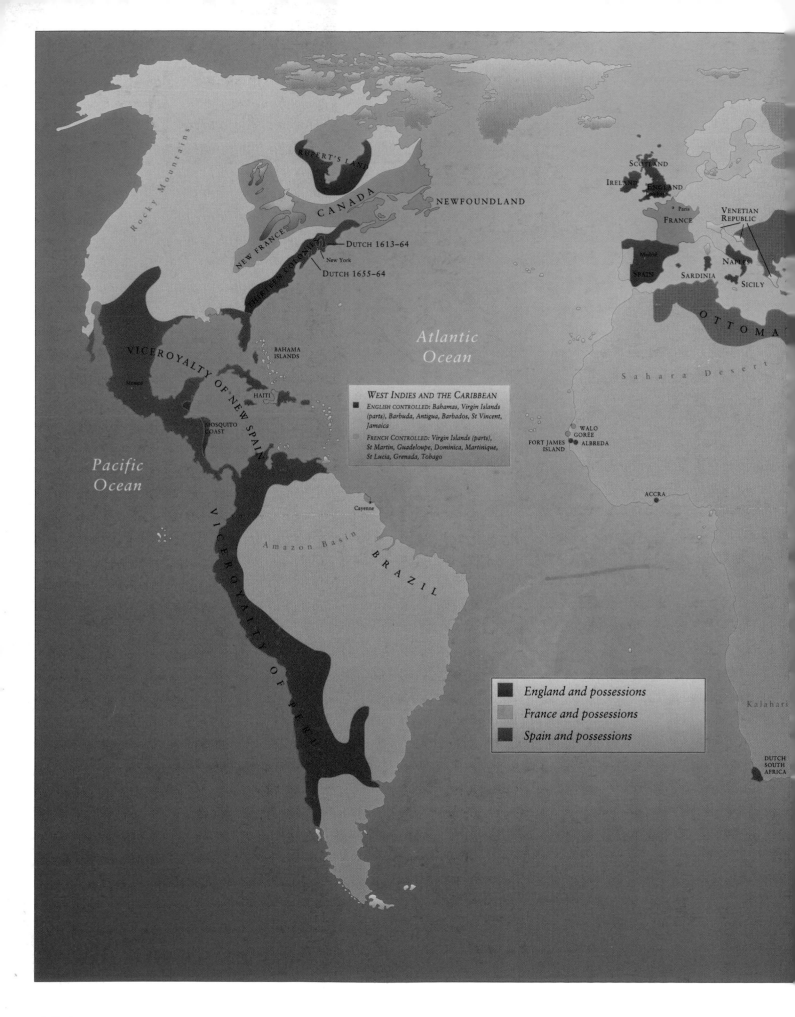

SCOTLAND

IRELAND
ENGLAND
London

Paris
FRANCE

VENETIAN
REPUBLIC

Madrid

SPAIN
SARDINIA
NAPLES

SICILY

O T T O M A

Rocky Mountains

RUPERT'S LAND

CANADA

NEWFOUNDLAND

NEW FRANCE

DUTCH 1613–64

New York

THIRTEEN COLONIES

DUTCH 1655–64

Atlantic
Ocean

Sahara Desert

VICEROYALTY OF NEW SPAIN

BAHAMA
ISLANDS

Mexico

HAITI

MOSQUITO
COAST

WALO
GORÉE
FORT JAMES
ISLAND
ALBREDA

Pacific
Ocean

ACCRA

WEST INDIES AND THE CARIBBEAN

■ ENGLISH CONTROLLED: *Bahamas, Virgin Islands (parts), Barbuda, Antigua, Barbados, St Vincent, Jamaica*

■ FRENCH CONTROLLED: *Virgin Islands (parts), St Martin, Guadeloupe, Dominica, Martinique, St Lucia, Grenada, Tobago*

Cayenne

Amazon Basin

B R A Z I L

VICEROYALTY OF PERU

Kalahari

■ England and possessions
■ France and possessions
■ Spain and possessions

DUTCH
SOUTH
AFRICA

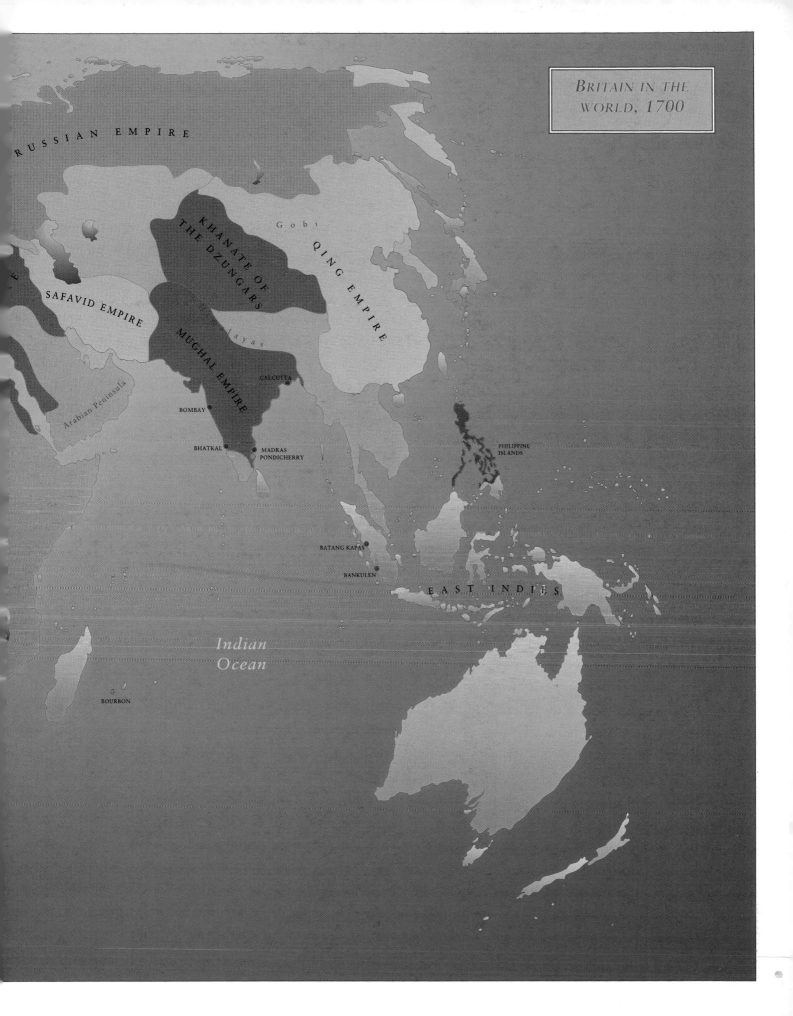

RUSSIAN EMPIRE

SAFAVID EMPIRE

KHANATE OF
THE DZUNGARS

Gobi

QING EMPIRE

MUGHAL EMPIRE

Himalayas

Arabian Peninsula

CALCUTTA

BOMBAY

BHATKAL
MADRAS
PONDICHERRY

PHILIPPINE
ISLANDS

BATANG KAPAS

BANKULEN

EAST INDIES

Indian
Ocean

BOURBON

The British also came to dominate North America as a result of their conquest of New France (Canada) in 1758–60. The crucial campaign was that of 1759 when the able and determined James Wolfe struck at Québec, his force convoyed up the St Lawrence by the navy. Wolfe arrived near Québec on 26 June, but his operations along the Beauport shore were initially unsuccessful. On 31 July an attack on French positions was repelled by Montcalm's larger army, with the British suffering 440 casualties to the French 60. As winter approached, it seemed increasingly likely that the British would fail. Wolfe risked a bold move. James Cook, later famous as the explorer of the Pacific, had thoroughly surveyed the St Lawrence and British warships had passed beyond Québec from 18 July onwards and made upriver raids on 8 August. The army was to follow. On 1–3 September, British troops left the Montmorency camp and moved along the southern bank of the river opposite Québec. On 10 September, Wolfe, having reconnoitred the river, decided to land at Anse au Foulon to the west of the city. After delays due to the weather, the British landed in the early hours of 13 September. Some 200 light infantry scaled the cliffs and successfully attacked a French camp of 100 men. The remainder of the British force, fewer than 4,500 men, then landed and advanced to the Plains of Abraham to the south-west of the city.

Montcalm, with a total of 13,000 men in the area, was in a strong position, with fresh troops approaching Wolfe's rear, but, instead of waiting on the defensive and uniting his forces, he chose to attack with the men immediately to hand. A member of Wolfe's force recorded:

> About 9 o'clock the French army had drawn up under the walls of the town, and advanced towards us briskly and in good order. We stood to receive them; they began their fire at a distance, we reserved ours, and as they came nearer fired on them by divisions, this did execution and seemed to check them a little, however they still advanced pretty quick, we increased our fire without altering our position, and, when they were within less than an hundred yards, gave them a full fire, fixed our bayonets, and under cover of the smoke the whole line charged.

Québec surrendered soon after the battle, and the remaining French force in Canada capitulated at Montréal the following year. Britain ended the Seven Years' War as the leading maritime power in the world. Her knowledge of the oceans was then greatly expanded by postwar exploration.

British imperial success was to be challenged in the 1770s, but the French attack in 1778 was possible only because the Thirteen Colonies had rebelled against George III in 1775. That rebellion, and the subsequent war (1775–83), which in 1779 broadened out to include Spain, lost Britain the Thirteen Colonies, Florida, and some possessions in the West Indies and West Africa. The bulk of the empire, including British India, Canada, Jamaica and Gibraltar, was held, however. Thomas Luny's panoramic paintings at Berrington Hall recorded Admiral Rodney's naval victories. Rodney insisted on oaks from the Powis Castle estate for his ships. Furthermore, there was no serious challenge to the government in the British Isles. There was no rebellion in Ireland or Scotland, although the Irish volunteers posed the threat of power slipping away to an ad hoc, non-governmental organisation, and failure abroad did not lead to an insuperable crisis at home. The fundamentals of the mid-century British achievement held. This was crucial to the way in which the population and economy of Britain expanded without political or social breakdown. The way was open to the Industrial Revolution.

Selected Further Reading

It is best to begin not with the writings of historians but with those of contemporaries. A selective list of the latter risks making invidious comparisons and leaving dangerous omissions, but let me begin by suggesting that the plentiful correspondence and diaries of the period should be the first port of call. Much has been published by the Historical Manuscripts Commission, but there are many more accessible volumes. Travel accounts are especially valuable and for that reason I begin with *The Illustrated Journeys of Celia Fiennes c. 1682–c. 1712* edited by Christopher Morris (London, 1982). Other published journeys include, most famously, Daniel Defoe's *Tour of the Whole Island of Great Britain* (London, 1724), and John Macky's *A Journey through England* (London, 1714). Modern works include Z. Dovey (ed.), *An Elizabethan Progress. The Queen's Journey into East Anglia 1578* (Stroud, 1999) and John Chandler, *Travels through Stuart Britain. The Adventures of John Taylor, the Water Poet* (Stroud, 1999). The accounts of foreign travellers throw an interesting light on British developments. They include C. de Saussure, *A Foreign View of England in the Reign of George II* (London, 1902) and P. Kalm, *Account of a Visit to England* (New York, 1892), and, for the close of the period, K. Morgan (ed.), *An American Quaker in the British Isles. The Travel Journals of Jabez Maud Fisher, 1775–1779* (Oxford, 1992).

The writings and correspondence of prominent literary figures offer a stimulating context. Among those of particular value, because of their direct engagement with contemporary issues, are D.F. Bond (ed.), *The Spectator* (Oxford, 1965) and *The Tatler* (Oxford, 1987), A. Ross and D. Woolley (eds), *Jonathan Swift* (Oxford, 1984) and W.B. Coley (ed.), *Henry Fielding. The True Patriot* (Oxford, 1987). The world of caricature is introduced in M. Duffy (ed.), *The English Satirical Print 1660–1832* (Cambridge, 1986).

The careful reading of sources offers much. Aside from the series *English Historical Documents*, there is also an edition of debates in William Cobbett (ed.), *A Parliamentary History of England* (London, 1806–20). Valuable editions of political material include John Brooke (ed.), *Horace Walpole. Memoirs of King George II* (New Haven, 1985).

Historical atlases of parts of Britain are very valuable. Especially worthy of note are Peter McNeill and Ranald Nicholson (eds.), *An Historical Atlas of Scotland c. 400–c. 1600* (St Andrews, 1975), D. Dymond and E. Martin, *An Historical Atlas of Suffolk* (Ipswich, 1988), *An Historical Atlas of County Durham* (Durham, 1992), M. Barke and R.J. Buswell (eds), *Newcastle's Changing Map* (Newcastle, 1992), and Joan Dils (ed.), *An Historical Atlas of Berkshire* (Reading, 1998). *The Journal of Historical Geography* contains much of interest, while the nature of regional identity is discussed in Charles Phythian-Adams (ed.), *Societies, Cultures and Kinship, 1580–1850, Cultural Provinces and English Local History* (Leicester, 1993), and Helen Jewell, *The North–South Divide: The Origins of Northern Consciousness* (Manchester, 1994). Agricultural regions in England and Wales are discussed in Eric Kerridge, *The Common Fields of England* (Manchester, 1992).

Another valuable approach is via regional history, especially the Regional History of England series, with volumes such as Peter Brandon and Brian Short (eds.), *The South East from AD 1000* (Harlow, 1990). A very different perspective is provided by J.M. Black, *Convergence or Divergence? Britain and the Continent* (London, 1994). For the empire, see Nicholas Canny (ed.), *The Origins of Empire* (Oxford, 1998) and P.J. Marshall (ed.), *The Eighteenth Century* (Oxford, 1998), both in 'The Oxford History of the British Empire'.

The fifteenth century can be best approached through A.J. Pollard, *The Wars of the Roses* (London, 1988). See also R.L. Storey, *The End of the House of Lancaster* (Stroud, 1999) and K. Dockray, *Edward IV. A Source Book* (Stroud, 1999).

For the Tudor period, Steven Gunn, *Early Tudor Government, 1485–1558* (London, 1995), Richard Rex, *Henry VIII and the English Reformation* (London, 1992), David Loades, *Power in Tudor England* (London, 1996), Diarmaid MacCulloch, *The Later Reformation in England, 1547–1603* (London, 1990), Susan Doran, *England and Europe in the Sixteenth Century* (London, 1998), J. Gwynfor Jones, *Early Modern Wales, c. 1525–1640* (London, 1994). Christopher Marsh, *Popular Religion in the Sixteenth Century* (London, 1998), and Michael Mullett, *Catholics in Britain and Ireland, 1558–1829* (London, 1998) are very useful for religious changes.

The best narrative account of the Stuart period is Mark Kishlansky, *A Monarchy Transformed. Britain 1603–1714* (London, 1996). Also on the political history of the century, Michael Young, *Charles I* (London, 1997), Ann Hughes, *The Causes of the English Civil War* (2nd edn., London, 1998), Ronald Hutton, *The British Republic, 1649–1660* (London, 1999), Paul Seaward, *The Restoration, 1660–1668* (London, 1991), Eveline Cruickshanks, *The Glorious Revolution* (London, 2000), Keith Brown, *Kingdom or Province? Scotland the Regal Union, 1603–1715* (London, 1992), J.S. Wheeler, *The Making of a World Power. War and the Military Revolution in Seventeenth-century England* (Stroud, 1999), and Craig Rose, *England in the 1690s* (Oxford, 1999).

Useful socio-economic accounts include Sybil Jack, *Towns in Tudor and Stuart Britain* (London, 1996), Helen Jewell, *Education in Early Modern England* (London, 1998), and Ian Whyte, *Scotland's Society and Economy in Transition, c. 1500–c. 1760* (London, 1997). For political thought, Glenn Burgess, *British Political Thought. From Reformation to Revolution* (London, 1999), A.P. Martinich, *Thomas Hobbes* (London, 1996) and W.M. Spellman, *John Locke* (London, 1997). On religion in the seventeenth century, John Craig, *English Parishioners 1500–1700* (London, 1999), Anthony Milton and J.F. Merritt, *Church and Religion in England, 1603–1642* (London, 1999) and John Spurr, *English Puritanism 1603–89* (London, 1998)

The eighteenth century can be approached through J. Black, *The Politics of Britain 1688–1800* (Manchester, 1993), *The Illustrated History of Eighteenth-Century Britain* (Manchester, 1996), *Britain as a Military Power 1688–1815* (London, 1999), and *Pitt the Elder: The Great Commoner* (Stroud, 1999). The best guide to its subject is Roy Porter, *English Society in the Eighteenth Century* (2nd edn., London, 1990), and, for a different angle, T. Hitchcock, *English Sexualities, 1700–1800* (London, 1997). The best for its subject is Murray Pittock, *Jacobitism* (London, 1998). Other important works include Paul Langford, *A Polite and Commercial People: England, 1727–1783* (Oxford, 1989), Alexander Murdoch, *British History 1660–1832. National Identity and Local Culture* (London, 1998), Murray Pittock, *Inventing and Resisting Britain. Cultural Identities in Britain and Ireland, 1685–1789* (London, 1997), John Rule, *The Vital Century. England's Developing Economy 1714–1815* (London, 1992), and John Shaw, *A Political History of Eighteenth-Century Scotland* (London, 1999). For Britain in the European context, J. Black, *Europe in the Eighteenth Century* (2nd edn., London, 1999). Newspapers of the period are plentiful and available in the reference divisions of many central libraries, including those of Bristol, Gateshead, Gloucester, Leeds, Newcastle, Reading, Sheffield and York.

Acknowledgements

The Author and the Publishers gratefully acknowledge permission to reproduce the following illustrations. Crown copyright material is reproduced by permission of English Heritage acting under licence from the Controller of Her Majesty's Stationery Office. Page numbers are given:

The Architectural Association, London: © Valerie Bennett 148
Ashmolean Museum, Oxford: 56, 105, 112
Reproduced by permission of the Marquess of Bath, Longleat House, Warminster, Wiltshire, Great Britain: 45
Bodleian Library, University of Oxford: 8, 9, 33 (4o R.I.Med.Seld), 44 (top) (Arch G. e. 37)
Bridgeman Art Library: Bearsted Collection, Upton House, Warwickshire, UK/Bridgeman Art Library 135; Belvoir Castle, Leicestershire, UK//Bridgeman Art Library 58; Photo: John Bethell/Bridgeman Art Library 182, 185: Blenheim Palace, Oxfordshire, UK/Bridgeman Art Library 151; British Library, London, UK/Bridgeman Art Library 14, 43, 87, 159; British Museum, London, UK/Bridgeman Art Library 144; Burghley House Collection, Lincolnshire UK/Bridgeman Art Library 5; Christie's Images, London, UK/Bridgeman Art Library 127; Essex Records Office, Chelmsford, UK/Bridgeman Art Library 11; Guildhall Art Gallery, Corporation of London/Bridgeman Art Library 190; Hermitage, St Petersburg, Russia/Bridgeman Art Library 133; Houses of Parliament, Westminster, London, UK/Bridgeman Art Library 176; Library of Congress, Washington DC, USA/Bridgeman Art Library 158; London, UK/Bridgeman Art Library 121; London Library, St James's Square, London, UK/Bridgeman Art Library 73; Loseley Park, Guildford, Surrey, UK/Bridgeman Art Library 59; Map House, London, UK/Bridgeman Art Library 95, 160; Philip Mould Historical Portraits, London, UK/Bridgeman Art Library 125; Museum of London, UK/Bridgeman Art Library 114; National Coal Mining Museum for England, Wakefield, UK/Bridgeman Art Library 48; New College, Oxford University, Oxford, UK/Bridgeman Art Library 162; Norfolk Museums Service (Norwich Castle Museum), UK/Bridgeman Art Library 171; O'Shea Gallery, London, UK/Bridgeman Art Library 10; Oxford University Musuem of Natural History, UK/Bridgeman Art Library 161; Palazzo Pitti, Florence, Italy/Bridgeman Art Library 175; Phillips, The International Fine Art Auctioneers, UK/Bridgeman Art Library 187; Prado, Madrid, Spain/Bridgeman Art Library 71; Private Collection/Bridgeman Art Library xii, 4, 60, 64, 85, 107, 122, 129, 164, 168, 174, 193; Royal Academy of Arts Library, London, UK/Bridgeman Art Library 120; Royal Albert Memorial Museum, Exeter, Devon, UK/Bridgeman Art Library 147; Royal Geographical Society, London, UK/Bridgeman Art Library endpapers, 52; RSA, London, UK/Bridgeman Art Library 183; Royal Society of Arts, London, UK/Bridgeman Art Library 55; Scottish National Portrait Gallery, Edinburgh, UK/Bridgeman Art Library 131; The Stapleton Collection, UK/Bridgeman Art Library 141; Victoria Art Gallery, Bath and North East Somerset Council/Bridgeman Art Library 154; Trustees of the Weston Park Foundation, UK/Bridgeman Art Library 12 (top)
British Library: frontispiece (Cott.Aug.i.i.9); vi (Roy 18 D111); 18 (Roy.15.E.VI), 75 (Maps.C.29.e.1), 82 (Cott.Aug.I.ii)
© British Museum: 118, 173
College of Arms: 76 (ms M6, f.41v)
© Crown copyright: reproduced courtesy of Historic Scotland: 99

© Crown copyright. NMR: 40

The Fotomas Index: 89

Humphrey Household Collection: 17 (both); 21; 24, 34, 36, 44 (bottom), 70, 72, 80 (both), 83, 104, 108 (both), 111, 116, 124, 163, 169, 177

Lincolnshire County Council, Lincolnshire Archives: 37 (MISC DEP 264/2)

Mary Evans Picture Library, London: 184

© Museum of London: 117

National Maritime Museum, Greenwich, London: 97

National Portrait Gallery, London: 16, 32, 188

National Trust Photographic Library: 12 (bottom); Matthew Antrobus 7, 30; Peter Aprahamian 153; Oliver Benn 128; Andrew Butler 77; Joe Cornish 38; John Darley 51; Dennis Gilbert 149; Fay Godwin 61; John Hammond 54, 90, 136, 156; Angelo Hornak 2; Brian Lawrence 31; Edward Leigh 94; Nadia MacKenzie 146; Nick Meers 78, 145; Erik Pelham 110; Magnus Rew 3; L.A. Sparrow 62; Rob Talbot/Talbot & Whiteman 39; Rupert Truman 67, 74; Andreas von Einsiedel 100, 165; Mike Williams 134; Derrick E. Witty 6; George Wright 25, 63

National Trust for Scotland: G. Satterley 57; 91, 179

The Royal Collection © 2000 Her Majesty Queen Elizabeth II: 181

Scottish National Portrait Gallery: 20

Society of Antiquaries of London: 26

The Marquess of Tavistock and the Trustees of the Bedford Estate: 68, 81

Geoffrey Williams, *Stronghold Britain* (Stroud, Sutton, 1999): 65

The Author and Publishers gratefully acknowledge permission to reproduce material from the following maps: page 27, Michael Bennett, *Battle of Bosworth* (Stroud, Sutton, 1985); page 35, H. Browning and Joan A. Dils, *An Historical Atlas of Berkshire* (Reading, Berkshire Records Society, 1998); pages 47 and 139, Roger Kain and William Ravenhill (eds), Helen Jones (cartography), *Historical Atlas of South-West England* (Exeter, University of Exeter Press, 1999); page 50, Joseph Boughey, *Hadfield's British Canals* (Stroud, Sutton, 1998); page 79, Roger Whiting, *The Enterprise of England: The Spanish Armada* (Stroud, Sutton, 1988); page 103, by permission of the editors, Stewart Bennett and Nicholas Bennett (eds), *An Historical Atlas of Lincolnshire* (Hull, University of Hull Press, 1993); page 123, Malcolm Falkus and John Gillingham (eds) *Kingfisher Historical Atlas of Britain* (London, Kingfisher, 1981); page 142, based on *British Isles: Parliamentary Representation Before 1832* from *The New Cambridge Modern History Atlas* (London, George Philip Ltd, 1970); page 150, David Dymond and Edward Martin (eds), *An Historical Atlas of Suffolk* (revised and enlarged edition, Ipswich, Suffolk County Council (Archaeology Service, Environment and Transport) and the Suffolk Institute of Archaeology and History, 1999); pages 166 and 167, E. Pawson, *Transport and Economy* (London, Academic Press Limited, 1977).

Index

Illustration captions are indicated by *italics*, maps by asterisks.

ANGLIA
hominū numero, rerumꝗ fere
omniū copijs abundans, sub mi-
tissimo Elizabethæ, serenissimæ
et doctissimæ Reginæ, imperio,
placidissima pace annos iam
viginti florentissima.

An. Dni
1579

OCEANVS

GERMA-

NICV-